Financial Management: Theory and Practice

Financial Management: Theory and Practice

Edited by Rory Nolan

Clanrye International
www.clanryeinternational.com

Clanrye International,
750 Third Avenue, 9th Floor,
New York, NY 10017, USA

ISBN: 978-1-64726-072-9

Cataloging-in-Publication Data

Financial management : theory and practice / edited by Rory Nolan.
p. cm.
Includes bibliographical references and index.
ISBN 978-1-64726-072-9
1. Finance--Management. 2. Business enterprises--Finance. 3. Corporations--Finance. I. Nolan, Rory.
HG4026 .F56 2022
658.15--dc23

For information on all Clanrye International publications visit our website at www.clanryeinternational.com

CLANRYE INTERNATIONAL

Contents

Preface

Financial management is a discipline that focuses on equities, ratios and debts. It is used for portfolio management, distribution of dividend, hedging and looking after fluctuations in foreign currency, capital raising and product cycles. It is also involved in the research and decisions related to the capital which should be obtained in order to fund the company's assets. It seeks to maximize the value of the firm for all the stakeholders. Financial management specifically deals with a company's financial strategy. It focuses on the ways to raise the capital and to allocate capital through capital budgeting. It also focuses on long and short term budgeting such as current liabilities. This book provides comprehensive insights into the field of financial management. It traces the progress of this field and highlights some of its key concepts and applications. This book aims to serve as a resource guide for students and experts alike and contribute to the growth of the discipline.

This book unites the global concepts and researches in an organized manner for a comprehensive understanding of the subject. It is a ripe text for all researchers, students, scientists or anyone else who is interested in acquiring a better knowledge of this dynamic field.

I extend my sincere thanks to the contributors for such eloquent research chapters. Finally, I thank my family for being a source of support and help.

Editor

1

The Effect of Corporate Governance Mechanism on Tax Aggressiveness With Earnings Management as Intervening Variable

Shelly Prahadian Putri[a] Mohamad Adam[b] Luk Luk Fuadah[c]

[a] Corresponding Author, Faculty of Economics, Sriwijaya University, Palembang, Indonesia, shelly.prahadian@gmail.com
[b] Prof., Faculty of Economics, Sriwijaya University, Palembang, Indonesia
[c] Ph.D., Faculty of Economics, Sriwijaya University, Palembang, Indonesia

Keywords
Corporate Governance, Tax Aggresiveness, Earnings Management.

Abstract
This study aims to analyze the effect of corporate governance mechanism on tax aggressiveness with earnings management as intervening variable. In this study, corporate governance is measured by institutional ownership and the proportion of independent board of commissioners. The sample used in this study is 43 manufacturing companies taken using purposive sampling technique. The type of data used is panel data while the data analysis used is path analysis model. The results of the study found that institutional ownership and the proportion of independent board of commissioners had a significant negative effect on earnings management and institutional ownership with significant negative impact on tax aggressiveness. The proportion of independent board of commissioners and earnings management are found to have significant positive effect on tax aggressiveness. The Sobel Test results show that earnings management variables are able to mediate the relationship of institutional ownership and proportion of independent board of commissioners to tax aggressiveness.

1. Introduction

Taxes are an important phenomenon and the focus of government. The government creates tax-related programs and regulations aimed at maximizing state revenues from the tax sector. However, in recent years the realization of tax revenue in Indonesia has not yet reached the target set by the government. The government's inability to achieve tax revenue target can be caused by various factors, one of which is the company's aggressive attitude toward taxes.

According to the Ministry of Finance, of a total of 12 million corporate taxpayers only 11% routinely report annual tax returns. This is evidenced by the low tax ratio of Indonesia which is only 10.3% compared to other countries such as Malaysia over 13%, and Vietnam and Singapore which has reached 16%. According to Suyanto & Supramono (2012), the company is considered more aggressive against taxes if more and more gaps are used. Companies tend to tax aggressiveness in order to minimize the tax burden to increase the company's net income (Chen *et al.,* 2010).

Corporate governance within the company is necessary to reduce the existence of tax aggressiveness so that it can have a positive impact on tax compliance. The Company implements corporate governance to create effective corporate performance and impact on decisions to be effective in determining policies related to the effective corporate tax rate (Pranoto & Widagdo, 2015). This research refers to research conducted by Nugroho & Firmansyah (2017), Prawira (2017), Hanna & Haryanto (2016), Cahyono *et al.,* (2016), Fadli (2016), Wulansari (2015), Pranoto & Widagdo (2015), Embree (2012), Suyanto & Supramono (2012), Khurana & Moser (2009), Badertscher *et al.,* (2009) that uses corporate governance, which is measured using institutional ownership and independent board of commissioners, have an impact on tax aggressiveness.

This study differs from the previous study as it uses institutional ownership and the proportion of independent board of commissioners in measuring corporate governance. These two corporate governance mechanisms are expected to make the management of the company better so that it will improve the company's performance and become an added value for the company. In addition, this study uses earnings management as an intervening variable. The act of tax aggressiveness that occurred closely related to the behavior of the management who tend to practice earnings management in order to minimize the tax burden of the company. Kim *et al.,* (2010) finds evidence that earnings management can be used as a tool for tax aggressiveness in order to reduce the tax burden.

1. Literature Review

1.1. Agency Theory

Jensen & Meckling (1976) describes the agency relationship in agency theory that the firm is a collection of contracts between the owner of the economic resources (principal) and the manager (agent) that takes care of the use and control of the resource. Differences of interests that occur between the management of the company as taxpayers with tax authorities as tax collectors to cause conflict between the two.

1.2. Positive Accounting Theory

Positive accounting theory was proposed by Watts & Zimmerman (1986). Positive accounting theory explains the factors that make the management has a motivation in choosing methods and accounting principles that can improve the welfare of the company. Watts & Zimmerman (1986) reveals three main hypotheses in positive accounting theory, namely: (1) Bonus Plan Hypothesis, (2) Debt Convenant Hypothesis, (3) Political Cost Hypothesis.

1.3. Hypothesis Development

1.3.1. The Effect of Institutional Ownership on Management Earnings

Institutional parties are considered sophisticated investors because the institutional can monitor the behavior and actions of management that will reduce the behavior of management to make earnings management (Midiastuty & Mahfoedz, 2003). This is in line with agency theory, which states that the ownership of shares by other institutions can reduce the conflicts of interest that occur and opportunistic behavior of management so as to reduce the potential likelihood of profit management practices (Jensen dan Meckling, 1976). This is also in accordance with the results of research Jao & Pagalung (2011) which shows that institutional ownership affects earnings management. Based on the description above, the proposed hypothesis is as follows:

H_1 : Institutional ownership has negative effect on the earnings management

1.3.2. The Effect of Proportion of Independent Board of Commissioners on Earnings Management

The independent board of commissioner is responsible for overseeing the activities of the company conducted by independent management who work for the company's interest in overseeing the process of preparing the financial statements. Therefore, the greater the proportion of independent board of commissioners the higher the supervision and expected to minimize opportunistic management behavior in the form of earnings management practices. Research conducted by Rahmawati (2013), Prastiti & Meiranto (2013), Jao & Pagalung (2011) indicate that independent board of commissioners have an influence on earnings management. Based on the description above, the proposed hypothesis is as follows:

H_2 : The proportion of independent board of commissioners has negative effect on earnings management

1.3.3. The Effect of Institutional Ownership on Tax Aggressiveness

It is believed that, the greater the ownership of shares owned by other institutions then they will have the ability to effectively control and supervise management and have the ability to influence the decisions and policies made by management (Easterbrook, 1984). Based on the agency theory, which states that by enlarging the ownership of shares by institutions outside the company can reduce the conflict of interest that occurred and opportunistic behavior of management so as to reduce the potential possibility of tax aggressiveness action. Research conducted by Nugroho & Firmansyah (2017), Cahyono *et al.,* (2016), Hanna & Haryanto (2016), Mahulae *et al.,* (2016), Prakosa (2014), Embree (2012), Badertscher *et al.,* (2009), Khurana & Moser (2009) show that institutional ownership has an influence on tax aggressiveness. Based on the description above, the proposed hypothesis is as follows:

H_3 : Institutional ownership has negative effect on tax aggressiveness

1.3.4. The Effect of Proportion of Independent Board of commissioners on Tax Aggressiveness

Independent commissioners in the board of commissioners contribute to supervising managers to not take tax aggressiveness. The greater the ratio of independent commissioners in the composition of the board of commissioners will minimize the possibility of corporate tax aggressiveness. Supervision of independent commissioners makes management more transparent in disclosing corporate information so that tax aggressiveness activities can be minimized and even eliminated. Research conducted by Nugroho & Firmansyah (2017), Prawira (2017), Fadli (2016), Wulansari (2015), Pranoto & Widagdo (2015), Richardson *et al.,* (2014), Fadli (2013), Armstrong *et al.,* (2012), Suyanto & Supramono (2012) indicate that independent board of commissioners influence tax aggressiveness. Based on the description above, the proposed hypothesis is as follows:

H_4 : The proportion of Independent board of commissioners has negative effect on tax aggressiveness

1.3.5. The Effect of Earnings Management on Tax Aggressiveness

Tax is believed to be the problem for the companies because paying taxes will lower their net profit. Therefore, the company will make earnings management to reduce the tax burden (Scott, 2009). Based on the political cost hypothesis in positive accounting theory, management tend to manipulate profits in order to avoid government regulation. One of the government regulations that directly relates to corporate profits is corporate income tax. Research conducted by Hashim *et al.,* (2016), Sari *et al.,* (2016), Tiaras & Wijaya (2015), Kamila (2014), Ohnuma (2013), Suyanto & Supramono (2012), Frank *et al.,* (2009) shows that earnings management has an influence on tax aggressiveness. Based on the description above, the proposed hypothesis is as follows:

H_5 : Earnings management has positive effect on tax agressivenss

1.3.6. The Effect of Institutional Ownership on Tax Aggressiveness through Earnings Management as Intervening Variable

Ownership of shares of companies by other institutions is one part of corporate governance that allegedly can solve conflicts of interest between shareholders and management and can reduce opportunistic management behavior in the form of earnings management practices because ownership of shares of companies owned by other institutions can align the various interests between the interests of holders shares with the interests of the management (Jensen & Meckling, 1976). With decreasing opportunistic management behavior in the form of earnings management practice, it is assumed that it can reduce the potential of tax aggressiveness. Based on the description above, the proposed hypothesis is as follows:

H_6 : Institutional ownership has positive effect on tax aggressiveness with earnings management as intervening variable

1.3.7. The Effect of Proportion of Independent Board of Commissioners on Tax Agressiveness through Earnings Management as Intervening Variable

Independent board of commissioners is one part of corporate governance. Supervision of independent commissioners makes management more transparent in disclosure of company information and is expected to minimize opportunistic behavior of management in the form of earnings management so the profits presented will be in accordance with actual company conditions so that the tax burden of the company will also be in accordance with the existing reality (Jao & Pagalung, 2011). Based on the description above, the proposed hypothesis is as follows:

H_7 : The proportion Independent board of commissioners has an impact on tax aggressiveness with earnings management as intervening variable

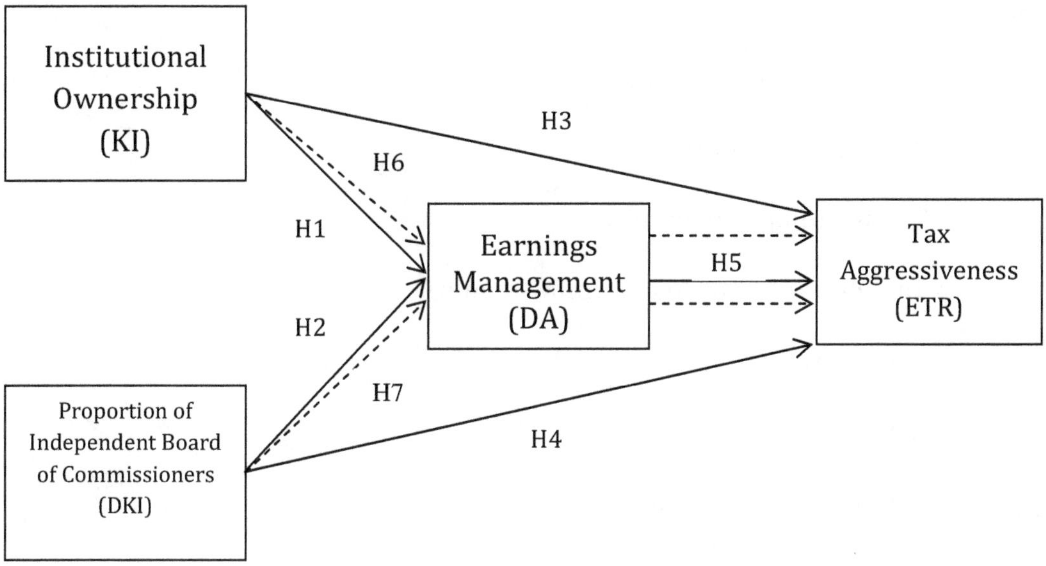

Figure 1. Research Framework

Notes:
⟶ : The effect of KI, DKI, DA, and ETR
------> : Mediating effect of KI, DKI and ETR

2. Methodology

2.1. Population and Sample

Population in this study is manufacturing companies listed in Indonesia Stock Exchange from 2012-2016 with the total of 152 companies. The sample selection used is purposive sampling method using the following criteria: (1) Not delisting during the observation periods, 2012-2016, (2) Using rupiah as the currency during the observation, (3) Earned profits successively during the study period.

2.2. Analytical Method

Regression method used in this research is panel data regression by using path analysis model. The structural equation in this research is as follows:

$$DA = \alpha + \beta_1 KI_{it} + \beta_2 DKI_{it} + \varepsilon_1 \qquad \text{...... (1)}$$

$$ETR = \alpha + \beta_3 KI_{it} + \beta_4 DKI_{it} + \beta_5 DA_{it} + \varepsilon_2 \qquad \text{...... (2)}$$

Notes:

DA = Earnings Management

ETR = Tax Agressiveness

KI = Institutional Ownership

DKI = Independent Board of Commissioners

i = Company - 1

t = Time - t

$\beta_1 - \beta_5$ = Regression coefficient

$\varepsilon_1 - \varepsilon_2$ = error

3. Result and Discussion

Data were analyzed by using panel data regression with path analysis model and to test the effect of mediation used sobel test. The following is the result of testing in this study by using EViews 9.

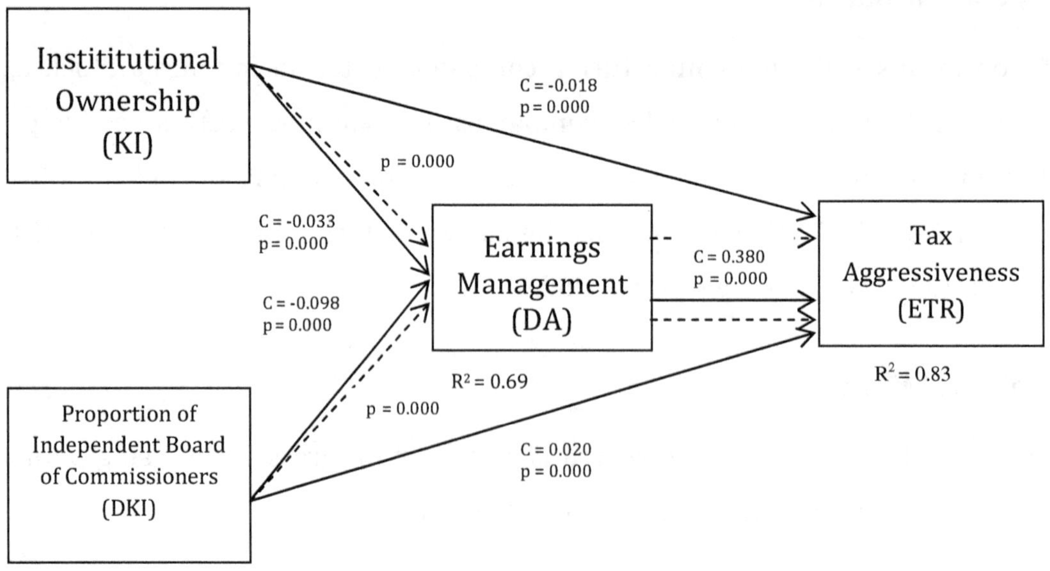

Figure 1. The Test Result

3.1. The Effect of Institutional Ownership on Management Earnings

Test results show that institutional ownership has a negative and significant impact on earnings management. This can be seen from the regression coefficient of institutional ownership showing the negative direction of -0.033 and the level of significance of institutional ownership of 0.000 smaller than 0.05 (α = 5%), which means H_1 accepted. The coefficient of institutional ownership has a negative sign which means that the greater the shares owned by the institutional then they will have the ability to control and supervise the management effectively and have the ability to influence the decisions and policies made by the management to reduce the possibility of occurrence profit management practices (Midiastuty & Mahfoedz, 2003). The results of this study in accordance with the theory of the agency, namely by enlarging the ownership of shares by the institutional then it can reduce the conflicts of interest that occur and opportunistic behavior management that can reduce the practice of earnings management. The results of this study are consistent with the Jao & Pagalung (2011) study indicating that institutional ownership affects earnings management.

3.2. The Effect of Proportion of Independent Board of Commissioners on Earnings Management

The test results show that the proportion of independent board of commissioners has a negative and significant effect on earnings management. This can be seen from the regression coefficient of the proportion of independent board of commissioners showing the negative direction of -0.098 and the level of significance of institutional ownership of 0.000 smaller than 0.05 (α = 5%), which means H_2 is accepted. The coefficient of independent board's proportion has a negative sign which means that the increasing number of independent board of commissioners along with the improved role of the independent board of commissioners, is able to reduce the management's chance to practice earnings management. This is because the greater the composition of the board of independent commissioners, the higher the supervision in the company will be, thus, it will make the manager be more careful and transparent in running the company which will encourage the realization of Good Corporate Governance. The results of this study are consistent with the research of Rahmawati (2013), Prastiti & Meiranto (2013), Jao &

Pagalung (2011) which indicate that the proportion of independent board of commissioners influences earnings management.

3.3. The Effect of Institutional Ownership on Tax Aggressiveness

The results show that institutional ownership has a negative and significant effect on tax aggressiveness. This can be seen from the regression coefficient of institutional ownership showing the negative direction of -0.018 and the level of significance of institutional ownership of 0.000 smaller than 0.05 ($\alpha = 5\%$), which means H_3 accepted. Coefficient value of institutional ownership has a negative sign, which means that if there is an increase in institutional ownership of shares it will decrease the chance of management to act aggressively against taxes. This shows that the size of the shares owned by the institutional will affect the amount of tax burden that must be paid by the company. By increasing institutional ownership, the higher the control of the management will be, thus, it will help to reduce the behavior of management to act aggressively against taxes. The results of this test in accordance with the theory of the agency, namely by increasing the institutional ownership, it can reduce the opportunity to act aggressively against taxes. Companies with higher institutional ownership tend to lower tax aggressiveness than companies with low institutional ownership (Badertscher *et al.*, 2009). The results of this study are consistent with the research of Nugroho & Firmansyah (2017), Hanna & Haryanto (2016), Cahyono *et al.*, (2016), Fadli (2016), Embree (2012), Khurana & Moser (2009) that found an effect of institutional ownership on tax aggressiveness.

3.4. The Effect of Proportion of Independent Board of Commissioners on Tax Aggressiveness

The results show that the proportion of independent board of commissioners has a positive and significant effect on tax aggressiveness. This can be seen from the regression coefficient of the proportion of the board of commissioners showing the positive direction of 0.020 and the significance level of the proportion of independent board of 0.000 that is smaller than 0.05 ($\alpha = 5\%$), which means H_4 is rejected. This is because the result of the research shows that the proportion of independent board of commissioner has a positive effect on tax aggressiveness, meaning that the greater proportion of independent board of commissioners will affect the amount of tax burden to be paid by the company. In this case, the independent board of commissioners has not been able to perform its role well since the independent board of commissioners actually increases the potential for tax aggressiveness due to the lack of oversight function of independent board members, it is assumed that the placement or addition of independent board members merely fulfills formal requirements, the granting of commissioners in Indonesia paid less attention to the competence and integrity of the commissioners, but tended as a tribute or reward only. This is also evidenced by the coefficient value of the proportion of independent board of commissioners that has a positive sign which means that the independent board of commissioners within a company can not dampen or reduce the management's behavior to act aggressively against taxes. The results of this study are consistent with Nugroho & Firmansyah (2017), Prawira (2017), Wulansari (2015), Pranoto & Widagdo (2015), Fadli (2013), Suyanto & Supramono (2012), which show that the proportion of independent board of commissioners influences tax aggressiveness.

3.5. The Effect of Earnings Management on Tax Aggressiveness

The test results show that earnings management has a positive and significant effect on tax aggressiveness. This can be seen from the earnings regression coefficient of earnings shows the positive direction of 0.380 and the level of significance of profit management of 0.000 is smaller than 0.05 (α = 5%), which means H_5 accepted. Coefficient value of earnings management has a positive sign which means that if earnings management practices improve then there is likely to increase the chances of management to act aggressively against taxes. This indicates that the amount of tax burden to be paid by the company is influenced by earnings management practices conducted by the management. Profit management is done for the purpose of tax savings. Effect of earnings management in the form of income decreasing against corporate tax aggressiveness can be explained, as the profit becomes the benchmark to measure the amount of corporate tax burden. Therefore, management will report profits tailored to its objective, namely using accounting options that reduce the income or income decreasing as a form of tax evasion. The results of this study in accordance with the political cost hypothesis in positive accounting theory, i.e. the management tends to manipulate profit in order to avoid government regulation, one of which is to avoid corporate income tax. The results of this study are consistent with Nugroho & Firmansyah (2017), Prawira (2017), Wulansari (2015), Pranoto & Widagdo (2015), Fadli (2013), Suyanto & Supramono (2012) which shows that earnings management has an effect on tax aggressiveness.

3.6. The Effect of Institutional Ownership on Tax Agressiveness through Earnings Management as Intervening Variable

The results of the sixth hypothesis testing (H_6) by using the test sobel show that earnings management is able to mediate the relationship between institutional ownership to tax aggressiveness. This can be seen from the results of the test sobel showing the significance value between the institutional ownership variable, tax aggressiveness, and earnings management, that is 0.000, which is smaller than 0.05 (α = 5%), which means H_6 is accepted. This suggests that the earnings management variable is able to mediate the relationship of institutional ownership to tax aggressiveness. The results of this study can be interpreted that the greater the shares owned by the institutional then it is able to reduce the opportunity of management to do earnings management practices so that if the practice of earnings management can be reduced it also can prevent the management behavior to be aggressive towards taxes.

3.7. The Effect of Proportion of Independent Board of Commissioners on Tax Agressiveness through Earnings Management as Intervening Variable

The results of the seventh hypothesis testing (H_7) show that earnings management is able to mediate the relationship between the proportion of independent board of commissioners to tax aggressiveness. This can be seen from the result of the test that shows the significance value between the independent proportion of board of commissioners, tax aggressiveness, and earnings management, that is 0.000, which is smaller than 0.05 (α = 5%), which means H_7 is accepted. This suggests that the earnings management variable is able to mediate the proportionate relationship of independent board of commissioners to tax aggressiveness. This can be interpreted that the increasing number of independent board of commissioners in a company will increase supervision on the management so that management makes more transparent in disclosure of company information and expected to minimize opportunistic behavior of management in form of earnings management. By minimizing the opportunity to practice earnings management, the profits presented will be in accordance with the actual conditions of the company so that the tax burden of the company will also be in accordance with the existing reality, which means it can reduce tax aggressiveness.

4. Conclusion

The result of regression testing of panel data proves that corporate governance mechanism as measured by institutional ownership and the proportion of independent board of commissioner have a significant negative effect to earnings management. This means that the greater the institutional share of ownership and the increasing number of independent commissioners can reduce the behavior of management to practice earnings management. The result also proves that institutional ownership has a significant negative effect on tax aggressiveness, which means that the greater the institutional share of ownership the more likely it is to reduce aggressive action against taxes. Meanwhile, the proportion of independent board of commissioner has a positive effect on tax aggressiveness, meaning that an increasing number of independent board of commissioners are unable to reduce tax aggressiveness. This study also proves that earnings management has a positive effect on tax aggressiveness, which means that one of the objectives of earnings management practice is to minimize the corporate tax burden or in other words to act aggressively against taxes.

In testing the effect of mediation using a sobel test found that earnings management mediated the institutional ownership relationship and the proportion of independent board of commissioners against tax aggressiveness. The greater the shares owned by the institutional then it will be able to reduce the opportunity of management to make earnings management so that if earnings management practices can be reduced, it will also reduce the behavior of the management to be aggressive towards taxes. Meanwhile, the higher the number of independent board of commissioners, the supervision of the management will also be increased, making management more transparent in the disclosure of company information and expected to minimize the opportunity to make earnings management. By minimizing the opportunity for management to make earnings management then the profits presented will be in accordance with the actual company conditions so that corporate tax burdens will also be in accordance with the existing reality, which means it can reduce to be aggressive towards taxes.

In addition, this study has several limitations and weaknesses, including the proxy of corporate governance used in this study is still limited to two variables, namely institutional ownership and the proportion of independent board of commissioners, and the independent variables used in this study only look in terms of non-financial factors that can affect the aggressiveness of taxes. Further research is expected to add other variables as a proxy of corporate governance mechanisms so as to further enrich the discussion of tax aggressiveness.

References

Armstrong, C. S., Blouin, J. L., Jagolinzer, A. D., & Larcker, D. F. (2012). *Corporate Governance, Incentives, and Tax Avoidance. Working Paper, University of Pennsylvania.*

Badertscher, B., Katz, S. P., & Rego, S. O. (2009). *The Impact of Private Equity Ownership on Corporate Tax Avoidance. Working Papers -- Harvard Business School Division of Research.*

Cahyono, D. D., Andini, R., & Raharjo, K. (2016). Pengaruh Komite Audit, Kepemilikan Institusional, Dewan Komisaris, Ukuran Perusahaan (Size), Leverage (DER) dan Profitabilitas (ROA) Terhadap Tindakan Penghindaran Pajak (Tax Avoidance) Pada Perusahaan Perbankan yang Listing BEI Periode Tahun 2011 - 2013. *Journal Of Accounting*, *2*(2).

Chen, S., Chen, X., & Cheng, Q. (2010). Are Family Firms more Tax Aggressive than Non-family Firms? *Journal of Financial Economics*, *95*(1), 1–56.

Easterbrook, F. H. (1984). Two Agency-Cost Explanations of Dividends. *The American Economic Review*, *74*(4), 650–659.

Embree, J. (2012). The Influence of Institutional Investment on Tax Aggressiveness. *SSRN Electronic Journal*, 1–46.

Fadli, I. (2016). Pengaruh Likuiditas, Leverage, Komisaris Independen, Manajemen Laba, dan Kepemilikan Institusional terhadap Agresivitas Pajak Perusahaan (Studi Pada Perusahaan Manufaktur yang Terdaftar Di Bursa Efek Indonesia Periode 2011-2013).

JOM Fekon, 3(1), 1205–1219.

Frank, M. M., Lynch, L. J., & Rego, S. O. (2009). Tax Reporting Aggressiveness and Its Relation to Aggressive Financial Reporting. *The Accounting Review, 84*(2), 467–496.

Hanna, & Haryanto, M. (2016). Agresivitas Pelaporan Keuangan, Agresivitas Pajak, Tata Kelola Perusahaan dan Kepemilikan Keluarga. *Jurnal Akuntansi, XX*(3), 407–419.

Hashim, H. A., Ariff, A. M., & Amrah, M. R. (2016). Accounting Irregularities and Tax Aggressiveness. *International Journal of Economics, Management and Accounting, 1*, 1–14.

Jao, R., & Pagalung, G. (2011). Corporate Governance, Ukuran perusahaan, dan Leverage Terhadap Manajemen Laba Perusahaan Manufaktur Indonesia. *Akuntansi & Auditing, 8*(1), 43–54.

Jensen, M. C., & Meckling, W. H. (1976). Theory of The Firm: Managerial Behavior, Agency Costs and Ownership Structure. *Journal of Financial Economics, 3*, 305–360.

Kamila, P. A. (2014). Analisis Hubungan Agresivitas Pelaporan Keuangan dan Agresivitas Pajak. *Finance and Banking Journal, 16*(2), 228–245.

Khurana, I. K., & Moser, W. J. (2009). Institutional Ownership and Tax Aggressiveness. *SSRN Electronic Journal*, (573), 0–42.

Kim, K. A., Nofsinger, J. R., & Mohr, D. J. (2010). *Corporate Governance* (3rd editio). Pearson (KNM).

Mahulae, E. E., Pratomo, D., & Nurbaiti, A. (2016). Pengaruh Kepemilikan Institusional, Kepemilikan Manajerial, dan Komite Audit terhadap Tax Avoidance. In *e-Proceeding of Management* (Vol. 3, pp. 1626–1633).

Midiastuty, Pranata Puspa Mahfoedz, M. (2003). Analisis Hubungan Mekanisme Corporate Governance dan Indikasi Manajemen Laba. In *Simposium Nasional Akuntansi VI. IAI.*

Nugroho, S. A., & Firmansyah, A. (2017). Pengaruh Financial Distress, Real Earnings Management, dan Corporate Governance terhadap Tax Aggressiveness. *Journal of Business Administration, 1*(2), 17–36.

Ohnuma, H. (2013). Tax Reporting Aggressiveness, Financial Reporting Aggressiveness, and Multinational Corporate Development-Evidence from Japan -. *SSRN Electronic Journal*, 1–31.

Prakosa, K. B. (2014). Pengaruh Profitabilitas, Kepemilikan Keluarga, dan Corporate

Governance terhadap Penghindaran Pajak di Indonesia. In *Simposium Nasional Akuntansi 17 Mataram, Lombok. Universitas Mataram.*

Pranoto, B. A., & Widagdo, A. K. (2015). Pengaruh Koneksi Politik dan Corporate Governance Terhadap Tax Aggressiveness. In *Seminar Nasional dan The 3rd Call for Syariah Paper* (pp. 472–486).

Prastiti, A., & Meiranto, W. (2013). Pengaruh Karakteristik Dewan Komisaris dan Komite Audit terhadap Manajemen Laba. *Jurnal Akuntansi, 2*(4), 1–12.

Prawira, I. F. A. (2017). Corporate Governance and Tax Aggresiveness, An Evidence on Manufacturing Companies in Indonesia. *International Journal of Accounting and Economics Studies, 5*(2), 134–140.

Rahmawati, H. I. (2013). Pengaruh Good Corporate Governance (GCG) Terhadap Manajemen Laba Pada Perusahaan Perbankan. *Accounting Analysis Journal, 2*(1), 1–10.

Richardson, G., Lanis, R., & Taylor, G. (2014). Financial Distress, Outside Directors and Corporate Tax Aggressiveness Spanning the Global Financial Crisis: An Empirical Analysis. *Journal of Banking and Finance, 52*, 112–129.

Sari, N. W., Pratomo, D., & Yudowati, S. P. (2016). Pengaruh Manajemen Laba Terhadap Agresivitas Pajak. In *e-Proceding of Management* (Vol. 3, pp. 1530–1535).

Scott, W. (2009). *Financial Accounting Theory* (Internatio). New Jersey: Prentice-Hall, Inc.

Suyanto, K. D., & Supramono. (2012). Likuiditas, Leverage , Komisaris Independen, dan Manajemen Laba Terhadap Agresivitas Pajak Perusahaan. *Jurnal Keuangan Dan Perbankan, 16*(2), 167–177.

Tiaras, I., & Wijaya, H. (2015). Pengaruh Likuiditas, Leverage, Manajemen Laba, Komisaris Independen dan Ukuran Perusahaan Terhadap Agresivitas Pajak. *Jurnal Akuntansi, XIX*(3), 380–397.

Watts, R. L., & Zimmerman, J. L. (1986). *Positive Accounting Theory*. New York: Prentice Hall.

Wulansari, R. (2015). Pengaruh Karakteristik Corporate Governance Terhadap Effective Tax Rate (ETR) (Studi Empiris Pada Perusahaan Perbankan yang Terdaftar di BEI Tahun 2011-2013). *Jom FEKON, 2*(2), 1–15.

2

Effect of Ownership Structure on Financial Performance of Listed Insurance Firms in Nigeria

Ohiani Danjuma Lawal[a] Eniola Samuel Agbi[b] Lateef O. Mustapha[c]

[a] Corresponding Author, Department of Accounting and Management, Nigerian Defence Academy, Kaduna, Nigeria, ohianidanjuma@gmail.com
[b] Department of Accounting and Management, Nigerian Defence Academy, Kaduna, Nigeria
[c] Department of Accounting and Management, Nigerian Defence Academy, Kaduna, Nigeria

Keywords
Ownership Structure, Financial Performance, Insurance Firms, Nigerian Stock Exchange.

Abstract
The study examines the effect of ownership structure on financial performance of listed insurance firms in Nigeria. Data was collected from the annual reports of 28 insurance firms listed in the Nigerian Stock Exchange for the periods of 2011 to 2016. The ex-post facto was employed by the study to examine the effect of ownership structure on financial performance of listed insurance firms in Nigeria. In addition to the descriptive statistics and correlation, multiple regression technique through panel data methodology was applied for model estimation. Data were subjected to pooled General Least Square, Fixed Effects, and Random Effects regression model to test the hypotheses of the study. Ownership structure proxied by managerial ownership, institutional ownership, and ownership concentration were adopted as independent variables. Firm financial performance as the dependent variables was proxied by Book value per Share. This study found ownership structure having significant positive effect on financial performance of the listed insurance firms except concentrated ownership with negative effect. However, in respect of size and growth of the firms, which form the control variables of the study, there were mixed evidence of their effects on financial performance. The study recommends that in order to enhance the financial performance, insurance firms in Nigeria should increase management equity-holding in the firms as this can stimulate the managers to maximize their efficiency and create more wealth for stakeholders.

1. Introduction

The financial performance of many organizations has been largely linked to their ownership structure over time as it provides funding through owner's equity. Normally, every business organization is saddled with the responsibility of making returns. This responsibility is important since the ability of a firm to make returns in the competitive market determines to a large extend its ability to survive in the future. Jensen and Meckling (1976) defined financial performance as a tool that measures how well a company uses its resources in generating profit thus make it a vital tool to several stakeholders in a company. Financial performance therefore is crucial to any business organization's survival and continuous patronage by investors, potential investors, creditors, and other stakeholders in the business world.

However, the type of ownership structure a firm adopts is engineered by the vision of the company. According to Jensen and Meckling (1976), ownership structure is defined by the distribution of equity with regards to votes and capital as well as the identity of the equity owners. Therefore, ownership structure of any company has been a serious factor for company's financial performance. The effect of managerial, institutional, and concentrated ownership on firm's financial performance measured by Book value per Share has been issue the researcher in the existing literature with mixed results. This has been widely tackled in the developed climes and more recently in emerging economies, but was less discussed in Nigeria context.

On top of the conflicting viewpoint, there has been very little interest on the ownership structure on financial performance of the insurance firms in Nigerian. The few studies in this area in Nigeria are those of Ibrahim (2012) and Benjamin, Love and Dandago (2014) that focused on the effect of managerial and institutional shareholding components of ownership structure on financial performance of the listed insurance firms between the periods 2001-2010. This study, however fill gap in literature by not only adding concentrated ownership on financial performance measured by Book value per Share of the listed insurance firms in the Nigerian Stock Exchange but also extend the work to cover most recent years of 2011-2016. This study therefore examines the effect of ownership structure on financial performance of the listed insurance firms in Nigeria from the period of 2011 to 2016. In order to achieve this objective, the following stated null hypothesis is formulated and tested:

Ho_1: Managerial ownership has no positive effect on the financial performance of the listed insurance firms in Nigeria.

Ho_2: Institutional ownership has no positive effect on the financial performance of the listed insurance firms in Nigeria.

Ho_3: Ownership concentration has no positive effect on the financial performance of the listed insurance firms in Nigeria.

Section 2 of this study reviews previous empirical literature on the effect of ownership structure on financial performance, the third section deals with the methodology that was adopted for the study. Section 4 presents the analysis of results, while the fifth section covers the conclusion and recommendations made by the researchers.

2. Literature Review

Concept of Ownership Structure

According to Jensen and Meckling (1976), ownership structure is described by the distribution of equity with respect to votes, capital, and also by the equity owners' identity. This was referenced in their study on how the nature of agency costs relates with equity where they aimed at incorporating concepts into the beginnings of a theory of corporate ownership structure. In the recent years, there have been renewed interests on ownership structures due to the increased dynamics of corporate ownership portfolios. Ownership structure, as a mechanism in corporate governance to facilitate increased efficiency of a firm, has been believed to have affected firm performance. For example, Adam Smith (1776) points out that the joint-stock companies are less efficient than private co-partner companies because the directors would not watch over other people's money" with the same anxious vigilance" as their own. Transaction cost theory considers a firm as an offer of contracts where the activities are cheaper internal than external. However, inside of the firm, there are conflicts between different parties. The principal-agent theory mentions the conflict between shareholders and management. The conflict is led by the different agendas of shareholders and managers, more specifically, the divergence between the control right and cash flow right. Therefore, ownership structure in this study includes managerial, institutional, and concentrated ownership.

i. Managerial Ownership

Managerial ownership refers to an ownership fraction or stake in a firm that is held by managers. Managerial ownership is not only meant to increase the equity of the organization but also to serve as incentives to managers to align managers' interests with those of the interests of the organization. Managerial ownership is measured by natural logarithm of equity held by managers as shareholders in a firm.

ii. Institutional Ownership

Institutional ownership refers to an ownership fraction or stake in a firm that is held by large financial organizations, pension funds or endowments. Institutions generally purchase large blocks of a firm's outstanding shares and can exert considerable influence upon its management. Therefore, institutional shareholders are usually professionals and they normally use their expertise in monitoring the management in ensuring that their interests align with those of the organization's interests. Institutional ownership is measured by natural logarithm of equity held by various institutions as investors in the firm.

iii. Ownership Concentration

Ownership concentration refers to an ownership fraction or stake in a firm that is held by shareholders with the controlling interest or with large stake. Ownership concentration affords the shareholders the motivation and ability to monitor and control management decisions. Therefore, concentrated shareholders use their large stake in reducing conflicts between managers and the organization by being more proactive in monitoring and protecting their investments. Ownership concentration is measured by natural logarithm of equity held by block holders as investors in the firm.

Concept of Financial Performance

Financial performance measures how well a firm uses its resources to make a profit and it is a vital tool to several stakeholders in a firm. These stakeholders include trade creditors, bond holders, investors, employees, and management. Each group has its own interest in tracking the financial performance of a firm. Analysts learn about financial performance from published annual reports. The report is a required legal document that must be published by all public firms. The purpose of the report is to provide stakeholders with accurate and reliable financial statements that provide an overview of the firm's financial performance. Financial performance can be measured in several ways. Some of them are Book Value per Share, Earnings per Share, Return on Assets, Dividend per Share, Return on Equity, etc. Therefore, financial performance in this study is measured in term of Book Value per Share. The justification for chosen Book Value per Share as measure of financial performance by this study is because effect of ownership structure has been tested on several other financial indicators as mentioned earlier on insurance firms in Nigeria with the exception of BPS.

Book Value per Share (BPS)

BPS is the shareholders' fund divide by the ordinary shares in issue and is expressed in naira or kobo. It indicates how much shareholder's fund attributable to every share of the firm. Shareholders' fund is a function of how effective and efficient money invested in the firm by shareholders are utilized. It helps in evaluating management commitment to wealth creation for shareholders. BPS is a combination of share capital, share premium, retained earnings, general reserve, and deposit for share.

Empirical Literature

The effect of ownership structure on financial performance has been widely researched and it produced very interesting debate in financial literature. The study focuses on some of the empirical studies conducted both locally and internationally on the effects of ownership structure on financial performance. Mwathi (2009) studied on the effects of commercial banks' financial performance and their ownership structure. She categorized them as private banks, government banks, foreign banks, and domestic banks. Using regression analysis, the study was centered on banks where the top 10 shareholders hold more than 50% of the shares for the period between 2004 and 2008 in Kenya. Using ROA as the financial performance measure, the study revealed that bank ownership structure had an insignificant positive influence on financial performance. The findings also showed that both private and state owned banks had a negative correlation with performance. She underscored that both banks that are foreign owned and those owned domestically had a positive correlation with performance. The study hypothesized that commercial banks owned by states perform dismally than the foreign or domestic commercial banks. The study concluded that widely held banks perform well than closely held ones.

Demsetz and Lehn (1985) provided evidence of the endogeneity of large US firm's ownership structure using a linear regression of an accounting measure of profit. In that model, the accounting measure of profit rate was assumed as a fraction of shares owned by the five largest shareholding interests and on a set of control variables in which ownership structure is treated as an endogenous variable. Their empirical study found no evidence of the relationship between profit rate and ownership concentration. Morck, Shleifer, and Vishny (1988) ignored the endogeneity issue altogether and re-examined the relation between corporate ownership structure and performance using Tobin's Q and accounting profit rate as alternative measures of performance. They found no significant relation in the linear regressions they estimated.

Demsetz and Villanonga (2001) in a research titled "ownership structure and firm performance," examined the effect of ownership structure of shareholders and firm performance in a sample including 233 companies in the United States. Demsetz and Villanonga hypothesized that the ownership is considered as multidimensional and as an endogenous variable, found no meaningful statistical relation between the ownership structure and performance of the firm. As it is said by these researchers, the results of this research conformed to this point of view that, while the unfocused ownership may lead to aggravate the agency problem but it has benefits which may solve too much problems (Demsetz & Villanonga, 2001). Lemmon and Lins (2003) used a sample of 800 firms in eight East Asian countries to study the effect of ownership structure on value during the region's financial crisis. The crisis negatively impacted firm's investment opportunities, raising the incentives of controlling shareholders to expropriate minority investors. The evidence is consistent with the view that ownership structure plays an important role in determining whether insiders expropriate minority shareholders.

Additionally, using a sample of 144 Israeli firms, Lauterbach and Tolkowsky (2004) found that Tobin's Q is maximized when control group vote reaches 67%. This evidence is strong when ownership structure is treated as exogenous and weak when it is considered endogenous. Kaserer and Moldenhauer (2005) addressed the question whether there is any empirical relationship between corporate performance and insider ownership. Using a data set of 245 Germen firms for the year 2003, they found evidence for a positive and significant relationship between corporate performance, as measured by stock price performance as well as by Tobin's Q and insider ownership. Mueller and Spitz (2006) analyzed the relationship between managerial ownership and performance of German SMEs with motivational hypothesis testing in their research. They used a sample of 356 firms in services sector that are associated with business in their research, for the years 1997 to 2000. The findings showed that performance of companies with managerial ownership percentage, above 40 percent, is being improved (Mueller & Spitz, 2006).

Karamu (2008) in the research entitled "Relationship between institutional owners and informational content of profit" collected evidences in connection with the supervisory role of institutional investors from the perspective that whether institutional ownership as effect on the informational content of reported profit. In this research, the different attitudes (the active monitoring hypothesis and the self-interest hypothesis) were examined about institutional investors. To test the relationship between informational content of corporate profit and institutional ownership, two models of multiple linear regressions were used. Based on the results of this research, the number of institutional ownership does not increase informational content of profit and may also degrade it, while the level of institutional ownership does not reduce the informational content of profit, but it is also possible to increase it (Karamu, 2008).

Numazu and Karamu (2008) analyzed the "impact of ownership structure on corporate performance of listed companies in Tehran Stock Exchange (TSE)". The main hypothesis of this research emphasized the existence of a significant relationship between ownership structure and performance. Research sample included 66 companies during 1382 and 1386. Statistical method used to test hypotheses in this research was "panel data". In this research, the ownership structure is divided into two institutional and private ownership categories that the private ownership also is divided into three categories including corporate, management, and external shareholders. The findings of this research indicated that there is a negative and meaningful relation between institutional ownership and firm performance and a positive and meaningful relation between the corporate ownership and firm performance. Managerial ownership has a negative meaningful influence on the performance and in the case of private ownership, no information indicating the ownership of external investors was observed in the sample companies. In the private ownership, it is also better that the main part of ownership is held by corporate investors. In general, there is a meaningful relation between the ownership structure and performance of the companies (Namazu & Karamu, 2008).

Alireza, Ali, and Kazem (2011) examined the effect of ownership structure on firm performance of listed firms in Tehran Stock Exchange between the period of 2001 and 2006. Using regression analysis, the study found that ownership concentration doesn't have any significant effect on firm performance but the effects of two other variables are significant: institutional ownership has positive and significant effect on firm performance whereas concentrated institutional ownership is negative. Abosede and Kajola (2011) investigated the relationship between firms' ownership structure and financial performance of listed companies in Nigeria between 2001 and 2008 respectively. Employing pooled OLS as a method of estimation and after controlling for four firm-specific characteristics, they found negative and significant relationship between ownership structure (director shareholding) and firm financial performance measured by ROE.

Ibrahim (2012) examined the effects of ownership structure on the financial performance of listed companies on the Nigerian Stock Exchange with the first finding showing a significant negative relationship between institutional ownership and firm financial performance measured in term of ROA and BPS and of course the second finding showed a significant positive effect between insider ownership and firm performance with firm growth as control variable having negative effect. Davis (2014) evaluated the effects of ownership structure on the financial performance of commercial banks in Kenya for the period 2009 and 2013. Using regression analysis, the study found that ownership structure positively affects the financial performance of commercial banks in Kenya.

Benjamin, Love, and Dandago (2014) examined the impact of ownership structure on the financial performance of listed insurance firms in Nigeria and they found a positive relationship between ownership structure and firm's performance measured by ROA and ROE for the period 2001 and 2010. Anthony (2014) investigated the effect of ownership structure on financial performance of listed companies in the Nairobi Securities Exchange during the period 2008 to 2013. Employing linear regression analysis, the study found a positive effect of ownership concentration on financial performance measured by ROE. Also, a positive effect of ownership identity on financial performance was identified.

Reem, Allam, and Wajeeh (2015) assessed the relationship between ownership structure dimensions and corporate performance of 42 out of 48 listed companies in Bahrain for the period 2007 and 2011. The first finding showed that ownership concentration has a negative relationship on company's performance measured by ROA and Tobin's Q. Second finding showed that institutional ownership has a positive relationship on company's performance. While the third finding showed that managerial ownership found a significance positive relationship with company's performance.

Stanley (2015) assessed the impact of ownership structure on financial performance of listed Chinese banks between the periods 2005-2013. Using correlation analysis, the results revealed that there is no significant difference in performance between the two types of ownership structure (state-owned and joint venture).Helen and Bature (2016) evaluated the impact of ownership structure on the financial performance of listed conglomerate firms in Nigeria from the year 2004 to 2013. Using regression analysis, they found a negative impact of both managerial and foreign ownership and financial performance measured by Earning per Share (EPS) within the study period, while firm size as control variable positively impacted the firms Earnings per Share.

Abdul (2016) examined the impact of ownership structure on firm performance in India in terms of textiles, oil marketing and distribution, and movies and entertainment industries registered in Bombay Stock Exchange (BSE). The research was carried out on 50 companies listed under BSE covering the period of 2011-2015. Using correlation statistical analysis, the study found that ownership structure measured by managerial, concentrate, institutional, and foreign shareholding has influence on companies' financial performance measured by ROA. Saseela and Thirunavukkarasu (2017) investigated the relationship between ownership structure and financial performance of listed beverage food and tobacco companies in Sri Lanka from the period of 2010 to 2015. The study also examined the impact of ownership structure on financial performance. Using Pearson's correlation and regression analysis, the results revealed that the ownership concentration and foreign ownership structure are positively correlated with the financial performance of the companies measured by Return on Equity (ROE). The study also found a significant impact of foreign ownership structure on financial performance.

Finally, the findings of the foreign studies are very vital only that, differences in political and economic conditions among the nations may hardly allow their findings applicable to Nigeria. However, the last review on this area was those of Benjamin, Love, and Dandago (2014) with a dataset ranges from 2001-2010, whereas this study is considering the review from 2011-2016 which earlier identified as gap in chapter one to be filled by this study by extending the year of assessment to 2016, a period considered most relatively current.

Theoretical Review

The Agency Theory

The agency theory was developed by Jensen and Meckling (1976). The theory states the relationship between principals such as shareholders, and agents such as a firm's senior managers. The principal delegates work to an agent. The theory attempts to deal with first, the agency problem where there is a conflict of interests between a firm's managers and firm's stockholders, and second, that the principal and agent settle for different risk tolerances. Therefore, there are two main agency relationships in a firm that are normally in conflicts; those between the firm's managers and stockholders and between the stockholders and the debt-holders. These agency conflicts have implications on corporate governance and business ethics. Such relationships have expensive agency costs that are incurred so as to sustain an effective agency relationship. Incentive fees paid to agents to encourage behavior consistent with the principal's goals are common examples of agency costs (Bowie & Edward, 1992).

One of the ways of reducing agency problems is debt financing which helps those problems that are normally related to free cash-flow and asymmetric information problems especially in the case of privately held debt. Secondly, conflicts of interests between managers and shareholders also arise from the divisions between ownership and control. Managerial ownership can align the interests between them and owners, hence; reduce the total agency costs. The relationship between managerial ownership and agency costs is linear and the optimal point for the firm is achieved when the managers acquire all of the shares of the company according to Jensen and Meckling (1976). Thirdly, ownership concentration is the other option of reducing agency costs by shareholders proactively taking active roles in monitoring. This is however dependent on the amounts of their equity stakes. The more the investor's stake, the more motivated they are to monitor and protect their investment according to Gilson and Lang (1990).

According to Aggrawal and Knoeber (1996), agents such as company managers will highly unlikely venture into behaviors that are strictly profit maximizing where shareholders are not strictly monitoring their activities. The implication therefore is that, if owner-controlled firms are highly performing than manager-controlled firms, the assumption is that concentrated ownership of insurance firms provides better monitoring which leads to better performance. Among the previous studies that adopted agency theory in explaining the effect of ownership structure on financial performance are those of Jensen and Meckling (1976), Benjamin, Love, and Dandago (2014), Helen and Bature (2016).

3. Methodology

The study adopts ex-post factor research design to examine the effect of ownership structure on financial performance of listed insurance firms in Nigeria. The population of this study is the listed insurance firms on the Nigerian Stock Exchange as at 31st December, 2016. As at the time of this study, there are 28 listed insurance firms in Nigeria. The entire population of the study was used based on the condition that the firms have complete data in their published annual reports for the periods under study. Multiple regression technique is used to analyze the panel data gathered for ownership structure and financial performance of listed insurance firms in Nigeria by means of STATA 12. A regression shows the effects one variable called independent has on the other variable called dependent which can either be positive or negative. The GLS regression is run to produce statistics for the coefficient of determination and f-test as well as t-test for results interpretation. The coefficient of determination (R^2) measures the explanatory power of the Independent Variables on the Dependent Variables. T-Test measures the individual significance of the estimated Independent Variables, while F-Test measures the overall significance.

Hausman's test is used to decide between the fixed effect and random effect estimates of the coefficients when there is present of heteroscedasticity in the results. Diagnostics test conducts by the study includes variance inflation factor (VIF) to test for multicolinearity which could mislead the results of the study. Hettest to test the error variances among variables so as the disturbances that could be appearing in the sampled firms are homoscedastics. The multiple regression model employed to determine the effect of ownership structure on the financial performance of listed insurance firms in Nigeria is as shown below:-

$$BPS_{it} = \alpha_0 + \beta_1 MGROWN_{it} + \beta_2 INSTOWN_{it} + \beta 3OWNCONCit + \beta_4 SIZE_{it} + \beta_5 GROWTH_{it} + \mu_{it}$$

MGROWN = Managerial Ownership, measured by natural log of equity held by managers.

INSTOWN = Institutional Ownership, measured by natural log of equity held by institutions.

OWNCONC = Ownership Concentration, measured by natural log of equity held by individuals with block vote.

SIZE = Firm Size, measured by natural log of total assets.

GROWTH = Firm Growth, measured by natural log of increase in total assets.

BPS = Book Value per Share, measured by shareholder's fund divided by ordinary shares.

α_0= Constant or Intercept;

β_1 - β_3= Coefficient of the explanatory Variables;

β_4 - β_5= Coefficient of control variables;

μ_{it} = error term of firm i for time period t;

it = firm i for time period t.

A priori expectations are $\beta_1, \beta_2, \beta_3, \beta_4, \ldots\ldots\ldots\ldots\ldots \beta_5$.

Theoretically, there are expectations of MGROWN, INSTOWN, OWNCONC, SIZE, and GROWTH, having no positive effect on BPS respectively.

4. Results and Discussion

Table 1 below presents the descriptive statistics of all the variables. The MGROWN, INSTOWN, and OWNCONC which are the proxies of ownership structure, range between minimum of 5.8982, 8.6358, 8.2842 and maximum of 9.3046, 9.7169, 9.5308 within the timeframe.

Table 1: Summary of Descriptive Statistics of the Variables

Variables	*Observations*	*Means*	*Std. Dev.*	*Minimum*	*Maximum*
BPS	168	0.8157	0.6357	1.6439	3.547
MGROWN	168	8.3085	0.6765	5.8982	9.3046
INSTOWN	168	9.2384	0.2635	8.6358	9.7169
OWNCONC	168	9.0744	0.2632	8.2842	9.5308
SIZE	168	10.0015	0.3413	8.807	10.8997
GROWTH	168	5.5684	6.9067	9.7382	10.333

Source: Descriptive Statistic Results Using STATA 12

From the Table above, the mean BPS of the firms over the year amounted to about N82 with minimum value of N164 and maximum value of N355 respectively. The standard deviation of about N64 shows the wide disparity in terms of ownership of the firms over the years. The table shows that the firms have a mean SIZE of about N1000 over the years under investigation. This shows that firms have enough assets to generate profit for the firms and owners of equity. The standard deviation of 34% indicates that there is considerable variation in the financial performance of the firms during the period under investigation. While some firms performed well and consistently reported good results, others performed poorly as they reported losses for some years. Also, the table shows that firms enjoy a mean GROWTH of about 6% over the period under study with a standard deviation of 7% showing the variation in the financial performance.

Table 2 shows the correlation between the dependent and independent variables. As evidenced from the table, the correlation coefficients are averagely good with highest 0.5232, which is the correlation between firm size and financial performance.

Table 2: Summary of Correlation Matrix of the Variables

	BPS	*MGROWN*	*INSTOWN*	*OWNCONC*	*SIZE*	*GROWTH*
BPS	1.0000					
MGROWN	0.0512	1.0000				
INSTOWN	0.0900	0.2037	1.0000			
OWNCONC	0.0779	0.4119	0.6372	1.0000		
SIZE	0.5232	0.4267	0.4072	0.5381	1.0000	
GROWTH	0.3802	0.1815	0.3047	0.2762	0.4401	1.0000

Source: Correlation Matrix Results Using STATA 12

Table 2 displays the correlation values between dependent and independent variables and also the relationship within the independent variables themselves. The values were gotten from the Pearson correlation.

The Table shows that there are positive relationships between the dependent variables measured by Book value per Share (BPS) and the independent variables measured by managerial ownership (MGROWN), institutional ownership (INSTOWN), and Ownership Concentration (OWNCONC). Positive relationships also occur within the independent variables themselves. Positive relationships equally found between the control variables and other variables of the study.

The Table 3 below presents the regression results. The coefficients of the independent variables (MGROWN, INSTOWN, OWNCONC, SIZE, GROWTH) which explain the power of ownership structure on financial performance alongside the probability values are provided in the table. The table also provides the analysis on the relationships between the dependent and the independent variables. The relationships within the variables themselves were also shown on the table as well as the overall relationship.

Table 3: Summary of Regression Results

Variables	*Coefficients*	*Standard Error*	*t-test*	*Significant values*
Constant	-5.1688	2.5269	-2.05	0.043
MGROWN	0.0324	0.1512	0.21	0.831
INSTOWN	1.7281	0.6775	2.55	**0.012**
OWNCONC	-1.3391	0.6216	-2.15	**0.033**
SIZE	0.1870	0.1896	0.99	0.326
GROWTH	0.0058	0.0044	1.31	0.191
R-Squared	0.3843			
Adjusted R-Squared	0.3653			
Durbin Watson	1.65			
F-Statistic	0.0000			

Source: Output of data analysis by author using STATA 12

The cumulative R^2 Overall (0.3843) which is the multiple coefficient of determination gives the proportion of the total variation in the dependent variable explained by the independent variables jointly. Hence, it signifies that 38% of the total variation in Book value per Share of listed insurance firms in Nigeria was caused by their managerial, institutional, and concentrated ownership respectively. Also, the regression results provided that Adjusted R^2 is 0.3653 (see appendix I). This means that ownership structure of the listed insurance firms contributes about 37% to firm's financial performance measured by BPS of the organization. This finding provides valid support of the contention that ownership structure can bring about a competitive advantage for a firm.

Discussion of Regression Results

Managerial Ownership and Financial Performance: The regression results revealed that the managerial ownership as depicted in Table 3 has a coefficient value of 0.0324 with a p-value of 0.831 which is insignificant at 5%. This indicates that managerial ownership though positive but insignificantly affected the Book value per Share of the listed insurance firms in Nigeria. This implies that for every one naira proportionate increase in managerial ownership of the firms, the BPS of the listed insurance firms in Nigeria will increase by 0.03 naira. This finding is in line with the studies of Benjamin, Love, and Dandago (2014).

Institutional Ownership and Financial Performance: The institutional ownership as depicted in table 3 above has a beta value of 1.7281 with a p-value of 0.012 which is significant at 5% significant level. This indicates that institutional ownership has positively and significantly affected the BPS of the listed insurance firms in Nigeria. This implies that for every one naira proportionate increase in institutional ownership of the firms under investigation, the BPS will increase by 1.73 naira. This finding is however in line with those of Reem, Allam, and Wajeeh (2015) and Numazu and Karamu (2008).

Ownership Concentration and Financial Performance: The concentrated ownership as depicted in table 3 above has a coefficient value of -1.3391 with a p-value of 0.033 which is significant at 0.05 level of significant. This indicates that institutional ownership is negatively and significantly affected the BPS of the listed insurance firms in Nigeria. This implies that for every one naira proportionate increase in ownership concentration of the firms under investigation, the BPS will decrease by 1.34 naira. This finding is however in line with those of Reem, Allam, and Wajeeh (2015) and Numazu and Karamu (2008).

The Hausman test: In ensuring greater results credibility and reliability, Hausman test was conducted by the researcher to decide between fixed effect and random effect. The results obtained from the Hausman test conducted indicate that fixed effect was decided against random effect (See Appendix I for the results).

5. Conclusion and Recommendations

Based on the empirical analysis, the researchers conclude that both managerial and institutional shareholding should be prioritized against block-holding (concentrated ownership) by insurance firms in Nigeria as this can increase the financial performance of the firms under investigation. This confirms to economic criterion, and could be supported by the work of Ibrahim (2012); he opined that an increase in managerial and institutional ownership could lead to an increase in the financial performance of an organization due to positive effects shown by his empirical analysis. It is therefore concluded that, organization's financial performance is dependent upon its managerial and institutional ownership structures as high managerial shareholding can stimulate management of an organization towards increased efficiency. Therefore, ownership by managers may be seen as a system of aligning the interests of managers with those of the shareholders in a way that enhances corporate performance.

However, this form of managerial ownership can also lead to entrenchment of managers, which is costly when they chose to pursue their self interests against the interest of the organization. It has been argued that the overall effect of managerial ownership on firm performance depends on how well the entrenchment effect and incentive alignment are balanced (Cubbin & Leech, 1982; Hansmann, 1988, 1996; Hill & Jones, 1982; Nickel, 1997). The findings therefore, suggest that when managers also double up as shareholders, they are motivated to work towards realization of the wealth creation objective of the shareholders of whom they are part. On the other hand, managers who are not shareholders are more likely to engage in insider dealings as a way of enhancing their personal wealth and prestige. The institutional ownership which has also been identified in the study to have shown positive effect on firms' financial performance was as a result of the fact that institutional investors are more sophisticated than other shareholders because they are more professional regarding capital markets, industries, and businesses and they are better informed. Apart from that, institutional shareholders have higher capabilities in taking actions and can therefore monitor managers more effectively and less costly (Hand, 1990).

From the conclusion drawn, it is imperative to recommend that:

1) there is dire need to reasonably increase managers' shareholding of the listed insurance firms in Nigeria as not only meant to increase the equity of the firms but as a way of motivating them towards increasing their operational efficiency. At the same time, the managers should be protected by the Board of Directors from unnecessary direct interference by other shareholders.

2) the institutional ownership is one of the identified ownership structures that has proven empirically positive to firm's financial performance in this study. This was linked by the researcher to the fact that institutional owners frequently deploy their professionalism and wealth of experience to the firms towards meeting corporate goals. Therefore, the institution ownership should be increased against concentrated ownership for better performance.

References

Abdul B. (2016). An assessment of the impact of ownership structure on firm performance in India. *Journal of Accounting and Financial Reporting, 4,* 345-476.

Abosede, A. J. & Kajola, S. O. (2011). An examination of the relationship between firms' Ownership structure and financial performance of listed companies in Nigeria. *Journal of Corporate Ownership and Control, 8,* 276-400.

Agrawal, A., & Knoeber, C. R. (1996). Firm performance and mechanisms to control agency problems between managers and shareholders. *Journal of Financial and Quantitative Analysis, 3,* 377-469

Alireza, F., Ali, T. H. & Kazem, M. (2011). An examination of effect of ownership structure on performance of listed firms in Tehran Stock Exchange. *Journal of Business and Management, 6,* 112-265

Anthony A. (2014). An investigation of effect of ownership structure on financial performance of listed companies in Nairobi Securities Exchange. *Journal of Accounting and Financial Reporting, 5,* 213-369

Benjamin, K. G., Love, O. A., & Dandago, K. I. (2014). The impact of ownership structure on the financial performance in Nigerian Insurance Firms. *Journal of Academic Research in Accounting, Finance, and Management Sciences, 4,* 409-416.

Berle, A. A., & Means, G. C. (1932). *The Modern Corporation and Private Property.* New York: Macmillan.

Cho, M. H. (1998). Ownership structure, investment and the corporate value: An empirical analysis. *Journal of Financial Economics, 47,* 103-121.

Claessens, S., & Djankov, S. (1999). Ownership concentration and corporate Performance in the Czech Republic. *Journal of Comparative Economics, 4,* 498-513.

Claessens, S., Djankov, S., & Lang, L. H. P. (2000). The separation of ownership and control in East Asian corporations. *Journal of Financial Economics, 58,* 81-112.

Coffee, J. C. (2005). A theory of corporate scandals: Why the U.S. and Europe differ. Columbia Law and Economics Working Paper No. 274.

Cubbin, & Leeh (1983). Manager-and owner-controlled companies and profitability. *Journal of Corporate Finance, 5,* 122-231.

Cyrus, W.N. (2013). Determinants of commercial banks profitability in Kenya: the case of Kenyan quoted banks. Unpublished MBA Project, University of Nairobi.

Davis, O. O. (2014). The effects of ownership structure on the financial performance of Kenyan listed commercial banks. Unpublished Research Project, University of Nairobi.

Dadson, S. (2012). Concentrated share ownership and financial performance of listed companies in Ghana. *Journal of corporate finance, 38,* 235-364.

Demsetz, H. (1983). The structure of ownership and the theory of the firm. *Journal of Law and Economics, 26,* 375-390.

Demsetz, H., & Villalonga, B. (2001). Ownership structure and corporate performance *Journal of Corporate Finance, 7,* 209-233.

Demsetz, H., & Lehn, K. (1985). The structure of corporate ownership: Causes and consequences. *Journal of Political Economy, 93,* 1155-1177.

Denis, D. K., & McConnell, J. J. (2003). International corporate governance. *Journal of Financial and Quantitative Analysis, 38,* 1-36.

Dlugosz, J., Fahlenbrach, R., Gompers, P., & Metrick, A. (2006). Large blocks of stock: Prevalence, size, and measurement. *Journal of Corporate Finance, 12,* 594-618.

Earle, J. S., Kucsera, C., & Telegdy, Á. (2005). Ownership concentration and corporate performance on the Budapest Stock Exchange: Do too many cooks spoil the goulash. *Corporate Governance, 13,* 254-264.

Ezazi, R. (2011). The effect of ownership structure on share price volatility of listed firms in Tehran Stock Exchange. *Journal of Corporate Finance, 4,* 122-231.

Fama, E. F., & Jensen, M. C. (1983). Separation of ownership and control. *Journal of Law and Economics, 26,* 301-325.

Grossman, S. J., & Hart, O. D. (1986). The costs and benefits of ownership: A theory of vertical and lateral integration. *Journal of Political Economy, 94,* 691-719.

Helen, A. A., & Bature, M. D. (2016).The impact of ownership structure on the financial performance of Nigerian listed conglomerate firms. Unpublished research paper in Kaduna State University. *The Business and Management Review, 7,*110-216.

Himmelberg, C. P., Hubbard, R. G., & Palia, D. (1999). Understanding the determinants of managerial ownership and the link between ownership and performance. *Journal of Financial Economics, 53,* 353-384.

Holderness, C. G. (2003). A survey of block-holders and corporate control. FRBNY Economic Policy Review, 9, 51-64.

Holderness, C. G., Kroszner, R. S., & Sheehan, D. P. (1999). Were the good old days that good? Changes in managerial stock ownership since the great depression. *Journal of Finance, 5,* 435-469.

Holderness, C., & Sheehan, D. (1988). The role of majority shareholders in publicly held corporations: An exploratory analysis. *Journal of Financial Economics, 20,* 317-346.

Ibrahim, R. (2012).The effect of ownership structure on the financial performance of listed companies in Nigeria. *Journal of Accounting and Finance, 5,* 213-298.

Jensen, M., & Meckling, W. (1976). Theory of the firm: Managerial behavior, agency costs, and ownership structure. *Journal of Financial Economics, 3,* 305-360.

Jensen, M. (1986). Agency costs of free cash flow, corporate finance and takeovers, American Economic Review, 76, 323-492.

Johnson, S., La Porta, R., Lopez-de-Silanes, F., & Shleifer, A. (2000). Tunneling. American Economic Review, 90, 22-27.

Karamu,K. (2008). Institutional ownership and profitability of listed Tehran firms in Tehran Stock Exchange. *Journal of Accounting and Finance, 4,* 213-237.

Kaserer, & Moldenhaner (2005). Insider ownership and corporate performance of listed German firms. *Journal of Corporate Finance, 4,* 101-214.

Kiruri, J. (2013). The effect of ownership structure on banks profitability in Kenya. *Journal of Accounting and Finance, 6,* 112-186.

Kole, S. R. (1995). Measuring managerial equity ownership: A comparison of sources of ownership data. *Journal of Corporate Finance, 1,* 413-435.

La Porta, P., Lopez-de-Silanes, F., & Shleifer, A. (1999). Corporate ownership around the world. *Journal of Finance, 54,* 471-517.

Lehmann, & Weigand (2000). Effect of large shareholders on profitability in Germany. An empirical analysis. *Journal of Accounting and Finance, 8,* 342-376.

Lins, K. (2002).Equity ownership and firm value in emerging markets, working paper, University of Utah.

Mueller, & Spitz (2006). Managerial ownership and financial performance of listed German SMEs. *Journal of Corporate Finance, 2,* 231-253.

Mwathi, H. (2009). Effect of commercial banks' financial performance and their ownership structure in Kenya. *Journal of Corporate Finance, 3,* 126-265.

McConnell, J., & Servaes, H. (1990). Additional evidence on equity ownership and corporate value. *Journal of Financial Economics, 27,* 595-612.

Morck, R., Shleifer, A., & Vishny, R. (1988). Management ownership and market valuation An empirical analysis. *Journal of Financial Economics, 20,* 293-315.

Numan, & Karamu (2008). Impact of ownership structure on corporate performance of listed companies in Tehran Stock Exchange, Tehran. *Journal of Corporate Finance, 2,* 123-214.

Ongore, Obonyo, & Martin (2011). The implication of shareholder types on the financial performance. *Journal of Accounting and Finance, 2,* 101-211.

Pedersen, T., & Thomsen, S. (2000). The causal relationship between insider ownership owner identity and market valuation among the largest European companies. Copenhagen Business School, working paper.

Reem, Allam, & Wajeeh (2015). The relation between ownership structure dimensions and corporate performance of listed companies. Evidence from Bahrain. *Australasian Accounting, Business, and Finance Journal, 9,* 38-56.

Sadegbi, Sharif, & Bahadori (2009). Investigating the effect of ownership structure on dividend pay-out ratio of listed companies in Tehran Stock Exchange, Tehran. *Journal of Corporate Finance, 3,* 212-215.

Saseela, B. & Thirunavukkarasu, V. (2017). An investigation of the relationship between ownership structure and financial performance of the listed Beverage Food and Tobacco companies in Sri Lanka. *Journal of Accounting and Financial Reporting, 7,*119-278.

Short, & Keasy (1999). Managerial ownership and financial performance of listed firms in Britain. *Journal of Corporate Finance, 9,* 235-311.

Shleifer, A., & Vishny, R. W. (1986). Large shareholders and corporate control. *Journal of Political Economy, 94,* 461-488.

Shleifer, A., & Vishny, R. W. (1997). A survey of corporate governance. *Journal of Finance, 52,* 737-783.

Stanley, J. I. (2015). An assessment of the impact of ownership structure on financial Performance of listed Chinese Banks. *Journal of Management Science and Business Administration, 1,* 26-33.

Stulz, R. (1988). Managerial control of voting rights. *Journal of Financial Economics, 20,* 25-59.

Thuku, T. (1992). The relationship between ownership structure and banks financial performance in Kenya. *Journal of Accounting and Finance, 1,* 98-121.

Xu, X., & Wang, Y. (1999). Ownership structure, corporate governance in Chinese stock companies. China Economic Review, 10, 75-98.

Zeitun, & Tian (2007). The effects of Ownership concentration on firm's performance. Literature of finance.

Zhou, X. (2001). Understanding the determinants of managerial ownership and the link between ownership and performance: Comment. *Journal of Financial Economics, 62,* 559-571.

```
. summarize bps mgrown instown ownconc size growth
```

Variable	Obs	Mean	Std. Dev.	Min	Max
bps	168	.8156643	.6356879	-1.6439	3.547
mgrown	168	8.308446	.6764584	5.8982	9.3046
instown	168	9.23841	.263507	8.6358	9.7169
ownconc	168	9.074395	.2632442	8.2842	9.5308
size	168	10.00152	.3412885	8.807	10.8997
growth	168	5.568394	6.906723	-9.7382	10.333

```
. sktest bps mgrown instown ownconc size growth
```

Skewness/Kurtosis tests for Normality

				joint	
Variable	Obs	Pr(Skewness)	Pr(Kurtosis)	adj chi2(2)	Prob>chi2
bps	168	0.3131	0.0000	17.63	0.0001
mgrown	168	0.0000	0.0000	45.80	0.0000
instown	168	0.8541	0.3174	1.05	0.5926
ownconc	168	0.0219	0.1218	7.13	0.0283
size	168	0.0024	0.0013	16.06	0.0003
growth	168	0.0000	0.2355	31.95	0.0000

```
. correlate bps mgrown instown ownconc size growth
(obs=168)
```

	bps	mgrown	instown	ownconc	size	growth
bps	1.0000					
mgrown	0.0512	1.0000				
instown	0.0900	0.2037	1.0000			
ownconc	0.0779	0.4119	0.6372	1.0000		
size	0.5232	0.4267	0.4072	0.5381	1.0000	
growth	0.3802	0.1815	0.3047	0.2762	0.4401	1.0000

```
. regress bps mgrown instown ownconc size growth

      Source |       SS       df       MS              Number of obs =     168
-------------+------------------------------           F(  5,   162) =   20.22
       Model |  25.9315649     5  5.18631298           Prob > F      =  0.0000
    Residual |    41.55298   162  .256499877           R-squared     =  0.3843
-------------+------------------------------           Adj R-squared =  0.3653
       Total |  67.4845449   167  .404099071           Root MSE      =  .50646

------------------------------------------------------------------------------
         bps |      Coef.   Std. Err.      t    P>|t|     [95% Conf. Interval]
-------------+----------------------------------------------------------------
      mgrown |  -.1477818   .0664148    -2.23   0.027    -.2789322   -.0166315
     instown |  -.1489436   .1973717    -0.75   0.452    -.5386967    .2408095
     ownconc |  -.5346214   .2180699    -2.45   0.015    -.9652476   -.1039953
        size |     1.2002   .1514503     7.92   0.000     .9011286    1.499271
      growth |   .0188744   .0063991     2.95   0.004      .006238    .0315109
       _cons |  -3.838051   1.714185    -2.24   0.027    -7.223078   -.4530237
------------------------------------------------------------------------------
```

```
. vif

    Variable |       VIF       1/VIF
-------------+----------------------
     ownconc |      2.15    0.466081
     instown |      1.76    0.567827
        size |      1.74    0.574893
      mgrown |      1.31    0.760955
      growth |      1.27    0.786296
-------------+----------------------
    Mean VIF |      1.65
```

```
. hettest

Breusch-Pagan / Cook-Weisberg test for heteroskedasticity
         Ho: Constant variance
         Variables: fitted values of bps

         chi2(1)      =     8.64
         Prob > chi2  =   0.0033
```

```
. xtset firm year
       panel variable:  firms (strongly balanced)
        time variable:  year, 2011 to 2016
                delta:  1 unit
```

```
. xtreg bps mgrown instown ownconc size growth, fe

Fixed-effects (within) regression               Number of obs      =       168
Group variable: firms                           Number of groups   =        28

R-sq:  within  = 0.0800                         Obs per group: min =         6
       between = 0.0272                                        avg =       6.0
       overall = 0.0292                                        max =         6

                                                F(5,135)           =      2.35
corr(u_i, Xb)  = -0.4165                        Prob > F           =    0.0443

------------------------------------------------------------------------------
         bps |      Coef.   Std. Err.      t    P>|t|     [95% Conf. Interval]
-------------+----------------------------------------------------------------
      mgrown |   .0324149   .1511756     0.21   0.831    -.2665639    .3313936
     instown |    1.72805   .6774646     2.55   0.012     .3882332    3.067866
     ownconc |  -1.339104   .6215905    -2.15   0.033    -2.568418   -.1097888
        size |   .1869576   .1895645     0.99   0.326    -.1879427    .5618579
      growth |   .0058136   .0044282     1.31   0.191     -.002944    .0145713
       _cons |  -5.168761   2.526878    -2.05   0.043    -10.16615   -.1713731
-------------+----------------------------------------------------------------
     sigma_u |  .63924974
     sigma_e |  .28283557
         rho |  .83628728   (fraction of variance due to u_i)
------------------------------------------------------------------------------
F test that all u_i=0:     F(27, 135) =    14.24             Prob > F = 0.0000
```

```
. xtreg bps mgrown instown ownconc size growth, re

Random-effects GLS regression                   Number of obs      =       168
Group variable: firms                           Number of groups   =        28

R-sq:  within  = 0.0442                         Obs per group: min =         6
       between = 0.3336                                        avg =       6.0
       overall = 0.2699                                        max =         6

                                                Wald chi2(5)       =     17.76
corr(u_i, X)   = 0 (assumed)                    Prob > chi2        =    0.0033

------------------------------------------------------------------------------
         bps |      Coef.   Std. Err.      z    P>|z|     [95% Conf. Interval]
-------------+----------------------------------------------------------------
      mgrown |   .0212628   .1028113     0.21   0.836    -.1802436    .2227692
     instown |   .4560684   .3565179     1.28   0.201    -.2426938    1.154831
     ownconc |  -.5188548   .3573183    -1.45   0.146    -1.219186    .1814762
        size |   .5226529   .1707322     3.06   0.002      .188024    .8572818
      growth |   .0065025   .0045031     1.44   0.149    -.0023235    .0153284
       _cons |   -4.12958   2.092101    -1.97   0.048    -8.230023   -.0291379
-------------+----------------------------------------------------------------
     sigma_u |  .40889529
     sigma_e |  .28283557
         rho |  .67638039   (fraction of variance due to u_i)
------------------------------------------------------------------------------


. hausman fe re

                 ---- Coefficients ----
             |      (b)          (B)            (b-B)     sqrt(diag(V_b-V_B))
             |      fe           re          Difference          S.E.
-------------+----------------------------------------------------------------
      mgrown |    .0324149     .0212628        .0111521        .1108328
     instown |     1.72805     .4560684        1.271981        .5760671
     ownconc |   -1.339104    -.5188548       -.8202487         .508624
        size |    .1869576     .5226529       -.3356954        .0823726
      growth |    .0058136     .0065025       -.0006888               .
------------------------------------------------------------------------------
                           b = consistent under Ho and Ha; obtained from xtreg
            B = inconsistent under Ha, efficient under Ho; obtained from xtreg

    Test:  Ho:  difference in coefficients not systematic

                  chi2(5) = (b-B)'[(V_b-V_B)^(-1)](b-B)
                          =       24.17
                Prob>chi2 =      0.0002
                (V_b-V_B is not positive definite)
```

3

Impact of Global Financial Crisis on Socially Innovative Microfinance Institutions in Pakistan

Ather Azim Khan[a] Faisal Mustafa[b] Ambreen Khursheed[c]

[a] Dr., Faculty of Management Studies, University of Central Punjab, Pakistan, ather.azim@ucp.edu.pk
[b] Dr., Faculty of Management Studies, University of Central Punjab, Pakistan, faisal.mustafa@ucp.edu.pk
[c] Corresponding Author, Faculty of Management Studies, University of Central Punjab, Pakistan, ambreen.khursheed@ucp.edu.pk

Keywords
Microfinance Institutions, Wilcoxon Signed Ranks Test, Descriptive Ratio Analysis.

Abstract
The wave of global financial crises (2007 – 2008) caused a surge in the capital flows of developed countries particularly, between developed and developing countries. The crisis has hit all financial sectors with unexpected severity and speed. This paper determines the impact of global financial crisis (2007 – 2008) on socially innovative microfinance institutions operating in Pakistan by using descriptive ratio analysis and the Wilcoxon Signed Ranks Test. This paper analyzes performance of MFIs for 15 years i.e., from 2000 – 2014 in three waves: before, during and after the financial crisis. The results show that financial crisis affected performance of all selected MFIs but Thardeep Rural Development Programme (TRDP) showed major changes in three waves of crises. The output of the Wilcoxon Signed Ranks Test confirms that the financial crisis worsened the operations of MFIs in Pakistan. This study will assist microfinance practitioners, policy makers, rural financial institutions, and microfinance institutions in maintaining and developing more effective strategies to survive in such crisis in the future.

1. Introduction

Microfinance (MF) is diffusing all over the world but at the same time it is rapidly changing with new innovative opportunities (Moro Visconti, 2012). In the present era technical or social innovation has a deep impact on microfinance institutions (MFIs) and it also contributes in reshaping their business model (Moro Visconti, 2014). For mitigating MF risk factors innovation works as an opportunity in view of its persistent impact on the risk factors (Holmes and Watts, 2009).

MFIs are considered as an effective and innovative measure of poverty alleviation as it provides various financial services to poor borrowers who require a small amount of money to finance their businesses (Kneiding, 2009). Therefore, microfinance can be recognized as an economic innovation with a goal to combat poverty (Jonker, 2009). At present thousands of microfinance institutions (MFIs) are operating with ranging from self-help groups to established commercial banks providing various financial services to millions of microbusinesses (Dokulilova, 2009). These MFIs are supported by not only the donor agencies, but also by many philanthropists, investors, network organizations, lenders, management consulting firms, and many other specialized businesses and all these organizations collectively form the flourishing global microfinance industry (Gonzalez, 2011).

Microfinance has developed as an essential tool for poverty alleviation from the past two decades and its idea was first launched in 1970 when Dr. Yunus of Grameen Bank (Nobel laureate) started interest free micro loans to poor people (Karanshawy, 2007). The beginning of microfinance sector in Pakistan can be drawn back to the early 1990s with two projects: The Aga Khan Rural Support Program (AKRSP) and the Orangi Pilot Project (OPP) (O'Donohoe, 2009). At present, a multitude of institutes are providing microfinance services in Pakistan including Non- Governmental Organizations (16) Microfinance Banks (10), Rural Support Programs (6), Non- Banking Financial Institutions (24) and others (16) (Pakistan Microfinance Network, 2014). According to Tahir and Che Tahrim (2014) microfinance institutions plays an important role in the financial sector of Pakistan by improving the living standards of poor households. Likewise, Chowdry (2011) explained that MFIs are a key sector being an operative and proven channel of credit delivery to the small and medium households of economy but due to the global financial crisis not only the financial sector but also the MFIs of Pakistan went through a very harsh period.

The economy of Pakistan showed an impressive growth during the first half of 2000s (Khawaja & Ghani, 2012). But in 2008 the world economy confronted its most dangerous catastrophe since the Great Depression of the 1930s (Chowdry, 2011).The crisis began in 2007, when in the United States sky-high home prices finally turned resolutely downward, spread rapidly, initially it effected entire financial sector of U.S. and then it reached financial markets overseas (Havemann, 2009). Among developing countries, Pakistan faced greater inflationary pressure in the crisis period due to an increase in food prices, severe power shortage and slowdown in the services and manufacturing sector and its microfinance sector also faced a shock in its balance sheet as on the liability side, all types of donors were badly influenced due to a sudden drop in liquidity and on the assets side, due to the worsening of macroeconomic conditions the loan delinquency and write offs also began to increase (Badiola, 2009). The crisis and recession also affected the poverty reduction goals of developing countries in East Asia as the crisis lead to rising unemployment and collapsing of financial institutions made it more difficult to tackle as compare to the past recession of 1980s (Littlefield, 2009).

In the past many researches have been done on this issue but still it is far from clear that how much the crisis affected performance of MFIs. The objective of this study is to evaluate the performance of the socially innovative MFIs against the background of global financial crisis and for this purpose, the study has examined some key performance measuring ratios for assessing the scalability, sustainability and outreach of MFIs. The study has applied Wilcoxon Signed Ranks Test for ranking MFIs primarily based on their performance. This study will assist policy makers, microfinance practitioners, rural financial institutions and microfinance institutions for meaningful analysis and developing strategies for being sustainable institutions.

2. Literature Review

In this part an overview of the literature on analysis of MFIs' performance is given and recommend that the thriving global industry of microfinance gives an opportunity to all researchers to make a difference in understanding this complex phenomenon of microfinance through research. Though in the past several studies have been conducted to evaluate performance of MFIs but still, no standardized method for evaluation of a microfinance programs performance has yet been established. The researchers like Wagner and Charlotte (2013), Krauss (2011), Silva and Chavez (2015), Gonzalez (2011) applied panel regression testing with correlation analysis for measuring the performance of MFIs on secondary data.

A few authors like Breza (2016) and Lavoie (2011) conducted qualitative research study based on primary data for measuring the performance of MFIs against the background of crisis. The researchers like Breza (2016), Aemiro and Mekonnen (2012) and Di Bella (2011) analyzed the ratios of gross loan portfolio (GLP), return on asset (ROA), return on equity (ROE) and portfolio at risk (PAR) for assessing performance of MFIs during and after the global financial crisis.

A number of authors like Lavoie (2011), Aemiro and Mekonnen (2012), Olson and Zoubi (2016) and Breza (2016) determined the impact of global financial crisis on the MFIs operating in the developing countries like Brazil, Ethiopia, Africa, Middle East and South East Asia (MENASA) and India. While Kollmann (2013) investigated the performance of MFIs using a two country model comprising of Europe and U.S. for assessing the impact of the global financial crisis. Whereas the study assessing MFIs' performance operating across the world was done by Beltratti (2012). Likewise, Schumacher (1973) encouraged "appropriate technology' i.e., the proper utilization of local resources for the benefit of poor.

Many researchers like Olson and Zoubi (2016), Breza (2016), Silva and Chavez (2015), Wagner and Charlotte (2013), Kollmann (2013), Bitrate (2012), Aemiro and Mekonnen (2012), Krauss (2011), Gonzalez (2011) and Lavoie (2011), assessed the performance of MFIs operating in the time period ranging from 1999 to 2011 and concluded that microfinance were efficiently providing different types of financial services including small deposits, micro-credit, payment services etc., to poor households but the global crises affected their operations badly.

Although in all previous researches the selected sample of MFIs was different but most of them like Olson and Zoubi (2016), Breza (2016), Silva and Chavez (2015), Aemiro and Mekonnen (2012), Kollmann (2013), Bitrate (2012) described a negative shift in the performance indicators of MFIs due to the global financial crisis mainly in year 2008 and also explained that MFIs were not stable enough to face the crisis without bearing some losses. While a few researchers like Mahinda and Wijesiri (2016), and Visconti and Roberto (2011) concluded that MFIs operating in developing countries were less affected by the crisis due the flexibility in their organizational structure to global shocks.

3. Methodology

The study employed quantitative approach on selected MFIs and the data is collected from Microfinance Information Exchange (MIX) database for the time period of 15 years that is, 2000-2014. The study analyzes the performance of those MFIs which offers wide range of socially innovative products/services and are more active in women empowerment programs. The study has applied two methodologies on the dataset which are descriptive ratio analysis and Wilcoxon Signed Ranks Test for assessing the performance before, during, and after the crisis of MFIs in Pakistan. The study comprises of all (non-profit) microfinance institutions providing services in Pakistan.

In this study 18 MFIs are sampled and the reason for selecting a small sample is to maintain the quality of results obtained from the Wilcoxon signed ranks test as this test requires small sample sizes for each phase of analysis. These MFIs are selected on the basis of provision of maximum socially innovative products/services to their clients and on their preference of providing maximum loans to female borrowers. As in the past researches, the promoters of microfinance has emphasized on providing more innovative services to the clients and considered women's empowerment as a social goal and an alternative way to evaluate the performance of MFIs (Badiola, 2009; Hermes et al., 2011)

Table 1. MFIs Selected on The Basis of their Socially Innovative Services and Average Loan Balance per Female Borrower

Serial No.	Names of Sampled MFIs in Pakistan	Average Loan Balance per Female Borrowing (Rs.)	Socially Innovative Products / Services of MFIs
1	Accion Microfinance Bank (AMFB)	27,827.87	• Small/ Larger Loans for Individuals • Fixed Asset Loan for Small Business Owners • Innovative Customized Overdraft • Group Loan • Support Programme for People Living with Impaired Disability • Education Based Loans for Schools • Savings Accounts, Brighta Socio-Investor Account • E-services (ATM Card)
2	Tameer Microfinance Bank (TMFB)	26,781.81	• Innovative services for micro loans, micro-credit and insurance • E-services (ATM Card)
3	Pak-Oman Microfinance Bank Ltd (POMFB)	24,769.19	• Group/ Individual Lending • Deposit Products, Product Brochures • Agriculture/ Enterprise Loan • Livestock Financing For • Milk Business Loan (MBL) • New Business Loan (NMBL)
4	Development Action For Mobilization & Emancipation (DAMEN)	23,843.10	• Non-Formal Education/Health Services. • Livestock Extension Service Program. • Training Capacity Building and Skill Development of Community Action Groups
5	The First Microfinance Ba nk (FMFB)	19,764.29	• Loans, Deposits and Insurance Services • Financial Literacy Program • Innovative Renewable Energy Product
6	Khushali Bank	19,321.90	• Innovative Agri Products & Services • Sarsabz Karobar Services • Khushhali Qarza Services • Khushhali Livestock Services • Khushhali Cash Sahulat Services • Khushhali Assan Qarza Services
7	Community Support Concern (CSC)	18,875.19	• Trainings: Provide Capacity Building Opportunities and Trainings
8	Kashf Foundation	17,345.89	• Micro-Credit, Micro-Insurance • Capacity Building Programs • Pilots and Research Trainings • Micro Deposits
9	Orix Leasing Pakistan Ltd.	15,338.23	• Astute savers invest in ORIX • Corporate Lease Service • Commercial Vehicle Leasing • Operating Lease Service • Islamic Finance Service • Innovative ORIX leasing Service • Micro Finance Service
10	Rural Community Development Society	13,704.40	• Agri Finance Service • Vocational Trainings • Provide Access to Justice Services

Serial No.	Names of Sampled MFIs in Pakistan	Average Loan Balance per Female Borrowing (Rs.)	Socially Innovative Products / Services of MFIs
	(RCDS)		• Women Training in Home Based Livestock Services • Network of water supply • Network of sanitation and conservancy services
11	Punjab Rural Support Programme (PRSP)	12,882.81	• Land use control services • Housing services • Urban or rural Infrastructure support services
12	The National Rural Support Programme (NRSP)	12,650.37	• Health insurance innovations for the poor in Pakistan • Livelihood improvement through agricultural and livestock innovations • Social sector services - education and health
13	Safco Support Foundation (SSF)	10,945.46	• Loan Product • Insurance Product • Special Project • PMIFL Loan • TUP Project (Innovative)
14	Akhuwat	10,910.30	Family Enterprise Loan, Liberation Loan, Education Loan, Health Loan, Emergency Loan, Housing Loan, Marriage Loan and a variety of innovative health services
15	Orangi Pilot Project (OPP)	10,860.44	• Micro Loans, Micro Credit and Innovative Loan Schemes
16	Thardeep Rural Development Programme (TRDP)	97,22.189	• Social Services • a. Health • b. Education • Innovation to cultivate crops during off-season • (Microfinance Programme (MFP) introduces a Branchless Banking service)
17	Sungi	88,39.18	• Micro Insurance, Loans for community infrastructure, Innovative services for sustainable livelihoods and disaster management.
18	Sarhad Rural Support Programme (SRSP)	79,37.56	• PEACE Project • Access to Justice Services • Legal Empowerment Services • Dispute Resolution Services • Aitebaar Awareness Raising Services • Strengthening Rule of Law In Malakand • Community Based Conflict Resolution Services • Livelihood Enhancement & Protection Project • Livelihood Enhancement & Enterprise Development Project • Livelihood Support & Promotion Of Small Community Infrastructure Projects • Innovative Green Project • Livelihood Strengthening Programme

*Source: (Mix Market, 2016 and Annual Reports of MFIs)

4. Ratio Analysis

In order to analyze performance of the selected 18 MFIs in Pakistan the following six key performance measuring ratios are used, in the past researches authors like Breza (2016), Aemiro and Mekonnen (2012), Di Bella (2011) and Llanto (2009) have also used some of the following ratios for measuring performance of MFIs.

Table 2: Variable Description

Serial No.	Variable	Description	Formula
1.	Dpsm	Depositors per staff member	Number of Depositors/Number of personnel
2.	Bpsm	Borrowers per staff member	Number of active borrowers/Number of personnel
3.	Lpsm	Loans per staff member	Adjusted number of loans outstanding/Number of personnel
4.	Wor	Write-off ratio	Value of loans write off/Average gross loan portfolio
5.	Albfb	Average loan balance per female borrowing	Average loan balance / Female borrowing
6.	Dasm	Deposit account per staff member	Number of deposit account/ Number of personnel

*Source: Author's Own Calculations

4.1 Wilcoxon Signed Ranks Test

The Wilcoxon Signed Ranks Test is applied on the secondary data with satisfying its four assumptions which are; use of two dependent samples for assessing differences in two time periods, independence of randomly selected paired observations, the inclusion of continuous dependent variable for ranking the differences according to their size and measurement of variables at ordinal level. Basically it is a non-parametric test used for examining significant differences between two scale/ordinal variables that can be matched, it also gives the descriptive statistics of the data and assign positive and negative ranks to the ratios of MFIs compared by using a standard normal distribution. In this study comparison and ranking of MFIs based on performance measuring ratios is done in three stages of time period; first comparison of ratios is done before and during the crisis period (2000-2006), second comparison is done between and during the crisis period (2007-2008) and third comparison is done before and after the crisis (2009-2014).

4.2 Results of Wilcoxon Signed Ranks Test

Table 3. Descriptive Statistics (before and during the crisis)

Descriptive Statistics					
Ratios	N	Mean	Std. Deviation	Minimum	Maximum
dpsm_b	18	1179.60	2662.44	.0000	10441.77
bpsm_b	18	609.62	524.18	36.08	2151.36
lpsm_b	18	512.37	421.63	36.08	1607.49
wor_b	16	.0652	.0904	.0000	.2881
dasm_b	18	572.04	1413.60	.00	5757.18
dpsm_d	14	80.40	88.88	.0000	214.34
bpsm_d	17	241.20	144.35	33.51	625.04
lpsm_d	16	252.13	155.28	37.22	625.04
wor_d	17	.0640	.0906	.0000	.3448
dasm_d	13	54.71	81.53	.00	214.34

The descriptive statistics obtained from the Wilcoxon Signed Ranks Test is depicted in above table which shows the value of mean and standard deviation along with maximum values attained by all ratios taken before the crisis is higher than during the crisis and the minimum values for all ratios taken before are comparatively lower then ratios during the crisis. The results of descriptive statistics showed that MFIs were performing well before the crisis as compare to the period of crisis that is, from 2007- 2008. The output obtained from Wilcoxon Signed Ranks Test is depicted below in Table 4.

Table 4. Wilcoxon Signed Ranks Test Results

Ranks				
		N	Mean Rank	Sum of Ranks
dpsm_d - dpsm_b	Negative Ranks	5[a]	6.20	31.00
	Positive Ranks	4[b]	3.50	14.00
	Ties	5[c]		
	Total	14		
bpsm_d - bpsm_b	Negative Ranks	14[d]	10.50	147.00
	Positive Ranks	3[e]	2.00	6.00
	Ties	0[f]		
	Total	17		
lpsm_d - lpsm_b	Negative Ranks	13[g]	10.00	130.00
	Positive Ranks	3[h]	2.00	6.00
	Ties	0[i]		
	Total	16		
wor_d - wor_b	Negative Ranks	7[j]	7.57	53.00
	Positive Ranks	6[k]	6.33	38.00

	Ties	1[l]		
	Total	14		
dasm_d - dasm_b	Negative Ranks	2[m]	5.00	10.00
	Positive Ranks	4[n]	2.75	11.00
	Ties	6[o]		
	Total	12		
albfb_d - albfb_b	Negative Ranks	5[p]	3.00	15.00
	Positive Ranks	0[q]	.00	.00
	Ties	0[r]		
	Total	5		

Table 4 depicts ranks obtained from Wilcoxon Signed Ranks Test Results which showed a greater number of positive ranks (representing ratios taken before crisis) as compare to negative ranks (representing ratios taken during crisis) with a significant difference between mean ranks for ratios measured before and during the crisis, with significant z-values for three ratios 'bpsm', 'lpsm' and 'albfb'. Thus, the output gives sufficient evidence to reject our null hypothesis and it is inferred from the results that performance of MFIs was badly affected by the global financial crisis in Pakistan.

4.3 Comparison between Ratios (during and after the crisis)

Table 5. Descriptive Statistics (during and after the crisis)

Descriptive Statistics					
	N	Mean	Std. Deviation	Minimum	Maximum
dpsm_d	14	80.40	88.88	.0000	214.34
bpsm_d	17	241.20	144.35	33.51	625.04
lpsm_d	16	252.13	155.28	37.22	625.04
wor_d	17	.064	.0906	.0000	.3448
dasm_d	13	54.71	81.53	.00	214.34
albfb_d	8	441.30	395.30	.0000	1149.75
dpsm_a	19	396.39	949.22	.0000	3996.64
bpsm_a	19	717.73	394.18	42.55	1600.41
lpsm_a	18	750.55	368.94	238.80	1600.41
wor_a	18	.1036	.13524	.0000	.5242
dasm_a	18	425.14	1056.62	.00	4365.17
albfb_a	18	28143.54	13333.06	7007.57	53563.63

The descriptive statistics shows higher value of mean and standard deviation for the ratios taken after the crisis showing that data is more dispersed after the crisis. The maximum values attained by all ratios taken during the crisis is higher than after the crisis and the minimum values for all ratios taken during are comparatively lower then ratios taken after the crisis. The output provide an evidence to state that the crises worsened the operations of microfinance institutions during the crises period.

Table 6. Wilcoxon Signed Ranks Test Results

Ranks				
		N	Mean Rank	Sum of Ranks
dpsm_a - dpsm_d	Negative Ranks	2[a]	3.00	6.00
	Positive Ranks	6[b]	5.00	30.00
	Ties	6[c]		
	Total	14		
bpsm_a - bpsm_d	Negative Ranks	1[d]	1.00	1.00
	Positive Ranks	16[e]	9.50	152.00
	Ties	0[f]		
	Total	17		
lpsm_a - lpsm_d	Negative Ranks	0[g]	.00	.00
	Positive Ranks	15[h]	8.00	120.00
	Ties	0[i]		
	Total	15		
wor_a - wor_d	Negative Ranks	5[j]	8.60	43.00
	Positive Ranks	11[k]	8.45	93.00
	Ties	0[l]		
	Total	16		
dasm_a - dasm_d	Negative Ranks	1[m]	1.00	1.00
	Positive Ranks	4[n]	3.50	14.00
	Ties	7[o]		
	Total	12		
albfb_a - albfb_d	Negative Ranks	0[p]	.00	.00
	Positive Ranks	8[q]	4.50	36.00
	Ties	0[r]		
	Total	8		

According to the Table 6 higher number of positive ranks (representing ratios taken after crisis) as compare to negative ranks (representing ratios taken during crisis) with a significant difference between mean ranks for ratios measured during and after the crisis and significant z value for four ratios which are 'dpsm', 'bpsm', 'lpsm' and 'albfb' provides sufficient proof to reject null hypothesis and proves that performance of MFIs was badly affected due to the crisis.

4.4 Comparison between Ratios (before and after the crisis)

Table 7. Descriptive Statistics (before and after the crisis)

Descriptive Statistics					
	N	Mean	Std. Deviation	Minimum	Maximum
dpsm_b	18	1179.60	2662.44	.0000	10441.77
bpsm_b	18	609.62	524.18	36.08	2151.36
lpsm_b	18	512.37	421.63	36.08	1607.49
wor_b	16	.0652	.0904	.0000	.288
dasm_b	18	572.04	1413.60	.00	5757.18
albfb_b	11	3173.86	4837.71	647.76	17247.73
dpsm_a	19	396.39	949.22	.0000	3996.64
bpsm_a	19	717.73	394.18	42.55	1600.41
lpsm_a	18	750.55	368.94	238.80	1600.41
wor_a	18	.1036	.13524	.0000	.524
dasm_a	18	425.14	1056.62	.00	4365.17
albfb_a	18	28143.54	13333.06	7007.57	53563.63

According to table 7 the mean values for ratios 'dpsm', 'dasm' and 'albfb' taken before the crisis is higher than the mean values of ratios taken after the crisis. While the mean value of 'bpsm', 'lpsm' and 'wor' taken after the crisis is greater than mean values of these ratios taken before the crisis. In case of standard deviation the ratios depicts more dispersion of data before the crisis as compare to after the crisis. The maximum values depicted by all ratios taken before the crisis is higher than values taken after the crisis and the minimum values for all ratios taken before crisis are comparatively lower then ratios taken after the crisis.

Table 8. Wilcoxon Signed Ranks Test Results

Ranks				
		N	Mean Rank	Sum of Ranks
dpsm_a - dpsm_b	Negative Ranks	8[a]	7.25	58.00
	Positive Ranks	5[b]	6.60	33.00
	Ties	5[c]		
	Total	18		
bpsm_a - bpsm_b	Negative Ranks	6[d]	7.17	43.00
	Positive Ranks	12[e]	10.67	128.00
	Ties	0[f]		
	Total	18		
lpsm_a - lpsm_b	Negative Ranks	3[g]	7.33	22.00
	Positive Ranks	14[h]	9.36	131.00
	Ties	0[i]		

	Total	17		
wor_a - wor_b	Negative Ranks	5[j]	10.00	50.00
	Positive Ranks	11[k]	7.82	86.00
	Ties	0[l]		
	Total	16		
dasm_a - dasm_b	Negative Ranks	6[m]	6.17	37.00
	Positive Ranks	5[n]	5.80	29.00
	Ties	6[o]		
	Total	17		
albfb_a - albfb_b	Negative Ranks	1[p]	1.00	1.00
	Positive Ranks	10[q]	6.50	65.00
	Ties	0[r]		
	Total	11		

The results depicted in table 8 shows difference between mean ranks for ratios measured before and after the crisis is significant with higher number of positive ranks (representing ratios taken before crisis) than negative ranks (representing ratios taken after the crisis) and significant test z values for three ratios which are 'bpsm', 'lpsm' and 'albfb'.Overall, the results gives sufficient evidence to reject null hypothesis and therefore, it is inferred that performance of MFIs is affected due to crisis.

5. Conclusion

The results of ratio analysis and the Wilcoxon Signed Ranks Test show that performance of all MFIs operating in Pakistan was badly affected by global financial crisis as a clear difference in the performance measuring ratios before, during, and after the crisis is observed by the analyses. The results of ratio analyses showed major changes in performance measuring ratios is depicted by TRDP as it showed highest ratio of Depositor per Staff Member 'dpsm' and Loan per Staff Member 'lpsm' among 18 selected MFIs before the crisis and depicted a major decrease in both the ratios 'dpsm' and 'bpsm' during the crisis. In case of Write-off Ratio 'wor', TRDP showed significant rise during the period of crisis, which shows performance of loan processing and collection departments working in TRDP was badly affected by the global financial crisis. After the crisis, TRDP showed a decrease in write off ratio, representing an improvement in its performance by stabilizing its loan disbursement process. But TMFB outperforms after the crisis in two ratios which are "bpsm' and 'albfb' as compare to TRDP by showing significant increase in opening of deposit accounts and allotment of average loan to their female borrowers. The results of Wilcoxon Signed Ranks Test showed significant z values and difference in mean ranks for most of the ratios compared. Thus, the results gives evidence to reject null hypothesis and the study concludes that performance of MFIs is badly affected due to crisis.

To our knowledge this study is the first attempt of its kind to analyze the impact of financial crunch on the performance of MFIs in Pakistan by using Wilcoxon Signed Ranks test as most of the previous researches have used fixed panel effects models or ratio analysis method. The findings of our study supports the results' findings of previous researches as Breza. K (2016) examined the performance of MFIs operating in the rural areas of India by using financial ratios (gross loan portfolio, average borrowers ratio) and found significant reduction in aggregate demand of MFIs during the crisis period. Similarly, Silva and Chavez (2015) examined the performance of MFIs by using fixed-panel regression model and revealed that performance of MFIs was severely affected by the financial crunch, they further exposed that efficient government polies for supporting MFIs can help them to survive in crisis period. On the similar lines, Wagner (2013) used key financial ratios like credit growth and portfolio quality and highlighted that MFIs are highly vulnerable to economic shocks. Likewise, Kollmann (2013) also confirmed the worst influence of (2007-2009) crunch on microfinance performance by conducting a research on two-country model and revealed 15% fall in the GDP of US and EA (euro area).

From the findings it is recommended that the methods of evaluating performance of MFIs should not be mere cost focusing rather it should consider the number of services provided by MFIs. This study shall help microfinance practitioners in evaluating performance MFIs more precisely and shall also assist them in maintaining financial and operational sustainability of MFIs by adopting appropriate strategies from TRDP as it survived efficiently after the crisis. Consequently, MFIs will be able to improve poor clients' welfare by maintain their sustainability and ensuring maximum outreach in terms of both directions i.e., outwards and downwards. In order to further enhance the understanding about ways of measuring performance of MFIs, future research is recommended to inspect on how MFIs can maintain their efficiencies during such crisis in the future.

References

Aemiro, T. (2012). The financial performance and sustainability of microfinance instituitions during the current financial crisis: The case of Amhara credit and saving instituition (ASCI) in Ethopia. *International Journal of Business and Public Management, 2*(2), 81-87.

Aemiro, T., & Mekonnen, D. (2012). The financial performance and sustainability of microfinance institutions during the current financial crisis: The case of Amhara Credit and Saving Institution (ACSI) in Ethiopia. *International Journal of Business and Public Management, 2*(2), 81-87.

Badiola, L. &. (2009). The impact of global financial crisis on rural and microfinance in Asia. *Philippine Institute for Development Studies.*

Beltratti, A. S. (2012). The credit crisis around the globe: Why did some banks perform better? *Journal of Financial Economics,, 105*(1), 1-17.

Blanchard, O. F. (2010). The impact effect of the crisis on emerging market countries. *estudio presentado en el panel de la Brookings sobre actividad económica el, 1*(1), 18-19.

Breza, & kinnan. (2016). Measuring the equilibrium impacts of credit: evidence from the indian microfinance crisis. *Manuscript, northwestern university, 1*(1), 1-44.

Chowdry, B. (2011). *NBFI and Modaraba: An important segment of financial industry.*

Di Bella, C. G. (2011). The impact of the global financial crisis on microfinance and policy implications. *IMF Working Papers,* 1-40.

Dokulilova, L. J. (2009). Sustainability of microfinance institutions in financial crisis. *MPRA,* 1-25.

Gonzalez, A. (2011). Lessons for strengthening microfinance institutions through financial crises, fluctuations in food and fuel prices, and other major risks. *MicroBanking Bulletin,* 1-14.

Havemann, J. (2009). *The financial crisis of 2008: Year in review 2008.*

IMF. (2009). *The Implications of the Global Financial Crisis for Low-income Countries.* International Monetary Fund.

Khawaja, I., & Ghani, E. (2012). Global Financial Crisis: Policy Implications for Pakistan. *NUML Journal of Management & Technology, 9*(1), 20-31.

Kneiding, C. E. (2009). Shedding Light on Microfinance Equity Valuation: Past and Present. *CGAP Occasional Paper, 14*(1), 1-40.

Kollmann, R. (2013). Global banks, financial Shocks, and international business cycles: Evidence from an estimated model. *Journal of Money, Credit and Banking, 45*(2), 159-195.

Krauss. (2011). Can microfinance reduce portfolio volatility? *Economic Development and Cultural Change, 58*(1), 85-110.

Karanshawy, H. (2007). Finance Plus: A model for the activation of microfinance and medium finance. *International Conference on Inclusive Islamic Financial Sector Development, University Brunei Darussalam.*

Latvia, & Russia, a. C. (2003). Microfinance in times of crisis: The effects of competition, rising indebtedness, and economic crisis on repayment behavior. *World Development, 31*(12), 2085-2114.

Lavoie. (2011). Challenges for inclusive finance expansion: The case of crediAmigo, a brazilian MFI. *Management international/International Management/GestiÃ³n Internacional, 15*(3), 57-69.

Littlefield, E. &. (2009). The global financial crisis and its impact on microfinance. *CGAP Focus nots, 52*(1), 1-8. Retrieved from Focus Note, World Bank.

Llanto, G. M. (2009). The impact of the global financial crisis on rural and microfinance in Asia *(No. DP 2009-24 (revised).*

Loncar, D., Novak, C., & Cicmil, S. (2011). Global recession and sustainable development: The case of microfinance industry in Eastern Europe. *CGAP, 22*(223), 1-10.

Mahinda, & Wijesiri. (2016). Weathering the storm: Ownership structure and performance of microfinance institutions in the wake of the global financial crisis. *Economic Modelling, 57*(1), 238-247.

Mendoza, R. U. (2008). From revolution to evolution: charting the main features of microfinance 2.0. *Perspectives on Global Development and Technology, 9*(3), 545-580.

Mix Market. (2016). Retrieved from Cross market analysis: https://reports.mixmarket.org/crossmarket

Moro Visconti, R. (2011). Global recession and microfinance risk governance in developing countries. *Risk Governance and Control Journal, 1*(3), 17-30.

Nguyen, H. (2011). *International crisis transmission and asymmetric recoveries.* Working Paper, World Bank.

O'Donohoe. (2009). Shedding light on microfinance equity valuation: past and present. *Available at SSRN 2619149*, 1-40.

Olson, D., & Zoubi, T. (2016). Convergence in bank performance for commercial and Islamic banks during and after the global financial crisis.,. *The Quarterly Review of Economics and Finance, 4*, 42.

(2014). *Pakistan Microfinance Network.* Retrieved from http://www.pmn.org.pk/assets/articles/e95eafccaaf580a11254137df5012ef7.pdf

Prasad, E. R. (2005). Effects of financial globalization on developing countries: some empirical evidence. In India's and China's Recent Experience with Reform and Growth. *Palgrave Macmillan UK*, 201-228.

Sahoo, S., & Mohapatro, D. (2013). Global economic turmoil—redefining microfinance institutions (MFIS) ELK. *Asia Pacific Journals, 4*(2), 1-7.

Shylendra, S. H. (2006). Microfinance institutions in Andhra Pradesh: crisis and diagnosis. *Economic and Political Weekly, 41*(1), 1959-1963.

Silva, A. C., & Chavez, A. G. (2015). Microfinance, country governance, and the global financial crisis. *Venture Capital, 2*(1), 191-213.

Srnec, K. H. (2009). Microfinance in developing countries and financial crisis. *Agricultura tropica et subtropica, 187-191*(4), 42.

Schumacher,E. F.,1973.Small is Beautiful: A Study of Economics as if People Mattered. Blond and Briggs, London.

Visconti, & Roberto, M. (2011). Global recession and microfinance risk governance in developing countries. *isk Governance and Control Journal, 1*(3), 43-61.

Wagner, & Charlotte. (2013). *Growth and crises in microfinance.* Frankfurt School of Finance & Management.

Wagner, Winkler, & Charlotte Adalbert. (2013). The vulnerability of microfinance to financial turmoil–evidence from the global financial crisis. *World Development, 51*(1), 71-90.

Appendix

Table 9. Data of Ratios (average) of 18 MFIs

MFI Name	Years	dpsm	bpsm	lpsm	wor	dasm	albfb
AMFB	2000-2006	175.25	7.42	36.08	0	74.31	112.54
	2007-2008	214.34	85.20	75.09	0.06	214.34	232.65
	2009-2014	258.97	42.55	0	0	0	0
Akhuwat	2000-2006	0	323.87	303.87	0.007	0	147.76
	2007-2008	164.97	164.97	0	0	0	0
	2009-2014	0	470.59	170.59	0.0062	0	117.27
Asasah	2000-2006	296.09	324.36	320.19	0	296.1	126.75
	2007-2008	157.47	150.42	150.42	0	0	0
	2009-2014	185.07	302.18	302.18	0.055	185.08	207.57
CSC	2000-2006	151.02	231.69	151.02	0	151.03	184.78
	2007-2008	112.41	86.107	86.10	0.19	0	172.40
	2009-2014	132.01	473.29	473.29	0.05	152.42	188.19
	2007-2008	131.25	349.24	349.24	0.02	125.46	198.52
	2009-2014	0	1081.14	1081.14	0.19	112.35	186.20
FMFB	2000-2006	122.52	294.88	287.45	0.01	383.31	137.18
	2007-2008	168.38	203.81	203.81	0.014	76.39	652.42
	2009-2014	221.67	710.85	711.60	0.25	121.67	328.58
KASFH	2000-2006	223.58	951.89	748.43	0.0074	126.27	871.19
	2007-2008	170.32	352.05	157.04	0.010	170.32	698.75
	2009-2014	131.18	935.75	200.89	0.163	131.19	391.78
Khushali Bank	2007-2008	0	535.70	219.98	0.149	0	155.83
	2009-2014	0	308.06	208.06	0.047	0	0
	2000-2006	110.95	106.31	107.97	0.257	1102.96	183.81
NRSP	2000-2006	46.23	674.68	528.98	0.050	13.28	0
	2007-2008	0	318.31	318.31	8.00E-04	114.23	0
	2009-2014	0	794.94	794.94	0.0698	125.62	253.74
ORANGI	2000-2006	0	133.48	125.70	0.1321	175.82	261.32
	2007-2008	124.52	300.63	300.63	0.0019	283.65	
	2009-2014	361.25	575.41	600.41	0.002	442.51	202.8
ORIX	2000-2006	124.24	984.06	104.60	0	332.14	
	2007-2008	147.85	625.04	225.04	0.018	114.25	
	2009-2014	125.68	1492.18	149.18	0.104	258.14	306.472
POMFB	2000-2006	0	90.59	90.59		332.14	
	2007-2008	182.54	143.02	143.02	0.049	182.54	
	2009-2014	134.94	238.80	238.80	0.524	646.45	495.38

MFI Name	Years	dpsm	bpsm	lpsm	wor	dasm	albfb
PRSP	2000-2006	120.34	719.29	127.34	0.236	1207.34	
	2007-2008				0	225.36	0
	2009-2014	0	441.76	141.76	0.005	265.89	257.62
RCDS	2000-2006				0.008	336.54	
	2007-2008	111.85			0.018	0	0.018
	2009-2014	0	526.84	226.8456	0.017	0	274.81
SRSP	2000-2006	104.77	578.39	170.1042	0.32	560.18	172.73
	2007-2008		333.52	133.52	0.149		
	2009-2014	0	553.74	253.74	0.001	0	175.13
SSF	2000-2006	114.75	730.78	161.86	0.017	127.45	129.66
	2007-2008	132.65	263.19	263.19	0.046	0	226.43
	2009-2014	165.24	690.34	190.34	0.083	0	210.93
Sungi	2000-2006	220.62	279.12	279.12	0	220.62	64.49
	2007-2008		33.51	37.22		215.98	
	2009-2014	0	692.19	192.19	0.032	0	178.35
TMFB	2000-2006	57.35	47.03	47.03		57.36	
	2007-2008	67.63	97.75	97.75	0.102	67.64	330.89
	2009-2014	399.64	713.05	113.05	0.012	436.17	535.62
TRDP	2000-2006	539.08	500.36	307.49	0.075	302.25	
	2007-2008	0	285.58	285.58	0.34	0	
	2009-2014	0	849.92	149.92	0.00	0	194.37

4

Taxpayers' Perception Of E-Filing System In Increasing Behavior Of Annual Reporting Of Tax Return (Indonesian Evidence)

Tiwi Aliffiani[a] Syamsurijal[b] Luk Luk Fuadah[c]

[a] Corresponding Author, Faculty of Economics, Sriwijaya University, Palembang Indonesia, twieonye@gmail.com
[b] Prof., Faculty of Economics, Sriwijaya University, Palembang Indonesia
[c] Ph.D., Faculty of Economics, Sriwijaya University, Palembang Indonesia

---

Keywords
E-filing, Taxpayer, Theory of Planned Behavior, Partial Least Square.

Abstract
The number of e-filing users, especially individual taxpayers has steadily been increasing, but this system has not been implemented by all registered taxpayers. This aims of this study are to examine the effect of attitude towards behavior, subjective norms, and perceived behavior control on intent to use e-filing by using the Theory of Planned Behavior. Furthermore, the effect of the intent to use e-filing on the behavior of individual taxpayer in reporting Annual Tax Return was included in the analysis. This research was conducted on 243 respondents who validly filled out the questionnaires within the period of May-June 2018 at the Primary Tax Office of Palembang Ilir Barat area. The collected data were analyzed by using Partial Least Square. The findings of the study reveal that the attitude towards behavior, subjective norms, and perceived behavior control have a positive and significant effect on the individual taxpayer's intent to use the e-filing system. In addition, the intent to use e-filing system has a positive and significant effect on the behavior of the individual taxpayers in reporting the annual tax return.

1. Introduction

Indonesia is classified as one of the developing countries in the Asian region with increasing economic growth. So it needs good sources of state revenue to finance the growth. The main source is the tax sector which is used to finance government expenditures and development. Based on the data on the realization of Indonesian state revenue in 2013-2017 presented on their website (www.bps.go.id), it is revealed that the proportion of the revenue from the tax sector is the largest domestic revenue of all state revenues, namely 86% on the average. Therefore, the state revenue from the tax sector should always be improved so that it can continue to finance the expenditures and the development of the country.

The Directorate General of Taxes has made various efforts to maximize tax revenues, among others, by conducting the tax revolution from the official assessment system to the self-assessment system, in which Indonesian citizens as taxpayers are given the trust to calculate, to assess and pay their own indebted taxes in the hope of facilitating the public to carry out their tax obligations, whereas in the official assessment system, levy responsibility lies entirely on the government as the ruler (Direktorat Jenderal Pajak, 2013).

To increase voluntary tax compliance, the taxpayers need to understand the main reason why they should pay and report taxes (Karanja, 2016). In addition, the taxpayers' motivation is very influential in improving tax compliance (Supriyati, 2012). The factors that affect the motivation of the taxpayers, among others, are external factors originating from all businesses and regulations issued by the Directorate General of Taxes to improve taxpayer's compliance. Whereas, the internal factors come from within the taxpayers themselves, namely how the taxpayers see how important it is to fulfil tax obligations (Budiarti & Sukartha, 2015).

The online system for tax filing (e-filing) and tax payments (e-billing) is launched by the Director General of Taxes with the purpose of facilitating the taxpayers to carry out their obligations. The data obtained from Primary Tax Office of Palembang Ilir Barat area. Ilir Barat area is one of the area in the city of Palembang that is located in South Sumatera, Indonesia. The data indicate that the number of e-filing users, especially individual taxpayers continues to increase since 2013-2017, although this system has not been applied by all registered taxpayers. For example in 2017, individual taxpayers who used e-filing consisted of 37% of the total number of individual taxpayers registered in the Primary Tax Office of Palembang Ilir Barat area. This mentioned ratio is lower than expected due to the fact that there were still many taxpayers who did not understand the e-filing system, so they still hesitated to use it in reporting tax liability. Based on the aforementioned finding, it is interesting to examine the perception of the individual taxpayers on the e-filing system in improving the behavior of reporting Annual Tax Return (SPT).

According to Susmita & Supadmi (2016) dan Tumuli et al. (2016), the implementation of e-filing system has a positive effect on the taxpayers' compliance. This proves that the better the quality of services provided with the application of the e-filing, the higher the compliance of the taxpayers will be. It means that the system will be able to improve the taxpayers' compliance. In addition, e-filing system will save taxpayers' time, especially for the taxpayers who already have a lot of experience in using it, whereas the taxpayers who are new to the e-filing system will require more time (Ibrahim, 2014).

The studies that have been done to analyze the individual acceptance of online tax filing services were done by Gupta et al., (2015); Sichone et al., (2017); Shao et al., (2015); Mustapha & Obid, (2015). The results of those studies show that the perceived ease of use has a significant mediation effect on the relationship between the quality of tax services and the online tax system, and the quality of tax services has a significant positive relationship with the online tax system.

The Theory of Planned Behavior used in the studies conducted by Aziz & Bani, (2017), Sichone et al., (2017), Soulange et al., (2017), and Gupta et al., (2015) revealed that the subjective norms, the perceived behavior control, and the taxpayers' attitudes over ease of use of e-filing affected the intention to use the e-filing system. Similarly, studies conducted by Karanja, (2016) and Saad, (2012) show that the attitudes of the taxpayers, the influence of co-workers, and the control of perceived behavior are the factors that are most influential in the behavior of non-compliance of the taxpayers.

Several studies have been undertaken with the aim at analyzing the taxpayers' intentions to comply with the tax regulations which become tax compliance behavior are the studies undertaken by Yusdita et al., (2017) and Damayanti et al., (2015). The results of the studies provide empirical evidence that the intention to obey has a positive effect on the tax compliance behavior. The study by Marthadinasyah et al.,(2014), in addition to analyzing the effect of the attitudes, the subjective norms, and the control of perceived behavior, shows an empirical evidence that moral obligation has a positive influence on the intention to comply with the annual filing of tax return.

Learning from the previous studies mentioned above, this study uses the Theory of Planned Behavior (TPB) to explain the factors that affect the perception of individual taxpayers to use of e-filing system. These factors include the tax reporting attitude, the subjective norms, the control of perceived behavior of the individual taxpayers' intent to use e-filing system. And it is also intended to know the influence of the individual taxpayers' intention to use e-filing system on the individual taxpayers' behavior in reporting Annual Tax Return.

Section 2 of this study presents a literature review of the factors affecting the perception of the individual taxpayers in the use of e-filing systems and the hypothesis development. Section 3 presents the methodology used in this study. Besides Section 4 presents the results and discussion. Finally section 5 of this study presents the conclusions, the limitations of this study, and the recommendation for further studies.

1. Literature Review And Hypothesis Development

1.1. Theory of Planned Behavior

The Theory of Planned Behavior (Ajzen, 1991) is one of the basic theories in psychology that has been used extensively to predict behavior. In the theory of planned behavior there are three main determinants of behavioral intention, namely attitude towards behavior, which is a reflection of a person's positive or negative feelings toward a predetermined behavior (Jogiyanto, 2007). According to Zikmund et al (2010) attitudes consist of three components: firstly emotion or feelings involved, secondly consciousness or knowledge, and thirdly behavior or tendency to act. An individual who has a positive belief will decide to accept a prescribed behavior (Ajzen, 1991).

Secondly, the subjective norm is the perception or an individual's views on the beliefs of others who will give effect to the intention to perform or not to do the behavior specified (Jogiyanto, 2007). The assessment of others which has significant influence is that which comes from the people such as parents, spouses, friends, and teachers. The subjective norm can be divided into two influences: interpersonal and external influences. Interpersonal influence is the influence of friends, family members, co-workers, bosses and experienced individuals known as potential adopters. While the external influence is the influence of external parties such as external reports of mass media, reports and expert opinions, and other non-personal information considered by individuals in conducting their behavior (Jogiyanto, 2007).

Thirdly, the control of perceived behavioral is the perception of an individual about his ability to perform certain behaviors (Ajzen, 1991). The perceived behavior control reflects the past experience and also anticipates the existing constraints. The greater the belief in the attitudes toward behavior, the subjective norms, and the greater perceived behavior control, the stronger the intention of an individual to perform a predetermined behavior (Jogiyanto, 2007).

The three aforementioned main determinants simultaneously will result in behavioral intention and which will lead to the behavior. Behavioral intention is an indication of an individual's desire to perform certain behaviors and is assumed to be a precursor to behavior. While the behavior is the actions or real activities undertaken by an individual (Jogiyanto, 2007). The decision of an individual to behave occurs on the will / control of the will of the individual. But not all behaviors are done in situations where an individual has full control over his behavior. A situation of loss of self-control occurs when the individual faces the limitations of the lack of resources used to carry out the behavior.

1.2. Previous Studies

Several previous researches have used the theory of planned behavior (TPB) in their studies, among others, Sichone et al. (2017) who conducted a study on the effects of perceived risk (security and information confidentiality), perceived benefits (cost savings and rate of return), and supporting condition (support and access to computers) of intent to adopt e-filing in Tanzania. The results of the study show that the risk of perception and supporting condition are negatively correlated and not significant with intent to adopt e-filing. While the benefits of perceptions are positively and significantly related to the intention to adopt e-filing.

The study conducted by Soulange et al. (2017) found that the use of perceived perceptions and perceived convenience influenced the intentions to adopt e-filing and the behaviors of the Mauritian taxpayers. However, the perceived security and perceived service do not affect the intentions of their e-filing adoption. In addition, according to Aziz et al. (2017) the use of perception is the most significant determinant of behavior for using e-LEJAR tax services. Perceived ease of use, although does not directly affect the behavior intention to use but it is the most significant variable that affects the attitude of the taxpayers to use e-LEJAR tax.

Many studies have been done about evaluating electronic taxation systems from the point of view of the taxpayers. On the contrary, Hammouri & Shanab (2017) evaluated the electronic taxation system in Jordan from an employee's perspective. Because the main factor affecting the success of the system is the level of employees' satisfaction with the use of electronic tax system. The study found that the ease of use of perceptions, the background of information technology, incentives, and social influences are key predictors of employees' satisfaction. While the use of perception is not significant in this relationship.

Then Olushola & Abiola (2017) conducted a study by reviewing the most recent theoretical model used in the study on information technology adoption. Using a literature review approach of more than 25 studies reviewed in the field of information adoption over the last 30 years and identifying the strengths and weaknesses of each theory used. The finding is that the technology acceptance model is so far the most widely used to support the study in this field followed by the theory of behavioral planning.

Karanja (2016) examined the factors affecting voluntary tax compliance in Kenya using the TPB. The result of this study is that the attitudes and perceptions of tax misuse, of politicians, co-workers and financial obligations and families have a positive influence on tax non-compliance. Likewise with the social norms and the income levels of respondents are the factors that most influential in affecting the non-compliance of tax payments. In addition, Damayanti et al. (2015a) examined the perception of trust in the government against taxpayers' intentions to behave obediently. The result of this study is that trust in government give positive influence to the taxpayers' intention to behave obediently, which is in accordance with the results of the study by Damayanti et al.,(2015b).

2.3. Hypothesis Formulation

2.3.1. The Effect of Attitude Towards Behavior on the Intent of Using an E-filing System

The attitudes towards tax reports are obtained from the belief / trust of the taxpayers on everything that is known, understood and experienced by the taxpayers regarding the implementation of tax laws. The taxpayers' beliefs about the behavior of online tax returns will result in a positive or negative attitude towards tax compliance that will ultimately shape taxpayer intentions to use or not to use e-filing systems.

Saad (2014) states that taxpayers with inadequate technical knowledge will regard the tax system as a complex and therefore the cause of non-compliance. The studies by Marthadinasyah et al.(2014) and Gupta et al.(2015) have found that attitudes toward behavior have a positive effect on trust or intention toward the behavior. The study undertaken by Aziz et al. (2017) states that the attitude of the taxpayer is one of the variables that has the most significant positive influence on the behavior of e-LEJAR tax usage. Saad (2012) also believes that the attitudes of the taxpayers have a positive effect on taxpayers' non-compliance behavior. Therefore, taxpayers who believe that doing obedient behavior in reporting the tax return will have a positive attitude so as to generate a positive intention toward the behavior. Therefore H_1 is formed as the folowing.

H_1: Attitude towards behavior has a positive effect on individual taxpayers' intentions to use e-filing system.

2.3.2. The Effect of Subjective Norms on the Intent of Using E-filing System

The subjective norm is the perception or the individual's view of the beliefs of others that will affect the intention to perform or not to do the behavior under consideration. Other people's judgments which have significant effect among others are those of the parents, the spouses, the friends, and the teachers. When a person believes in a reference that motivates him to obey and thinks he should behave in a manner, it is said to have accepted social pressure to do that behavior. And conversely, someone who believes that the references that motivate them to obey but do not agree to conduct a behavior will have subjective norms that put pressure on them to avoid doing such behavior.

In accordance with Chaouali et al. (2016) who states that the aspects of social influence, except descriptive norms, and multi-dimensional beliefs have a significant effect on the behavior of e-filing in Tunisia. In addition, the social norms pressure is also one of the variables that positively affect employees' satisfaction behavior (Hammouri & Shanab, 2017). According to Lu et.all (2010) the taxpayer's perception of online tax reporting will be influenced by a stronger external environment. For example, governments are forcing taxpayers to use tax reporting online, or taxpayers want to adjust to the surrounding environment like family, friends, and neighbors. The above perceptions can be classified as social norms, since the intention to behave in an individual is influenced by the pressure of society (Ajzen, 1991).

In addition, the intention to behave in an individual is influenced by moral norms, in which an individual who decides to engage in a behavior will be affected by internal (Randall & Gibson, 1991). The more an individual has a positive internal moral norm, such as reporting the actual tax, approving government policy, the more that trust directly affects the subjective norm of the individual towards taxation. Hence H_2 is formed as follows.

H_2: The subjective norm positively affects the intent of individual taxpayers to use e-filing system.

2.3.3. The Effect of Perceived Behavioral Control on Intent of Using an E-filing System

Perceived Behavioral Control is an individual's perception of his ability or level of perceived control to engage in certain behaviors (Ajzen, 1991). This belief is gained not only by past experience with behavior, but it is also influenced by information from the experiences of friends and other factors that enhance and reduce perceptions of behavioral difficulties. The more resources and opportunities the individual has and the fewer obstacles that must be anticipated the greater the trust of control over behavior. In accordance with Gupta et al. (2015) higher perceived behavior and perception controls are associated with higher intentions in the behavior of adopting online tax filing.

When taxpayers have a positive perception of online tax reporting, it means that they have enough understanding and can operate the system and have confidence that the system is profitable such as being fast, accurate, easy service without having to queue. So that the perceived behavior is positively influenced and behavioral intentions will also increase. Taxpayers will be able to know that there is a positive behavior intent behind the advantages and benefits of the online tax reporting system provided by governments (Lu et al., 2010). So H_3 is formed as the folowing.

H_3: Perceptive behavior control positively affects individual taxpayers' intent to use e-filing system

2.3.4. Effect of Intent to Use an E-filing System on Individual Taxpayers' Behavior Report of Annual Income Tax Through E-filing

Intention is a desire to do a behavior according to the will of the individual. Intentions can be related to behavior or actions and can be predicted with high level of accuracy (Jogiyanto, 2007). If a taxpayer has the perception that his tax obligations will have many advantages, he will have a positive intention to tax liabilities and will affect his taxpayer behavior (Juniati et al., 2014). Behavior is a real and observed response in certain situations with respect to the given target (Ajzen, 1991). A person's behavior is determined by his intention to engage in a behavior and is a function of his attitude toward his subjective behavior and norm. Therefore H_4 is formed as the folowing.

H_4: The intentions of the individual taxpayers to use e-filing system have a positive effect on the individual taxpayers' behavior in reporting Annual Tax Return through e-filing

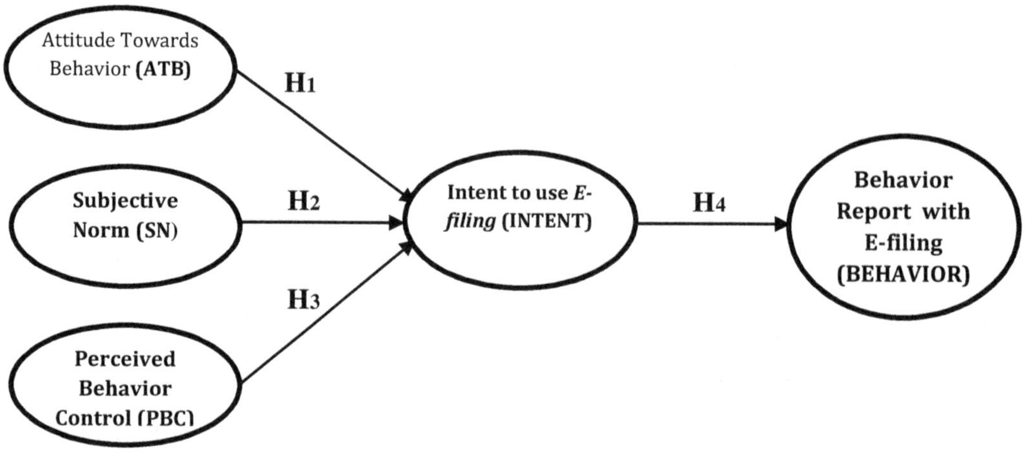

Figure 1: Conceptual Framework

3. Research Methods

This study uses descriptive method by using cross sectional data. This study is conducted at Primary Tax Office of Palembang Ilir Barat area. The data used are primary data of the year 2018. The subjects of the study are the individual taxpayers, entrepreneurs and professional people registered at the Primary Tax Office of Palembang Ilir Barat area. The data were gathered by means of a series of questionnaires submitted by the author which were then filled out by the respondents. The population of this study is all taxpayers, entrepreneurs and professional people registered at the Primary Tax of Palembang Ilir Barat area. The sample size of the population was determined by Slovin's formula. The formula of Slovin is given as follows.

$$n = \frac{N}{1 + Ne^2}$$

Where:

n = a sample size

N = population size

e = desired margin of error (percent allowance for non-precision)

In this research, the total number of samples required with 5% *allowance* for non-precision is 392 respondents.

This study uses the technique of data analysis of Partial Least Square (PLS) which is one of the statistical methods of Structural Equation Modeling (SEM). The structural equation in this study is as follows:

Model I :

INTENT = $\gamma_1 ATB + \gamma_2 SN + \gamma_3 PBC + \varepsilon_1$ I

Model II :

BEHAVIOR = $\gamma_1 ATB + \gamma_2 SN + \gamma_3 PBC + \gamma_4 INTENT + \varepsilon_2$ II

4. Results and Discussion

4.1. Distribution of Research Questionnaires

Data collection in this study was conducted through the distribution of questionnaires directly to the respondents in this case, the taxpayers of private entrepreneurs and professionals. The questionnaires were distributed throughout May-June 2018 and 263 answered questionnaires were returned, 129 were not returned, 20 were invalid, so the number of valid questionnaires was 243, with the level of response of 62%.

The questionnaire was divided into 5 sections consist of 3 independent variables and 2 dependent variables, which are attitude towards behavior (ATB), subjective norms (SN), perceived behavior control (PBC), individual taxpayers' intent to use an e-filing system (INTENT), and individual taxpayers' behavior in reporting tax return through e-filing (BEHAVIOR). Indicators that were used to measure the variables taken from previous study (See Appendix 9).

4.2. The Results of Evaluation of Measurement Model (Outer Model)

4.2.1. Measurement Model (Outer Model) with Convergent Validity

The value of factor loadings is presented in Table 1. Most indicators have values above 0.7. However there are 3 indicators that have a value below 0.7, namely ATB2 of 0.001; SN4 of 0.622; and PBC2 of -0.223. According to Abdillah & Jogiyanto (2015), if the value of factor loadings is below 0.5 then this indicator can be removed from the variable because this indicator is not loaded to the variable that represents it. But if the value of factor loadings is between 0.5 - 0.7, it should not be removed if the AVE value is greater than 0.5. The AVE (Average Variance Extracted) value is presented in Table 2.

Table 1: Factor Loadings Value of Each Indicator before Estimating

No	Variables	Indicator	
		Symbol	Value of *Factor Loadings*
1	Attitude towards behavior (ATB)	ATB1	0.795
		ATB2	***0.001***
		ATB3	0.866
		ATB4	0.755
		ATB5	0.885
		ATB6	0.884
2	Subjective norm (SN)	SN1	0.842
		SN2	0.840
		SN3	0.862
		SN4	***0.622***
3	Perceived behavior control (PBC)	PBC1	0.878
		PBC2	***-0.223***
		PBC3	0.877
		PBC4	0.881
4	The intent of individual taxpayers to use e-filing (INTENT)	INTENT1	0.869
		INTENT2	0.916
		INTENT3	0.939
		INTENT4	0.937
		INTENT5	0.897
5	Individual Taxpayers' Behavior in Reporting Annual Tax Return through e-filing (BEHAVIOR)	BEHAVIOR1	0.901
		BEHAVIOR2	0.894
		BEHAVIOR3	0.914
		BEHAVIOR4	0.907

Table 2: AVE (Average Variance Extracted) Value before Estimation

No	Variables	AVE	Result
1	Attitude towards behavior (ATB)	0.586	Valid
2	Subjective norm (SN)	0.636	Valid
3	Perceived behavior control (PBC)	0.592	Valid
4	The intent of individual taxpayers to use e-filling (INTENT)	0.832	Valid
5	Individual Taxpayers' Behavior in Reporting Annual Tax Return through e-filing (BEHAVIOR)	0.817	Valid

The subjective norm variable (SN) shows a value above 0.5, so the SN4 indicator with the factor loadings value of 0.622 should not be removed. As for the indicator ATB2 and PBC2 which have the value of factor loadings below 0.5 will be re-estimated by removing the indicator. The small value of factor loadings is likely due to the bias on the questionnaire's question given to the respondents.

After the indicator ATB2 and PBC2 are excluded then the result of factor loadings and AVE values after re-estimation can be seen in Table 3 and Table 4 below. The value of AVE after estimation on the variable Attitude report of individual taxpayers (ATB) and perceived behavior control (PBC) has increased. While the AVE values for other variables remain.

Table 3: Factor Loadings Value of Each Indicator after Estimation

No	Variables	Indicator	
		Symbol	Value of *Factor Loadings*
1	Attitude towards behavior (ATB)	ATB1	0.795
		ATB3	0.866
		ATB4	0.755
		ATB5	0.885
		ATB6	0.885
2	Subjective norm (SN)	SN1	0.842
		SN2	0.840
		SN3	0.862
		SN4	0.622
3	Perceived behavior control (PBC)	PBC1	0.878
		PBC3	0.880
		PBC4	0.880
4	Individual taxpayers' intent to use e-filling (INTENT)	INTENT1	0.869
		INTENT2	0.916
		INTENT3	0.939
		INTENT4	0.937
		INTENT5	0.897
5	Individual taxpayers' behavior in Reporting Annual Tax Return through e-filling (BEHAVIOR)	BEHAVIOR1	0.901
		BEHAVIOR2	0.894
		BEHAVIOR3	0.914
		BEHAVIOR4	0.907

The value of factor loadings as presented in Table 3 show a positive result. All the variables have values above 0.7 except for SN4 that is between 0.5 - 0.7. This value is acceptable considering the AVE value on Table 4 below.

Table 4: AVE (Average Variance Extracted) Value after Estimation

No	Variables	AVE	Result
1	Attitude towards behavior (ATB)	0.704	Valid
2	Subjective norm (SN)	0.636	Valid
3	Perceived behavior control (PBC)	0.773	Valid
4	Individual taxpayers' intent to use e-filling (INTENT)	0.832	Valid
5	Individual taxpayers' behavior in Reporting Annual Tax Return through e-filling (BEHAVIOR)	0.817	Valid

Based on the results above, it is shown in Table 4 that all variables have AVE value above 0.5. Therefore, it is concluded that all variables fulfill the rule of thumb in terms of the convergent validity test.

4.2.2. Measurement Model (Outer Model) with Discriminant Validity

Cross loading values after re-estimation are presented in Table 5. cross loading values of each indicator in a variable will be different from indicators in other variables and accumulates on the variables in question. So it can be concluded that all variables meet the requirements of discriminant validity test.

Table 5: Cross Value Loading after Estimation

	ATB	SN	PBC	INTENT E-FILING	REPORT BEHAVIOR
ATB1	*0.795*	0.579	0.607	0.562	0.548
ATB3	*0.866*	0.576	0.626	0.669	0.609
ATB4	*0.755*	0.526	0.536	0.538	0.442
ATB5	*0.885*	0.628	0.587	0.684	0.604
ATB6	*0.885*	0.556	0.546	0.625	0.603
SN1	0.725	*0.842*	0.560	0.674	0.644
SN2	0.441	*0.840*	0.478	0.422	0.495
SN3	0.532	*0.862*	0.474	0.502	0.505
SN4	0.384	*0.622*	0.560	0.393	0.448
PBC1	0.658	0.625	*0.878*	0.700	0.707
PBC3	0.512	0.531	*0.880*	0.662	0.633
PBC4	0.652	0.551	*0.880*	0.644	0.600
INTENT1	0.752	0.636	0.688	*0.869*	0.798
INTENT2	0.634	0.611	0.763	*0.916*	0.731
INTENT3	0.677	0.563	0.702	*0.939*	0.721
INTENT4	0.662	0.565	0.658	*0.937*	0.733
INTENT5	0.630	0.582	0.653	*0.897*	0.702
BEHAVIOR1	0.589	0.665	0.683	0.714	*0.901*
BEHAVIOR2	0.605	0.570	0.588	0.682	*0.894*
BEHAVIOR3	0.570	0.572	0.735	0.777	*0.914*
BEHAVIOR4	0.670	0.621	0.652	0.750	*0.907*

4.2.3. Measurement Model (Outer Model) with Reliability Test

Reliability test shown uses two methods, namely Cronbach's alpha and composite reliability. In this study the values of Cronbach's alpha and composite reliability are presented in Table 6.

Table 6: Cronbach's Alpha and Composite Reliability Value after Estimation

No	Variabel	*Cronbach's alpha*	*Composite reliability*	Information
1	Attitude towards behavior (ATB)	0.894	0.922	Reliable
2	Subjective norm (SN)	0.806	0.873	Reliable
3	Perceived behavior control (PBC)	*0.853*	0.911	Reliable
4	Individual taxpayers' intent to use e-filling (INTENT)	0.949	0.961	Reliable
5	Individual taxpayers' behavior in Reporting Annual Tax Return through e-filling (BEHAVIOR)	0.925	0.947	Reliable

Figure 2: Path Diagram Model of Individual Taxpayers' Behavior in Tax Return Reporting with E-filing after Estimation

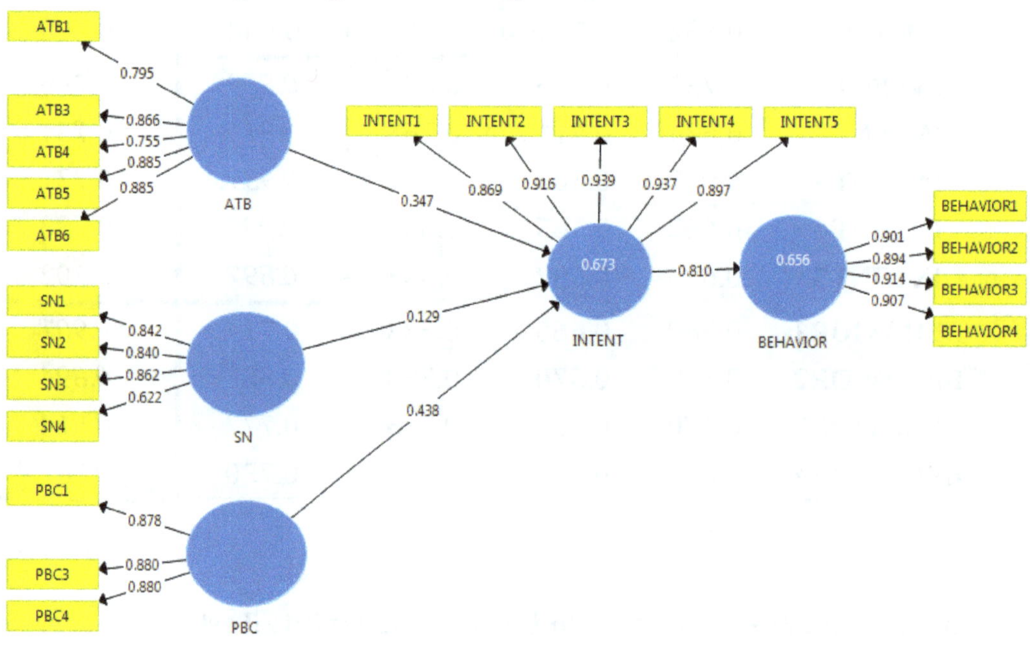

4.3. Evaluation of Structural Model (Inner Model)

The structural model is made to ensure that the constructed structural model is well constructed and accurate. Inner model evaluations are viewed in several ways, namely by using the coefficient of determination (R Square), prediction relevance (Q^2) and Goodness of Fit (GoF).

4.3.1. Inner Model Evaluation with R^2 (R-Square)

The value of R^2 is used to measure the level of variation of the independent variable changes against the dependent variable. The higher the value of R^2, the better the prediction model of the proposed research model (Abdillah & Jogiyanto, 2015) The value of R^2 (R-Square) can be seen in table 7 below.

Table 7: R-Square Value after Estimation

No	Dependent Variables	R-*Square*
1	Individual Taxpayers' intent to use e-filling (INTENT)	0.673
2	Individual Taxpayers' Behavior in Reporting Annual Tax Return through E-filling (BEHAVIOR)	0.656

The variable of individual taxpayers' intent to use e-filling (INTENT) has variance which can be explained by three independent variables, namely taxpayers' report attitude of individual person (ATB), subjective norm (SN) and perceived behavior control (PBC) of 67.3 %, while the remaining 32.7% is explained by other factors.

The variable of individual taxpayers' behavior in reporting the Annual Tax Return through e-filing has the variance that can be explained by the three independent variables, namely the report attitude of individual taxpayers (ATB), subjective norm (SN), perceived behavior control (PBC) and Individual taxpayers' Intent variable to use e-filling (INTENT) of 65.6%, while the remaining 34.4% is explained by other factors.

4.3.2. Inner Model Evaluation with Q^2 (Prediction relevance)

The value of Q^2 is used to measure how good is the value of observation generated by the model and also the parameter estimation. The model is said to be feasible and has a relevant predictive value if it has a value of Q^2 greater than zero ($Q^2 > 0$). To calculate Q^2 we can use the following formula:

$$Q^2 = 1 - (1 - R_1^2)(1 - R_2^2) \ldots\ldots\ldots (1 - R_p^2),$$

$$Q^2 = 1 - (1 - 0.671)(1 - 0.656)$$

$$Q^2 = 0.887$$

Based on the above calculation, it can be concluded that the value of $Q^2>0$, namely 0.887, it can be said that the proposed structural model is relevant.

4.3.3. Inner Model Evaluation with GoF (Goodness of Fit)

To obtain the GoF value of the model, calculation is done manually because the PLS does not provide special menu to calculate GoF (Abdillah & Jogiyanto, 2015). According to Tenenhaus et al. (2004), GoF PLS can be measured using the following formula:

$$GoF = 0.707$$

$$GoF = \sqrt{\overline{AVE} \ x \ \overline{R^2}}$$

$$GoF = \sqrt{0.752 \ x \ 0.665}$$

According to to Tenenhaus et al. (2004), small GoF value = 0.1, medium GoF value = 0.35, and large GoF value = 0.38. Based on results of the testing of R Square, Q^2 and GoF, it can be concluded that the model formed in this study is good and accurate.

4.4. Hypothesis Testing

Hypothesis testing proposed can be seen on t-statistics after data processing. Statistical estimation results are presented in Table 8.

Table 8: Estimation of Parameters and Significance of Path Test

	Original Sample	Sample Mean	Standard Deviation	t-Statistics	P Values
ATB -> INTENT	0.347	0.342	0.079	4.412	0.000
SN -> INTENT	0.129	0.134	0.061	2.118	0.035
PBC -> INTENT	0.438	0.436	0.075	5.808	0.000
INTENT -> BEHAVIOR	0.810	0.807	0.045	17.821	0.000

4.4.1. The Effect of Tax Report Attitudes on Intent to Use an E-filing System

The first hypothesis states that the tax report attitude has a positive effect on the intention of individual taxpayers to use e-filing system. It can be seen in the original value of the sample which shows that there is a positive effect of 0.347, in which each addition of 1 point of tax report attitude will increase an intention of e-filing of 0.347 point. While the level of significance is seen at the value of t-statistics which is greater than 1.96 (>1.96) of

4.412 and the value of the p-value is smaller than 0.05, namely 0.000, so that the results of this study accept the first hypothesis (H_1). So that it can be concluded that the report attitude of the individual taxpayers has a positive and significant impact on the individual taxpayers' intent to use e-filing system. The higher the taxpayers' trust about reporting the annual tax return by e-filing, the more positive the attitude of the taxpayers that will ultimately shape the taxpayers' intent to use the e-filing system. Conversely, the lower the trust/attitudes of the taxpayers to use e-filing, the lower the intention to use it.

Therefore, the Directorate General of Taxation should continue to conduct activities/socialization to increase the taxpayers' belief / trust in tax compliance. The results of this study are consistent with the results of the studies conducted by Gopi & Ramayah, (2007), Lu et al. (2010), Saad (2012), Saad (2014), Moorthy et.al (2014), Marthadinasyah et al.(2014), Gupta et al.(2015), Damayanti et.al (2015b), Karanja (2016), Soulange et al. (2017) dan Aziz et al. (2017).

4.4.2. The Effect of Subjective Norms on Intent to Use E-filing System

The second hypothesis states that the subjective norm positively affect the intention of individual taxpayers to use e-filling system. It can be seen in the original value of the sample that shows that there is a positive influence of 0.129, in which each addition of 1 point of subjective norms will increase e-filing intention of 0.129 points. While the level of significance is seen at the value of t-statistics which is greater than 1.96 (>1.96) of 2.118 and the value of p-value which is smaller than 0.05, namely 0.035, so that the results of this study accepted the second hypothesis (H_2). So it can be concluded that the subjective norm has a positive and significant effect on the intention of individual taxpayers to use e-filing system. The higher the taxpayers' trust in others who motivate them (e.g parents, spouses, friends, government) to use e-filing, the higher their intention to use e-filing system. On the contrary, the lower the taxpayers' trust in others around him to use e-filling, the lower their intention to use it. The result of this study is consistent with the results of the studies conducted by Randall & Gibson (1991), Gopi & Ramayah, (2007), Lu et.al (2010), Damayanti, et.al (2015), Gupta et al.(2015), Shao et.al (2015), Chaouali et al. (2016), Karanja (2016) dan Hammouri & Shanab (2017).

4.4.3. The Effect of Perceived Behavior Control on the Intent to Use E-filing System

The third hypothesis states that the control of perceived behavior has a positive effect on the intention of individual taxpayers' intent to use e-filing system. It can be seen that in the original value of the sample there is a positive effect of 0.438, in which each addition of 1 point of the control of the perceived behavior will increase the e-filling intention of 0.438 points. While the level of significance is seen at the t-statistic value which is greater than 1.96 (>1.96) namely 5.808 and the p-value is less than 0.05, namely 0.000. So that the results of this study accept the third hypothesis (H_3). So that, it can be concluded that perceived behavior control has a positive and significant effect on the individual taxpayers' intention to use e-filling system. The higher the ability and the opportunity owned by the taxpayers, the higher the trust of the individual taxpayers' intent to use e-filling system. On the contrary, the lower the ability and the opportunity owned by the individual taxpayers, the lower the intention of the individual taxpayers to use e-filling system. The result of this study is consistent with the results of the studies done by Gopi & Ramayah, (2007), Lu et al., (2010), Gupta et al. (2015), dan Chaouali et al. (2016).

4.4.4. The Effect of the Intent to Use E-filing System on the Individual Taxpayers' Behavior Reports of Annual Tax Return Through E-filing

The fourth hypothesis states that the intention of the individual taxpayers to use e-filing system has a positive effect on the behavior of the individual taxpayers in reporting Annual Tax Return through e-filing. It can be seen at the value of the original sample which shows that there is a positive effect of 0.810, in which each addition of 1 point of intent for e-filing will increase the behavior of individual taxpayers' behavior in reporting the annual tax return of 0.810 points. Whereas the significance level is seen at the t-statistic value which is greater than 1.96 (>1.96), namely 17.821 and the p-value is less than 0.05, namely 0.000. So, the results of this study accept the fourth hypothesis (H_4). So it can be concluded that the intention of using e-filing system has a positive and significant effect on the behavior of individual taxpayers' behavior in reporting annual tax return through e-filing. The higher the taxpayers' intent to use the e-filing, the higher the individual taxpayers' behavior to report the annual tax return through e-filing. Conversely, the lower the intention of the individual taxpayers to use e-filing the lower the taxpayers' behavior to report the annual tax return through e-filing. The results of this study are consistent with the results of the studies conducted by Gopi & Ramayah, (2007), Lu et al. (2010), Juniati et al.,(2014), Damayanti, et.al (2015), dan Damayanti et.al (2015b).

5. Conclusion

The results of this study revealed that there is a positive effect of the tax reporting attitude, the subjective norm, the perceived behavior control on the personal taxpayers' intention to use e-filings system. And the independent variables can explain the intention of using e-filing system as much as 67.3% while the remaining 32.7% is explained by other factors. In addition, there is also a positive effect of the individual taxpayers' intention to use e-filing system on the behavior of the individual taxpayers in reporting the annual tax return. And the behavior of the individual taxpayers in reporting the annual tax return can be explained by the attitude of tax reports, the subjective norms, the control the perceived behavior, and intent of using the e-filing system as much as 65.6%, while the remaining 34.4% is explained by other factors. So all the hypotheses formed within the study are accepted.

This study has some limitations, among others, are as follows: Firstly, the independent variables used in this study are limited to three variables based on the Theory of Planned Behavior, namely the tax reporting behavior, the subjective norms and the perceived behavior control. Secondly, the sample collection period for this study was conducted for 2 months only, from May to June 2018. To improve these limitations, the author suggests that for further studies, the researcher can extend the period of sample gathering to obtain maximum results. In addition, the researcher is suggested to add independent variable, so that he can do more in-depth examination about taxpayers' behavior.

References

Abdillah, W., & Jogiyanto. (2015). *Partial Least Square Alternatif Structural Equation Modeling dalam Penelitian Bisnis* (Pertama). CV Andi Offset.

Agarwal, R., & Karahanna, E. (2000). Time Flies When You're Having Fun: Cognitive Absorption And Beliefs About Information Technology Usage'. *MIS Quarterly, 24*(4), 665–694.

Ajzen, I. (1991). The theory of planned behavior. *Orgnizational Behavior and Human*

Decision Processes, 50, 179–211.

Aziz, S. A., & Bani, M. A. A. (2017). Tax E-Lejar Service : Determinants of Behavioral Intention among Individual Taxpayers in Kuala Lumpur. *ICoEC 2017 Proceedings I*, (September 2017), 90–98.

Budiarti, K. M., & Sukartha, P. D. Y. (2015). Faktor Eksternal dan Internal yang Memengaruhi Motivasi dalam Memenuhi Kewajiban Perpajakan. *E-Jurnal Akuntasi Universitas Udayana, 11*(1), 29–43.

Badan Pusat Statistik. (2017). Realisasi Penerimaan Negara. Retrieved from https://www.bps.go.id

Chaouali, W., Yahia, I. Ben, Charfeddine, L., & Triki, A. (2016). Understanding citizens' adoption of e-filing in developing countries: An empirical investigation. *Journal of High Technology Management Research, 27*(2), 161–176.

Chin, W. W., Marcolin, B. L., & Newted, P. R. (2003). A Partial least Squares Latent Variable Modeling Approach For Measuring Interaction Effects: Results From a Monte Carlo Simulation Study and Voice Mail Emotion/Adoption Study. *Proceedings of the Seventeenth International Conference on Information Systems*, 21–41. https://doi.org/10.1287/isre.14.2.189.16018

Damayanti, T. W., Sutrisno, Subekti, I., & Baridwan, Z. (2015a). The Role of Taxpayer's Perception of the Government and Society to Improve Tax Compliance. *Accounting and Finance Research, 4*(1).

Damayanti, T. W., Sutrisno, Subekti, I., & Baridwan, Z. (2015b). Trust and Uncertainty Orientation: An Efforts to Create Tax Compliance in Social Psychology Framework. *Procedia - Social and Behavioral Sciences, 211*(September), 938–944.

Direktorat Jenderal Pajak, K. K. R. I. (2013). Undang-Undang PPh dan Peraturan Pelaksanaannya (p. 707).

Gopi, M., & Ramayah, T. (2007). Applicability of theory of planned behavior in predicting intention to trade online: Some evidence from a developing country. *International Journal of Emerging Markets, 2*(4), 348–360. https://doi.org/10.1108/17468800710824509

Gupta, G., Zaidi, S. K., Udo, G. J., & Bagchi, K. K. (2015). The Effect of Espoused Culture on Acceptance of Online Tax Filing Services in an Emerging Economy. *Advances in*

Business Research, *6*(1), 14–31.

Hammouri, Q., & Shanab, E. A. (2017). Exploring the factors influencing employees' satisfaction toward e-tax systems. *International Journal of Public Sector Performance Management*, *3*(2), 169–190.

Ibrahim, I. (2014). The Compliance Time Costs of Malaysian Personal Income Tax System: E-filers vs. Manual-filers. *Procedia - Social and Behavioral Sciences*, *164*(August), 522–527.

Jogiyanto. (2007). *Sistem Informasi Keperilakuan* (II). CV Andi Offset.

Juniati, Liya ; Zirman ; Hariyani, E. (2014). Analisis Faktor-faktor yang Berpengaruh terhadap Tax Compliance Penyetoran dan Pelaporan SPT Masa PPN (Survei pada PKP yang Terdaftar Di KPP Pratama Tampan Pekanbaru). *JOM FEKON*, *1*(2), 1–17.

Karanja, E. K. (2016). Factors Affecting Voluntary Tax Compliance On Rental Income : Acase Study Of Nairobi Landlords. *The Strategic Journal of Business & Change Management*, *3*(3 (12)), 201–222.

Lu, C., Huang, S., & Lo, P. (2010). An empirical study of on-line tax filing acceptance model : Integrating TAM and TPB. *African Journal of Business Management*, *4*(May), 800–810.

Marthadinasyah ; Meutia, Inten ; Mukhtaruddin ; Saputra, D. (2014). Taxpayer Compliance in Tax Filing at Palembang City. *Jurnal InFestasi*, *10*(2), 01–09.

Moorthy, M. K., Samsuri, A. S. B., Hussin, S. B. M., Othman, M. S. B., & Chelliah, M. K. (2014). E-Filing Behaviour among Academics in Perak State in Malaysia. *Technology and Investment*, *5*(2), 79–94.

Mustapha, B., & Obid, S. N. B. S. (2015). Tax Service Quality: The Mediating Effect of Perceived Ease of Use of the Online Tax System. *Procedia - Social and Behavioral Sciences*, *172*, 2–9.

Olushola, T., & Abiola, J. O. (2017). The Efficacy of Technology Acceptance Model: A Review of Applicable Theoretical Models in Information Technology Researches. *Quest Journals Journal of Research in Business and Management*, *4*(11), 70–83. Retrieved from www.questjournals.org

Randall, D. M., & Gibson, A. M. (1991). Ethical Decision Making in the Medical Profession : An Application of the Theory of Planned Behavior. *Business Ethics*, *10*(2), 111–122.

Saad, N. (2012). Tax Non-Compliance Behaviour: Taxpayers View. *Procedia - Social and*

Behavioral Sciences, 65(ICIBSoS), 344–351.

Saad, N. (2014). Tax Knowledge, Tax Complexity and Tax Compliance: Taxpayers' View. *Procedia - Social and Behavioral Sciences, 109*(1), 1069–1075.

Sentosa, I., & Mat, N. K. N. (2012). Examining a Theory of Planned Behavior (TPB) and Technology Acceptance Model (TAM) in Internetpurchasing Using Structural Equation Modeling. *Journal of Arts, Science & Commerce, 3*(2), 62–77.

Shao, B., Luo, X., & Liao, Q. (2015). Factors influencing e-tax filing adoption intention by business users in China. *Electronic Government, an International Journal, 11*(4), 283. https://doi.org/10.1504/EG.2015.071408

Sichone, J., Milano, R. J., & Kimea, A. J. (2017). The Influence of Facilitating Conditions, Perceived Benefits, and Perceived Risk on Intention To Adopt E-Filing in Tanzania. *Business Management Review*, (July-Dec), 50–59.

Soulange, M. L., Soondram, H., Jugurnath, B., & Seedoyal, A. B. (2017). E-Filing Behaviour among Mauritian Taxpayers. *Proceedings of Annual South African Business Research Conference*, (May).

Supriyati. (2012). Dampak Motivasi Dan Pengetahuan Perpajakan Terhadap Kepatuhan Wajib Pajak. *Jurnal InFestasi, 8*(2), 171–178.

Susmita, P. R., & Supadmi, N. L. (2016). Pengaruh Kualitas Pelayanan, Sanksi Perpajakan, Biaya Kepatuhan Pajak, Dan Penerapan E-Filing Pada Kepatuhan Wajib Pajak. *E-Jurnal Akuntansi Universitas Udayana*, (Februari), 1239–1269.

Taylor, S., & Todd, P. A. (1995). Understanding information technology usage: A test of competing models. *Information Systems Research*.

Tenenhaus, M., Amato, S., & Vinzi, E. V. (2004). A global goodness-of-fit index for PLS structural equation modelling. *The XLII SIS Scientific Meeting*, 739–742.

Tumuli, A. K., Sondakh, J. J., & Wokas, H. R. . (2016). Analisis Penerapan E-Spt Dan E-filling Dalam Upaya Peningkatan Kepatuhan Wajib Pajak. *Jurnal EMBA, 4*(3), 102–112.

Yusdita, E. E., Subekti, I., & Adib, N. (2017). Peran Persepsi Wajib Pajak Atas Keadilan Sistem Perpajakan Dalam Meningkatkan Kepatuhan Pajak. *EKUITAS (Jurnal Ekonomi Dan Keuangan), 1*(3), 361.

Zikmund, W. G., Babin, B. J., Carr, J. C., & Griffin, M. (2010). *Business Research Methods.*

Appendix

Table 9: Operational Definition and Measurement of Variables

No	Variable	Measurement	Scale
Independent Variables			
1	Attitude toward behavior (ATB): positive or negative feelings/ belief of a taxpayer when having to conduct the behavior of reporting the annual tax return through e-filing	Measured by using criteria developed in the studies by Taylor & Todd (1995), Agarwal & Karahanna (2000), Chin et al (2003), Lu et al., (2010) ,and Sentosa & Mat (2012)namely: - ATB1 = using e-filing of 2017 - ATB2 = confusing e-filing system - ATB3 = improved performance - ATB4 = reduces errors - ATB5 = simplify the tax report - ATB6 = more flexible time	Ordinal
2	**Subjective norm (SN):** a person's belief to approve or disapprove of performing an act of reporting the Annual Tax Return through e-filing, which is influenced by assessment of others who are significant	Measured by using the criteria developed in the studies by Taylor & Todd (1995), Lu et al., (2010), and Sentosa & Mat (2012) namely: - SN1 = the Director General of Taxation suggests the use of e-filing system - SN2 = the family expect the use of e-filing system - SN3 = friends expect to use e-filling system - SN4 = tax officer helps in using e-filling system	Ordinal
3	**Perceived** behavior control (PBC): the beliefs a person has about his or her ability and opportunities to anticipate the barriers he faces in performing the behavior of reporting the annual tax return through e-filing.	Measured by using the criteria developed in the studies conducted by Taylor & Todd (1995), Lu et al., (2010) ,and Sentosa & Mat (2012) namely: - PBC1 = able to use e-filing system - PBC2 = cannot report with e-filing - PBC3 = share expertise and knowledge of e-filing system - PBC4 = taxpayer can control data to e-filing system	Ordinal

No	Variable	Measurement	Scale
Dependent Variables			
4	Individual taxpayers' intent to use an e-filing (INTENT) system: a taxpayer's desire to perform the behavior of reporting the Annual Tax Return through e-filing.	Measured by using the criteria developed in the studies by Agarwal & Karahanna (2000), Chin et al., (2003), Lu et al., (2010) , and Moorthy et al., (2014) namely: - INTENT1 = intend to use e-filing system - INTENT2 = trying to share expertise and knowledge about e-filing - INTENT3 = advise and invite other taxpayers to use e-filing - INTENT4 = recommend e-filling system to family members - INTENT5 = recommend e-filling system to friends	Ordinal
5	Individual taxpayers' behavior in reporting tax return through e-filing (**BEHAVIOR**): action or concrete activities undertaken by the taxpayers to report the Annual Tax Return using e-filing.	Measured by using the criteria developed in the studies conducted by Lu et al., (2010) ,Sentosa & Mat (2012), and Moorthy et al., (2014) namely: - BEHAVIOR1 = service and quality of e-filing system information is good - BEHAVIOR2 = tax report is faster by using e-filing system - BEHAVIOR3 = share your expertise and knowledge about e-filling - BEHAVIOR4 = Being secure to use e-filling system	Ordinal

Intellectual Capital and Stock Market Performance of Retail Trade and Property and Real Estate Industry in Indonesia

Harry Anugerah Pradana[a] Sulaeman Rahman Nidar[b] Zaenal Aripin[c]

[a] Corresponding Author, Faculty of Economics and Business, University of Padjadjaran, Indonesia, harrypradana.bpkp@gmail.com
[b] Faculty of Economics and Business, University of Padjadjaran, Indonesia, sulaeman.rachman@fe.unpad.ac.id
[c] Faculty of Economics and Business, University of Padjadjaran, Indonesia, zaenal_ariep@yahoo.com

Keywords
Intellectual Capital, Stock Market Performance, Retail Trade, Property and Real Estate, Indonesia.

Abstract
This study aims to analyze the influence of intellectual capital on the value of company. Intellectual capital as an independent variable is measured using the Value Added Intellectual Capital (VAIC) component. On the other hand, company value as a dependent variable is proxied with Price to Book Value (PBV). 28 companies are selected based on purposive sampling method that come from retail trade and property & real estate sectors listed on Indonesia Stock Exchange (BEI) from 2014 to 2016. Both panel data procedure analysis and statistical criteria test were conducted. The findings show that the Value Added Capital Employed (VACA), Value Added Human Capital (VAHU), and Structural Capital Value Added (STVA) significantly influence the Price to Book Value (PBV), where VACA has significant positive effect on PBV, while VAHU and STVA have no significant positive effect on PBV.

Introduction

The growth of innovation and remarkable advances in information technology is a sign that the world economy has grown rapidly. The introduction of internet-based technologies to the business environment caused production factors such as land, labor and capital, no longer fully reliable in the face of highly competitive business competition (Maciocha & Kisielnicki, 2011). The increasingly tight business competition requires corporate leaders to change their business patterns, initially from a traditional business pattern that is centered solely on physical capital into knowledge-based business pattern (Yuskar & Novita, 2014). This is to ensure that companies can continue to compete and create value for the company and provide sustainable competitive advantage.

It is said that, the implementation of knowledge based business system has an impact on company's financial reporting. There is a lot of information that needs to be presented in the company's financial statements that will add value to the company. Herdyanto (2013) stated that the added value can be innovation, invention, knowledge, employee development, and good relationship to consumers known as intellectual capital. Companies that can understand the concept of intellectual capital will tend to be more successful in achieving their goals because they will continue to update their knowledge and ability to compete with other companies (Feimianti & Anantadjaya, 2014). Therefore, intellectual capital is important because it creates sustainable benefits in business competition and makes a company different as compared to other companies. This condition explains that there is a business shift phenomenon that initially focuses on tangible assets to intangible assets. Śledzik (2012) states that in an economy based on knowledge of intellectual capital, it becomes more important to add value than to tangible assets.

The value of a company is not only in formed of its tangible assets, but also formed by its intangible assets. This is evident from the number of companies that have greater market value than the book value of assets. The market gives a higher price because they believe that the company has intangible assets in the form of intellectual capital. Intellectual capital owned by the company into consideration of investors in appreciating the company's shares, thus forming the market value of the company. To find out how far the influence of intellectual capital on investor's decision making, the intellectual capital needs to be measured in a reliable way, through VAIC method. Each dimension of the intellectual capital including the Value Added Capital Employed (VACA), the Value Added Human Capital (VAHU) and the Structural Capital Value Added (STVA) must be correctly identified so as to provide unbiased explanations. The relationship between VACA, VAHU and STVA on corporate performance shows diversity and differences when compared to existing theories. The relationship can be seen in Table 1.

Table 1: The VAIC relationship to PBV

FIRM	YEAR	VACA	VAHU	STVA	VAIC	PBV
Ace Hardware Indonesia Tbk.	2014	0,47	2,50	0,60	3,58	6,16
	2015	0,45	2,15	0,53	3,14	5,73
Matahari Putra Prima Tbk.	2014	0,27	1,93	0,48	2,67	6,19
	2015	0,19	1,23	0,19	1,61	3,42
Duta Pertiwi Tbk.	2014	0,11	4,24	0,76	5,12	1,48
	2015	0,10	3,71	0,73	4,54	1,76
Summarecon Agung Tbk.	2014	0,17	5,32	0,81	6,30	4,00
	2015	0,12	4,09	0,76	4,97	3,25

(Source: Processed from www.idx.co.id)

Based on the table, the relationship of VACA, VAHU and STVA to company performance (PBV) does not always have a positive relationship. This can be seen from the condition of PT. Duta Pertiwi Tbk. Because there is still a difference between the theory and the existing facts, as well as the results of previous research, researchers are interested to examine again about the influence of intellectual capital components on the value of companies listed on the Stock Exchange. This research is a replication of previous studies. In contrast to previous research, this study was conducted on two types of corporate sectors simultaneously as the object of research in the form of retail trade sector companies and property & real estate sector. Based on Global Industry Classification Standard (GICS) in Woodcock and Whiting (2009), retail trading companies are classified as Low-IC Intensive Industries, while property & real estate firms are part of the High-IC Intensive Industries classification, intellectual capital.

Literature Review

Some definitions of intellectual capital have been put forward by several scholars. For instances, Riahi-Belkaoui (2003) defines intellectual capital as an intellectual property asset that includes knowledge, trade secrets, copyrights, patents and various types of design rights that establish legal mechanisms to protect corporate assets. According to Anatan (2010), intellectual capital is defined as intellectual material that can be utilized to achieve welfare. The intellectual material in question includes knowledge, experience and information. In other words, intellectual capital is also categorized intangible assets as all related to data, technology, contract, consumer, personal capital, location, goodwill, and marketing processes.

On the other hand, Murti (2010) states that intellectual capital is operationally an intellectual capital that is formulated, extracted and enhanced to produce higher asset values. Similarly, Uniariny (2012) states that intellectual capital is all processes and wealth that are not normally shown in the balance sheet and all the intangible assets that have been considered in modern accounting methods. The amount of knowledge of organizational members and knowledge that has been translated into the organization's practical activities is also included as intellectual capital.

Scholars have developed many concepts about methods to measure the intellectual capital held by companies (Sawarjuwono & Kadir, 2003). The techniques are continuously being developed by scholars by continuously trying to apply the concept of competitive advantage (Murti, 2010). One well-known method is the Pulic's Model, commonly referred as VAICTM. In Basyar (2012) the Value Added Intellectual Coefficient (VAIC) is proposed by Pulic (1998) to provide information about the efficient creation of value from the company's tangible and intangible assets. Basyar (2012) states some of the main reasons that support the use of VAIC, among others, are (1) VAIC obtained from audited data, of course the result will be more objective and verificative; (2) VAIC provides a consistent and standardized measure. From the financial statements will be obtained a standard number, so it will be more effective in comparative analysis; and (3) VAIC is an analytical procedure that allows to evaluate and monitor value-added efficiency with total resources and each major resource section. In this case, value added is the difference between income and expense.

Chen et al (2005) examined all listed companies on Taiwan Stock Exchange (TSH) which consisted of 4,254 companies from 1992 to 2002. Using linear correlation and linear regression analysis, Chen et al (2005) examined the relationship between capital (VAIC, VACA, VAHU, STVA), development expenditure and advertising expenses on market to book value ratio of equity and financial performance. The results showed that VAIC, VACA, VAHU, and STVA had positive and significant relationship with the market value of the company. Mehralian et al (2012) used 19 pharmaceutical companies listed on the Iranian Stock Exchange Organization from 2004 to 2009. The study used descriptive statistical analysis, correlation analysis and multiple linear regression analysis (VAIC, VACA, VAHU, STVA) for testing intellectual capital relationships on the value of pharmaceutical companies. The results indicated that there was no statistically significant relationship between intellectual capital and market value of pharmaceutical companies. Kartika and Hatane (2013) conducted research on all banking companies listing on BEI from 2007 to 2011. The study examined the effect of intellectual capital on corporate profitability. Using multiple linear regression analysis techniques, the study proved that VAHU was negative but had no effect on profitability, then STVA and VACA had positive effect on profitability.

Methodology

Research Hypotheses

The company's ability to manage its resources in the form of capital asset is defined as VACA. If the company can properly manage its assets and then be able to reduce operational costs of course it will be able to provide more value so that the performance, income, and value of the company increased. Thus, it can be concluded that VACA has an influence on firm value and positive relationship.

H1. Value Added Capital Employed (VACA) has a positive and significant effect on price to book value (PBV).

VAHU is a human resource that has the skills, knowledge, and superior competence. The company provides salaries and benefits to employees to encourage employees to improve the company's performance. When a company is able to maximize knowledge, expertise, and networking, it certainly creates more value for the company. Thus, VAHU influence on firm value is positive.

H2. Value Added Human Capital (VAHU) has a positive and significant effect on price to book value (PBV).

Capital required by the company so that the company's routine activities can run and optimal performance can be achieved defined as STVA. These routine activities include the company's operating system, manufacturing process, management philosophy, organizational culture, and all intellectual property of the company. Companies that are able to manage STVA well will help improve the company's performance so as to increase profit and value of the company. Therefore, in conclusion the influence of STVA on firm value is positive.

H3. Structural Capital Value Added (STVA) has a positive and significant effect on price to book value (PBV).

Regression Models

The following analysis model is used in this research:

$PBV_{it} = \alpha_0 + \alpha_1 VACA_{it} + \alpha_2 VAHU_{it} + \alpha_3 STVA_{it} + \varepsilon$

PBV	= price to book value
α_0	= constants
$\alpha_1, \alpha_2, \alpha_3$	= variable coefficients
VACA	= Value Added Capital Employed
VAHU	= Value Added Human Capital
STVA	= Structural Capital Value Added
i	= the number of cross section data
t	= the number of time series data
"ε"	= error term

Variables

a) Dependent Variable

Price to Book Value or PBV is formulated by comparison between price and book value of equity. An increasingly large ratio indicates that the market is increasingly believing with the company's performance going forward.

b) Independent Variables

There are 3 independent variables tested in this study, namely the Value Added Capital Employed, Value Added Human Capital and Structural Capital Value Added.

Value Added Capital Employed (VACA)

VACA is an indicator for VA created by a unit of capital employed. This ratio shows the contribution made by each unit of CE to the value added organization (Basyar, 2012).

$$\text{VA} = OUT - IN$$

$$\text{VACA} = \frac{Value\ Added}{Capital\ Employed}$$

Value Added = *Difference between Output and Input.*

Output (OUT) =*Total sales and other revenue.*

Input (IN) = *Expenses and costs (except employee expenses).*

Capital Employed = *Book value of net assets.*

Value Added Human Capital (VAHU)

VAHU is the ratio of the VA can be generated with funds spent for labor. This ratio shows the contribution made by each rupiah invested in human capital (HC) to the value added of the organization (Basyar, 2012).

$$\text{VAHU} = \frac{Value\ Added}{Human\ Capital}$$

Human Capital = *Employee expenses.*

Value Added = *Difference between Output and Input.*

Structural Capital Value Added (STVA)

STVA is this ratio measuring the amount of SC needed to generate 1 rupiah from VA and is an indication of how SC's success in value creation (Basyar, 2012).

$$\text{STVA} = \frac{\textit{Structural Capital}}{\textit{Value Added}}$$

Structural Capital = Value Added – Human Capital.

Value Added = Difference between Output and Input.

Sample Selection

The population in the study are all companies listed on the BEI from 2014 to 2016 but focuses on retail and property and real estate sectors. Companies are selected based on purposive sampling method and able to meet the following criteria: 1) The retail and property & real estate sector companies are listed consecutively during the observation period from 2014 to 2016; 2) The company did not report negative equity during the observation period; 3) The company did not report negative earnings during the observation period; and 4) Complete stock trading data in the observation period. Based on the sample selection process, 28 companies are obtained per year and the total during the research period is 84 companies shown in Table 2.

Table 2: Determination of Samples Number

No	Criteria	Amount
1	Retail trade sector companies listed on the BEI period 2014-2016	23
2	Property & real estate sector companies listed on BEI period 2014-2016	50
3	The companies reported negative equity during the observation period.	(0)
4	The companies reported negative earnings during the observation period.	(15)
5	Incomplete stock trading data during the observation period.	(30)
6	Companies that meet the study criteria.	28
	Total sample (3 years observation)	**84**

(Source: Processed from www.idx.com)

Results

The hypothesis in this study are tested using panel data procedure analysis and statistical criteria test. The following are statistical descriptive data for all variables used in the study.

Table 3: Description of Statistics

	N	Minimum	Maximum	Mean	Std. Dev.
VACA	84	0.014825	0.474662	0.147880	0.094312
VAHU	84	1.231208	18.04149	4.489497	3.280825
STVA	84	0.187789	0.944572	0.654856	0.216884
PBV	84	0.150000	6.960000	1.870833	1.543036
Valid N	84				

Table 3 illustrates statistical descriptions for each of the variables used. From the table, it can be seen that the retail sector and property and real estate sector has an average VACA of 1.147880; VAHU of 4.489497; STVA of 0.654856; and PBV of 1.870833. Analysis of panel data includes 4 steps as follows:

a. Common Effect Model Estimation

The Common Effect Model is the simplest model, in which timeout data (historical) and cross-section are combined.

Table 4: Common Effect Model Estimation Results

Variable	Coefficient	Std. Error	t-Statistic	Prob.
C	0.143758	0.491388	0.292555	0.7706
VACA	13.33679	1.151720	11.57989	0.0000
VAHU	0.118611	0.046083	2.573861	0.0119
STVA	-1.187559	0.774560	-1.533204	0.1292

The equations in the Common Effect Model are:

PBV = 0.143758 + 13.33679*VACA + 0.118611*VAHU - 1.187559*STVA

b. Fixed Effect Model Estimation

With the Fixed Effect Model, each research object will have a constant for various time periods and has the same regression coefficient for all objects and the magnitude remains over time.

Table 5: Fixed Effect Model Estimation Results

Variable	Coefficient	Std. Error	t-Statistic	Prob.
C	-0.917390	0.566466	-1.619497	0.1113
VACA	16.70005	4.041305	4.132342	0.0001
VAHU	0.018713	0.044845	0.417290	0.6782
STVA	0.358246	1.088100	0.329240	0.7433

The equations in the Fixed Effect Model are:

PBV = - 0.917390297736 + 16.7000532635*VACA + 0.0187132454536*VAHU + 0.358245751291*STVA

c. Chow Test

Chow test can be done by looking at the probability value of Cross-section Chi-square.

Table 6: Chow Test Results

Effects Test	Statistic	d.f.	Prob.
Cross-section F	9.268417	(27,53)	0.0000
Cross-section Chi-square	146.517555	27	0.0000

Based on Chow Test results show that the probability value of cross-section Chi-square is 0.0000. The value is smaller than alpha (5%), so H_0 is rejected. So, the model used is Fixed Effect Model.

d. Random Effect Model Estimation

Data processing with Eviews 9 shows estimation results with Random Effect Model as follows.

Table 7: Random Effect Model Estimation Results

Variable	Coefficient	Std. Error	t-Statistic	Prob.
C	-0.559636	0.495185	-1.130154	0.2618
VACA	14.52377	1.425626	10.18764	0.0000
VAHU	0.050197	0.035898	1.398320	0.1659
STVA	0.087545	0.714337	0.122555	0.9028

The equations in the Random Effect Model are:

$$PBV = -0.559635578928 + 14.5237671217*VACA + 0.050196791472*VAHU + 0.0875453793458*STVA$$

e. Hausman Test

This test is performed to select the model, whether Fixed Effect Model or Random Effect Model to be used for analysis.

Table 8: Hausman Test Results

Test Summary			
	Chi-Sq. Statistic	Chi-Sq. d.f.	Prob.
Cross-section random	2.693495	3	0.4413

The Hausman Test results show that the value of Prob. Cross-section random is 0.4413. Therefore, the value is greater than alpha (5%), so H_0 is accepted. So, the model chosen is the Random Effect Model.

f. Lagrange Multiplier (LM) Test

After performing Hausman test, it is necessary to ensure that the Random Effect Model is more appropriate than the Common Effect Model by using the Lagrange Multiplier Test. Test Lagrange Multiplier can be done by looking at Prob value. Breusch-Pagan (BP).

Table 9: Lagrange Multiplier (LM) Test Results

	Test Hypothesis		
	Cross-section	Time	Both
Breusch-Pagan	41.81713	0.376170	42.19330
	(0.0000)	(0.5397)	(0.0000)

Based on the Lagrange Multiplier Test results show that the value of Prob. Breusch-Pagan (BP) of 0.000. Because the value is smaller than alpha (5%), then the model chosen is Random Effect Model.

Coefficient of Determination (R^2)

The coefficient of determination (R^2) is used to see how far an independent variable determines the change of dependent variable value can be known. The magnitude of the coefficient of determination is 0 to 1. The closer to zero, the magnitude of the coefficient of determination (R^2), the smaller the influence of independent variable on dependent variable and vice versa.

Table 10: Coefficient of Determination (R^2) Test Results

R-squared	0.614914	Mean dependent var	0.590961
Adjusted R-squared	0.600473	S.D. dependent var	0.678189

Based on table 10, the coefficient of determination (R-square) is 0.6149. The value explained that the variable of Value Added Capital Employed (VACA), Value Added Human Capital (VAHU), and Structural Capital Value Added (STVA) give influence to Company Value (PBV) equal to 61,5%, while the rest equal to 38,5% influenced by other variables outside the model.

F-Test

The F statistic test is performed to see the effect of the overall independent variable together with the dependent variable.

Table 11: F-Test Results

S.E. of regression	0.428671	Sum squared resid	14.70068
F-statistic	42.58195	Durbin-Watson stat	1.733396
Prob(F-statistic)	0.000000		

Based on the F test statistic table above, the regression output shows the value of Prob (F-statistic) 0,0000 < 0,05 so it can be concluded that Together VACA, VAHU, and STVA variables significantly influence the PBV variable.

T-Test

T-test is done to determine the level of significance of each independent variable influence on dependent variable partially.

Table 12: T-Test Results

Variable	Coefficient	Std. Error	t-Statistic	Prob.
C	-0.559636	0.495185	-1.130154	0.2618
VACA	14.52377	1.425626	10.18764	0.0000
VAHU	0.050197	0.035898	1.398320	0.1659
STVA	0.087545	0.714337	0.122555	0.9028

From the test results presented in Table 12, the regression equations that can be formed in this study are as follows:

$$PBV = -0{,}559635578928 + 14{,}5237671217*VACA + 0{,}050196791472*VAHU + 0{,}0875453793458*STVA$$

In general, the relationship between a company's ability to manage its capital asset (known as VACA) with firm value is significant indicating that companies engaged in the retail sector and property and real estate sectors have been effective and efficient in managing their physical assets and intellectual assets. Such good management will contribute to the value of the company. Companies in the retail and property sectors and real estate sectors are characterized by large inventory assets. Both sectors of the company make a high inventory turnover, which means the company can be actively operating and the results can be quickly absorbed by the market, resulting in revenue for the company and increase the value of the company. A positive relationship between a company's ability to manage its capital asset and company value can be explained that when a company can properly manage its capital asset, it will create a competitive advantage for the company, thereby increasing the company's value.

The relationship of human resources (VAHU) with insignificant corporate value indicates that the company has not been able to manage human resources optimally. This can be seen from the lack of training activities for employees, the lack of relationships between companies and educational institutions, and no one has allocated corporate funds for research through cooperation with educational institutions. Although nominally the allocation of funds for high employee salaries, it has not been able to describe the management of good human resources, because it may be small paid employees perform better than employees who are paid more. When the human resources are managed less than optimal, of course it will not boost the company's value. Another indication is that the company does not have good systems and procedures in managing its human resources, so the amount of rupiah spent on employees is inefficient and economical in creating value for the company. This condition also indicates that investors in assessing the company is more dominant considering only physical assets than human capital or lack of investor knowledge about the human capital. A positive relationship between VAHU and company value can be explained that when a company can properly manage its human resources then it will certainly be able to raise the value of the company.

The capital required to run the company's routine activities (STVA) is not significant indicates that the company has not been able to process effectively and efficiently in the company's operating system, corporate culture, and intellectual property processing. For example, in building a network with suppliers, banks, and potential buyers is still a regular routine, the company has not been able to create innovations that can add value to the company. Positive relationship between STVA and company value can be explained that when the company can properly manage capital to run the company's routine activities, then it certainly will be able to support employee productivity in generating profit and value added company, so that will raise the value of the company.

Conclusions

In conclusion, it can be concluded that the Value Added Capital Employed (VACA) has a significant effect and positive influence toward company value. Meanwhile, Value Added Human Capital (VAHU) and Structural Capital Value Added (STVA) have no significant effect on company value. Yet, based on the measurements of collectively on the three components of intellectual capital show a significant influence on company value. However, the results of this study are limited only for 28 companies in retail and property and real estate industry. There is possibility of different result produce when adding the number of longer periods or use variety industrial sectors. In addition, further research is also can be done to determine whether the characteristics of the industry play a role in testing the influence of intellectual capital on the company.

References

Anatan, L. (2010). Manajemen Modal Intelektual: Strategi Memaksimalkan Nilai Modal Intelekstual dalam Technology Driven Business. Jurnal Manajemen Maranatha, 5(2), pp-46.

Basyar, F. (2012). Pengaruh Modal Intelektual (Intellectual Capital/IC) terhadap Return On Asset Perusahaan Perbankan yang Terdaftar di Bursa Efek Indonesia (BEI) Tahun 2007–2009.

Bontis, N. (1999). Managing organisational knowledge by diagnosing intellectual capital: framing and advancing the state of the field. International Journal of technology management, 18(5-8), 433-462.

Bontis, N. (2001). Assessing knowledge assets: a review of the models used to measure intellectual capital. International journal of management reviews, 3(1), 41-60.

Celenza, D., & Rossi, F. (2012). The relationship between intellectual capital (IC) and stock market performance: Empirical evidence from Italy. Journal of Modern Accounting and Auditing, 8(11), 1729.

Chen, M. C., Cheng, S. J., & Hwang, Y. (2005). An empirical investigation of the relationship between intellectual capital and firms' market value and financial performance. Journal of intellectual capital, 6(2), 159-176.

Dessler, G. (2009). Manajemen SDM buku 1. Jakarta: Indeks.

Entika, N. L., & Ardiyanto, M. D. (2012). Pengaruh Elemen Pembentuk Intellectual Capital Terhadap Nilai Pasar dan Kinerja Keuangan pada Perusahaan Perbankan yang Terdaftar di Bursa Efek Indonesia (BEI) (Doctoral dissertation, Fakultas Ekonomika dan Bisnis).

Feimianti, E., and Anantadjaya, S.P.D. (2014). Value Creation of Intellectual Capital: Financial Performance Analyses in Indonesian Publicly Listed Consumer Goods Industry. Review of Integrative Business & Economics Research Volume 3 No.1 (pp. 99-113).

Gujarati, D. N. (2009). Basic econometrics. Tata McGraw-Hill Education.

Herdyanto, I., & Nasir, M. (2013). PENGARUH INTELLECTUAL CAPITAL PADA FINANCIAL PERFORMANCE PERUSAHAAN (Studi Empiris pada Perusahaan Infrastruktur, Utilitas, dan Transportasi yang Terdaftar di Bursa Efek Indonesia Tahun 2009-2011) (Doctoral dissertation, Fakultas Ekonomika dan Bisnis).

Indonesia, I. A. (2009). Pernyataan standar akuntansi keuangan. Salemba Empat. Jakarta.

Kartika, M., & Hatane, E. S. (2013). Pengaruh Intellectual Capital pada Profitabilitas Perusahaan Perbankan yang Terdaftar di Bursa Efek Indonesia pada Tahun 2007-2011. Business Accounting Review, 1(2), 14-25.

Maciocha, A and Kisielnicki, J. (2011). Intellectual Capital and Corporate Performance. The Electronic Journal of Knowledge Management Volume 9 Issue 3 2011 (pp. 271-283)

Madhani, P. M. (Ed.). (2009). Resource Based View: Concepts and Practices. Icfai University Press.

Mathis, R. L., & Jackson, J. H. (2006). Human Resources Management (Manajemen Sumber Daya Manusia) Terj: Diana Anggelica. Salemba Empat. Jakarta.

Mehralian, G., Rajabzadeh, A., Reza Sadeh, M., & Reza Rasekh, H. (2012). Intellectual capital and corporate performance in Iranian pharmaceutical industry. Journal of intellectual capital, 13(1), 138-158.

Murti, A. C. (2010). Analisis Pengaruh Modal Intelektual Terhadap Kinerja Perusahaan (Studi pada Perusahaan yang Terdaftar di Bursa Efek Indonesia). Semarang: Fakultas Ekonomi Universitas Diponegoro.

Nachrowi, D. N., & Usman, H. (2006). Pendekatan Populer dan Praktis Ekonometrika Untuk Analisis Ekonomi dan Keuangan. Jakarta: Lembaga Penerbit Fakultas Ekonomi Universitas Indonesia.

Pulic, A. (1998). Measuring the performance of intellectual potential in knowledge economy. In 2nd McMaster Word Congress on Measuring and Managing Intellectual Capital by the Austrian Team for Intellectual Potential.

Putra, I. G. C. (2012). Pengaruh Modal Intelektual pada nilai perusahaan Perbankan yang Go Public di Bursa Efek Indonesia. JINAH (Jurnal Ilmiah Akuntansi dan Humanika), 2(1).

Rachmawati, A. S. (2011). Pengaruh Aktiva Tetap Tak Berwujud (Intangible Assets) terhadap Financial Distress (Studi pada: Perusahaan Manufaktur di Bursa Efek Indonesia Periode 2007-2010. Jakarta: Universitas Indonesia.

Riahi-Belkaoui, A. (2003). Intellectual capital and firm performance of US multinational firms: a study of the resource-based and stakeholder views. Journal of Intellectual capital, 4(2), 215-226.

Sawarjuwono, T., & Kadir, A. P. (2003). Intellectual Capital: Perlakuan, Pengukuran dan Pelaporan (Sebuah Library Research). Jurnal Akuntansi dan Keuangan, 5(1), pp-35.

Śledzik, K. (2012). The Intellectual Capital Performance of Polish Banks: An Application of VAIC™ Model.

Syarifin, M. T. (2014). Pengaruh Intangible Asset berupa Intellectual Capital terhadap Nilai Perusahaan Industri Properti dan Real Estate yang Terdaftar di Bursa Efek Indonesia Periode 2012-2013. Bandung: Universitas Padjadjaran.

Uniariny (2012). Pengaruh Struktur Modal dan Modal Intelektual terhadap Nilai Perusahaan Sektor Perbankan yang Terdaftar di Bursa Efek Indonesia Periode 2006-2010. Jakarta: Universitas Indonesia.

Wigati, I. R., & Haryanto, H. (2013). Pengaruh Intellectual Capital Terhadap Kinerja Keuangan Perusahaan Konstruksi Dan Real Estate Yang Listing Di Bei Tahun 2009-2011 (Doctoral dissertation, Fakultas Ekonomika dan Bisnis).

Woodcock, J., & Whiting, R. H. (2009). Intellectual capital disclosure by Australian companies. Paper Accepted for Presentation of The AFAANZ Conference. Adelaide, Australia.

Yuskar and Novita, D. (2014). The Influence of Intellectual Capital on Firm Value Through Financial Performance as an Intervening Variable. The Journal of Management and Business Sriwijaya Volume 12 No. 4

6

The Mediating Effect of Sustainability Disclosure on the Relationship between Financial Performance and Firm Value

Yossi Diantimala[a]

[a] University of Syiah Kuala, Banda Aceh, Indonesia, ydiantimala@yahoo.com

Keywords
Financial Performance, Firm Value, Sustainability Disclosure, Jakarta Islamic Index.

Abstract
The purpose of the study is to examine the effect of financial performance on sustainability disclosure and then to examine the effect of sustainability disclosure on firm value. Sustainability disclosure is treated as a mediating variable, therefore an investigation of the indirect effect of financial performance on firm value is required to accomplish the mediating effect. It is predicted that lower leverage and higher firm size, higher liquidity, as well as higher profitability will motivate companies' management to convey more their sustainability disclosure. This action should increase firm value. The sample used in this study is companies listed on the Jakarta Islamic Index (JII) for the period 2013 – 2015. The study uses path analysis to examine the hypothesis.

The results present that higher liquidity emboldens management to convey more sustainability disclosure. Higher sustainability disclosure increase firm value significantly. However, the effect of leverage, profitability, and firm size is not significant. Regarding the indirect effect of financial performance on firm value, the results show that leverage and profitability have a positively indirect effect on firm value. However, size and liquidity have no indirect effect on firm value. This means that the increase of leverage and profitability will encourage management to publish more sustainability disclosure and it will increase firm value of companies listed on the Jakarta Islamic Index.

Introduction

The Jakarta Islamic Index (JII) is a stock market index on the Indonesia Stock Exchange, which aims to provide guidance for investors who wish to invest in shares in accordance with Islamic Sharia. Since JII was established on July 3, 2000, JII has progressed rapidly. At the end of the fourth quarter of 2015, sharia shares listed on the JII have controlled 35.65% of the total stock market capitalization listed on the stock exchange. Every year, the market capitalization of sharia stocks keeps increasing, although the value tends to fluctuate year to year. The development of JII over the past year is shown in Figure 1.1 and the development of market capitalization of sharia stocks in JII is shown in Figure 1.2 below.

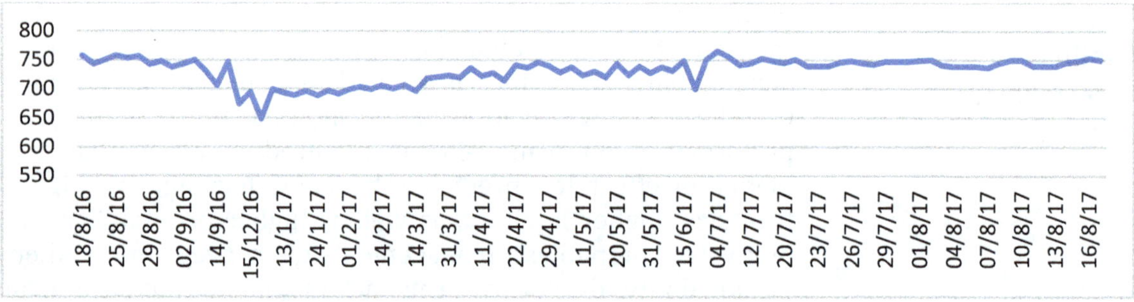

Figure 1.1. Jakarta Islamic Index from August 2016 until August 2017

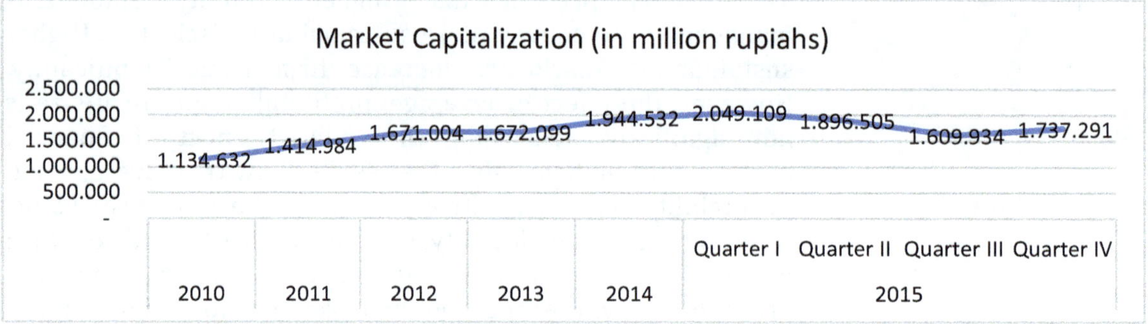

Figure 1.2. Market Capitalization of Shariah Stock of Jakarta Islamic Index

Resource: Report of Otoritas Jasa Keuangan Indonesia.

The increase in market index and market capitalization of sharia stocks shows an increase in corporate value. The condition indicates that investors' interest in sharia stocks is getting higher. To attract investor concern, the company discloses financial and non-financial information about company's prospects and future corporate performance.

Sustainability disclosure is one of the information that can influence investors' decision to buy the company's shares (Fazzini and Maso, 2016; Saka and Oshika, 2014). It is indicated by a variation of companies' stock prices when the companies publish their sustainability disclosure (Klerk et al., 2015; Klerk and Villiers, 2012).

The regulatory[1] and financial accounting standards[2] in Indonesia recommend public companies to disclose corporate sustainability. This disclosure is very crucial to describe the company's sustainability and to explain the company's concern for the social and environmental aspects. Companies that have run their business with the assumption of sustainability can be seen from the disclosure of the sustainability of the company. This sustainability disclosure consists of reports on social responsibility (Corporate Social Responsibility) and the environment. Sustainability disclosure is not the same as social responsibility reporting (CSR). The CSR report only focuses on social and environmental disclosure while the sustainability report which includes the concept of sustainable development covers a broader area of economic, social and environmental aspects (Hubbard, 2008).

Although there is a regulation requiring sustainability disclosure, not all companies listed on the stock exchange prepare the disclosure. This maybe because, there is no sanction for the companies which do not convey sustainability disclosure, or the company does not engage in activities related to corporate responsibility to the environment, or the company's commitment for the environment is low (Clarkson et al., 2007). Also, may be it is due to the fact that the company's financial performance is bad. Dienes et al. (2016) assert that firm size, profitability, capital structure, firm corporate governance structure, ownership structure, and firm age affect firms propensity to make sustainability disclosures or not. Better the indicators of financial performance lead the companies to convey sustainability disclosures (Weber, 2017).

---

[1] Law No. 40 of 2007 Article 66 Paragraph 2 regarding to Perseroan Terbatas.

[2] PSAK No. 1 Paragraph 31.

Theory and Hypothesis Development

Stakeholder Theory

I use Stakeholder Theory to explain the motivation of managers or organizations for sustainability disclosure. Stakeholder theory is motivated by organizational responsibility to stakeholders. This theory explains that the existence of an organization is strongly influenced by the support of groups and individuals who have relationships with the organization (Freeman, 1984). Stakeholders are groups and individuals who can influence or be influenced in the process of achieving the goals of an organization.

The sustainability reporting can be used as a tool by stakeholders to assess the extent of the company's role in addressing social and environmental issues. Firms that communicate their sustainability disclosure can also improve their corporate accountability and transparency. The sustainability reporting is the responsibility of the company not only to investors and owners but also to all stakeholders (Donaldson dan Preston, 1995; Laan, 2009).

Financial Performance and Sustainability Disclosure

Sustainability disclosure takes into account the balance between people, planet, and profit or the so-called Triple Bottom Line (TBL) concept (Hubbard, 2008), which shows a balance between economic (profit), environmental (planet), and social aspects (people). If these three aspects can be well executed, then the company can produce sustainability performance so that the company will continue to grow stably (Dainiene and Lina, 2015). If one of the three aspects is not met, it will be difficult for the company to keep growing. Preparing sustainability disclosure is one way to implement the Triple Bottom Line concept in a company. The sustainability disclosure reveals the information about the most important impact of an organization (whether positive or negative) on the environment, society, and economy.

There are seven determinants that drives management to convey their sustainability disclosure (Dienes et al., 2016). They are firm size, profitability, capital structure, media visibility, corporate governance structure, ownership structure, firm age. One indicator for firm size is total assets. The indicators for profitability are ROA, ROE, etc. The indicators for capital structure is book value of debt to book value of equity ratio (DER ratio) and book value of debt to total assets ratio (leverage). Firm size positively affects sustainability disclosure (Wang, 2017; Kend, 2015; Shamil et al., 2014). Larger firms are more likely to publish their sustainability disclosure.

Research findings regarding the effect of leverage on sustainability disclosure are contrary. Drilling et al. (2010) as well as Ho and Taylor (2007) show that leverage negatively affects sustainability disclosure. However, Wang (2017) and Li et al. (2013) show that leverage positively impact the sustainability disclosure. From liquidity side, a company with higher liquidity ratio indicates a strong financial position. The company usually considers the certain level of liquidity as an indicator of their credibility. Consequently, as liquidity ratio matchs with their expectation, the companies will publish the sustainability disclosure. From the profitability side, there is a positive relationship between profitability and sustainability disclosure. The more profitable the companies, the more they are able to finance their voluntary reporting (Dienes et al., 2017).

H_{1a}: Leverage negatively affects sustainability disclosure of companies listed in JII.

H_{1b}: Firm size positively affects sustainability disclosure of companies listed in JII.

H_{1c}: Liquidity positively affects sustainability disclosure of companies listed in JII.

H_{1d}: Profitability positively affects sustainability disclosure of companies listed in JII.

Sustainability Disclosure and Firm Value

The companies convey sustainability disclosure to the public in order to increase their firm value (Fazzini and Maso, 2016; Klerk et al., 2015; Saka and Oshika, 2014; Klerk and Villiers, 2012; Haggard et al., 2008). The research of Saka and Oshika (2014) show that environmental disclosure could increase the value of firms in Japan. Fazzini and Maso (2016) explain that the disclosure of the environment is an information that has value relevance and positively significant affects the value of companies in Italy. In Indonesia, the findings related to the effect of sustainability disclosure on firm value is mostly carried out in manufacturing and mining companies listed on the BEI.

Burhan and Rahmanti (2012) conduct a study on all companies, except financial companies listed on the BEI during the period 2006-2009. During the observation period, only 32 companies convey sustainability disclosure. The results show that sustainability reporting had an effect on the company performance. Conversely, Gunawan and Mayangsari (2015) also carry out a research on the effect of sustainability reporting on firm value with investment opportunity set as a moderating variable. The sample of this research is 18 companies listed on BEI with observation year 2011-2013. The result of the research shows that sustainability disclosure has no effect on company value.

H2: Sustainability disclosure positively affects firm value of companies listed in JII

H3: Financial performance of companies listed in JII affects firm value indirectly.

Research Method

Population and Sample

The population used in this study is non-financial companies listed on the Jakarta Islamic Index (JII) year 2013-2015. JII Companies consist of 30 companies that are evaluated every 6 months. Companies that do not qualify for Islamic sharia will be excluded from the index and other qualified companies will be added instead. Sample companies are companies that deliver continuous disclosures continuously for 3 consecutive years. Based on these criteria, there are 14 non-financial companies listed on the JII in the period 2013 to 2015 that deliver sustainability disclosure for 3 years. The number of observations from 2013 to 2015 is 42 companies – years.

Data Collection Techniques

The data about financial performance are taken from company's annual report. The data about market value is acquired from the website of Indonesian Stock Exchange. The data about sustainability index is constructed by checking the conformity of the information submitted in companies' sustainability reporting with the information items required by the GRI (Global Reporting Initiative). The way to construct the index is explained in operationalization of variables below.

Operationalization of Variables

Definition and operationalization of all variables are exhibited in Table 3.1.

The Sustainability Disclosure

One of the organizations that set up sustainability disclosure guidelines is the GRI. According to the GRI, sustainability reporting is the practice of measuring, disclosing and accountability efforts of organizational performance in achieving sustainable development goals to the stakeholders both internal and external. GRI is an independent organization that prepares sustainability reporting guidelines and is based in the Netherlands. The GRI guidelines are internationally recognized and widely used in many countries. According to the GRI, 92% of the world's 250 largest companies use the GRI guidelines in preparing company sustainability reports. The latest GRI guide is GRI G4. GRI G4 was launched in May of 2013.

The sustainability reporting consists of 3 aspects, these are economics, environmental, and social. All these aspects contain individual items. These items are taken under the guidelines of the GRI. The GRI Index is an index commonly used by companies to measure the level of corporate sustainability disclosure. The sustainability disclosure index (SDI) is measured by looking at the items in the sustainability reporting. The GRI Index used in this study is the GRI G4 Index. Each item disclosed will be scored. If the value is 0 (no), there is no disclosure of the item and if the value 1 (yes) otherwise. If the company does not disclose the item of sustainability disclosure because the incident does not occur in the company, it will be given the code N / A. After the scoring is done then the score is summed to get the overall score for each company. The formula used to measure the sustainability disclosure index is as follows:

$$\text{SDI} = \frac{\text{The amount of items disclosed}}{\text{The amount of items must be disclosed}} \text{ or } \frac{\text{Yes}}{\text{Yes + No}}$$

Table 3.1 Operationalization of All Variables

Research Variables	Operational Definition	Indicator	Symbol	The Expected Correlation
Dependent Variable				
Firm Value	Tobins' Q	Market value of equity + debt divided by total assets.	FV	
Intervening Variable				
Sustainability Disclosure	Sustainability Disclosure Index	$\text{SDI} = \frac{\text{The amount of items disclosed}}{\text{The amount of items must be disclosed}}$ or $\frac{\text{Yes}}{\text{Yes + No}}$	SDI	
Independent variable				
Leverage	A measurement of the amount of assets that is financed with debt.	Total debt to total assets Ratio = Total Debt / Total Assets	LEV	(-)
Size	Size of the company can be stated in total assets,	The ratio of total assets Size = Ln (Total assets)	SIZE	

	sales and market capitalization. The greater the value of company's total assets, or sales or market capitalization then the larger will be the size of a company.			(+)
Liquidity	The availability of fund so that company can afford the payment of current liabilities	The ratio of current assets to current liabilities. Liquidity = Current Assets/ Current Liabilities	LIQ	(+)
Profitability	The ability of the company with all their capital in their company to generate income	The ratio of net operating income to total equity. ROE= Net Operating Income / Total book value of equity	ROE	(+)

Hypothesis Testing Design

In order to examine and analyze the indirect impact of financial performance includes leverage (LEV), size (SIZE), liquidity (LIQ), and profitability (ROE) on firm value with sustainability disclosure (Y) as intervening variable. The hypothesis testing in this research uses path analysis method. Path analysis can be used to test the indirect effect of financial performance on firm value and direct effect of sustainability disclosure on firm value. To analyze the relationship between the variables it needed to construct two substructures as follows. The model is described in Figure 3.1.

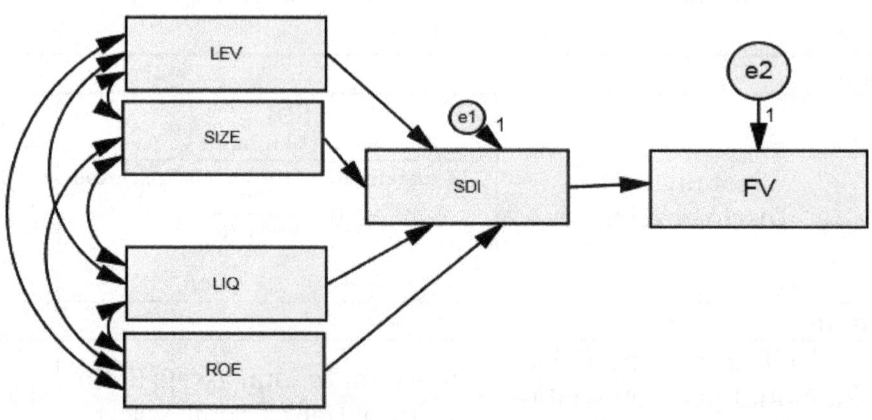

Figure 3.1 The Development of Path Diagram

Substructure I

The first substructure is related to hypothesis 1a, 1b, 1c, 1d. The effect of these variables is determined through path coefficient with the structural equation.

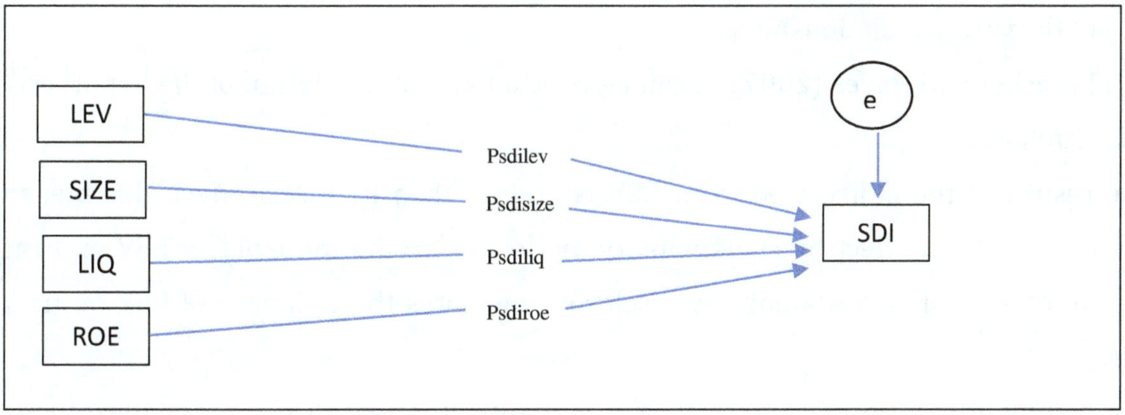

Figure 3.2. Substructure I: SDI = P_{sdilev}LEV + $P_{sdisize}$SIZE + P_{sdiliq}LIQ + P_{sdiroe}ROE + e_1

Notes: LEV is leverage, SIZE is firm size, LIQ is liquidity, ROE is profitability, and SDI is sustainability disclosure. e_1 is the influence of other variable that is not involved in this research model.

Substructure II

Second substructure is the impact of sustainability disclosure (SDI) on firm value (FV).

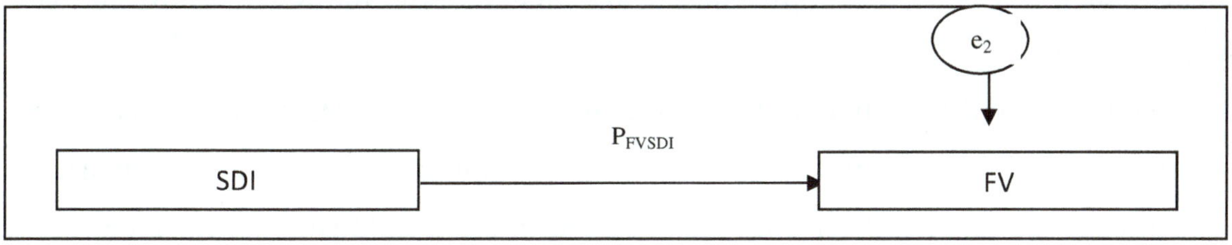

Figure 3.3. Substructure II: FV = P_{fvsdi}SDI + e_2
Notes: SDI is sustainability disclosure, and FV is firm value. e_2 is the influence of other variable that is not involved in this research model.

Mediation Hypothesis testing

Preacher et.al (2007) state that mediation or an indirect effect occur when the causal effect of an independent variable (X) on a dependent variable (Y) is transmitted by a mediator (M). In other words, X affects Y because X affects M, and M, in turn, affects Y. Mediation effect and indirect effect are often used interchangeably Analysis on direct effect, indirect effect and total effect are used to see the power of influence between constructs, either directly, indirectly, or the total effect. Direct effect is the coefficient of all lines with one end dart. While the indirect effect is the effect that arises through intervening variable. Intervening variable in this research is sustainability disclosure. The total effect is the influence of the various relationships.

Based on Preacher and Hayes (2007), it can be concluded that the design of the hypothesis testing is as follows:

1. If the results of the indirect effect of LEV is greater than its direct effect, this means there is an indirect effect by sustainability disclosure on the influence of LEV on firm value. In other words, sustainability disclosure mediates the influence of LEV on firm value.
2. If the results of the indirect effect of SIZE is greater than its direct effect, this means there is an indirect effect by sustainability disclosure on the influence of SIZE on firm value. In other words, sustainability disclosure mediates the influence of SIZE on firm value.
3. If the results of the indirect effect of LIQ is greater than its direct effect, this means there is an indirect effect by sustainability disclosure on the influence of LIQ on firm value. In other words, sustainability disclosure mediates the influence of LIQ on firm value.
4. If the results of an indirect effect of ROE is greater than its direct effect, it means there is an indirect effect by sustainability disclosure on the influence of ROE on firm value. In other words, sustainability disclosure mediates the influence of ROE on firm value.

Results and Discussion

Statistic Descriptive

Figure 4.1 below reveals fluctuations in corporate value and sustainability disclosure. The abscissa line describes the company code, whereas the ordinate line explains the value. At most points, this indicates an increase in sustainability disclosure followed by an increase in corporate value and a decrease in sustainability disclosure followed by a decline in firm value. This indicates that if the company delivered the sustainability disclosure to the public, the value of the company will be changed.

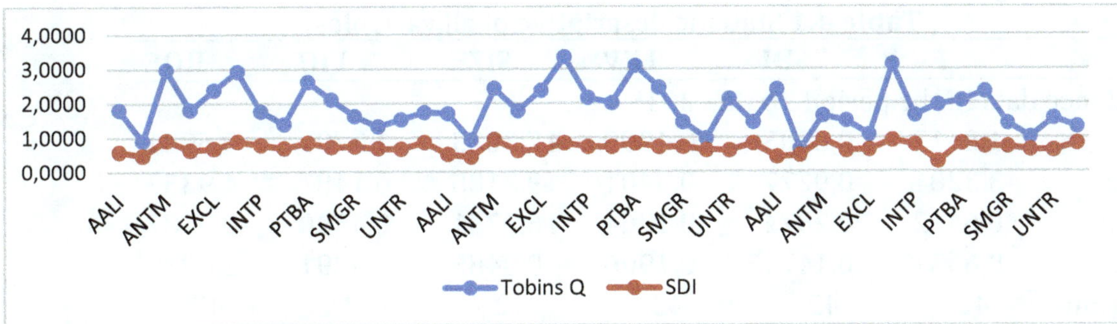

Figure 4.1 Firm Value and Sustainability Disclosure

The average (mean), maximum, and minimum values of firm value, sustainability disclosure index, and other variables can be seen in Table 4.1. The company's average value of 1.8617 explains that the market value of equity and debt is 187% of the company's total assets. This value is relatively high. The company's lowest value is 64.52% and the highest is 332.81%. The average of sustainability disclosure index (SDI) 0.6905 indicates the information items disclosed by the company regarding sustainability of 69.05% of all information items they should disclose under GRI G4 guideline. Minimum value of sustainability disclosure index 28.74% and maximum 92.77%. The difference between this minimum and maximum value is relatively high which causes the average value of the disclosure index to be low.

The average value of variable financial performance, i.e. leverage (LEV) 0.4999 explains that companies' total debt is 49.99% of 100 total assets. The highest leverage is 84.01% and the lowest is 13.64%. Firms with leverage 13.64% better than firms with leverage 84.01% due to lower leverage indicate a lower level of financial risk. The average value of liquidity 1.7791 explains that companies' current assets is 177.91% of their 100 current liability. The highest value of liquidity is 614.81% and the lowest 45%. Higher liquidity values are better than smaller liquidity. The average profitability of 0.6931 explains that companies' earnings before taxes 69.31% of their 100 book value of equity. The lowest value of -0.0787 shows the company's profit (loss) of 7.87% of the book value of equity. Negative values indicate there are companies that suffered losses during the year of observation but still deliver sustainability reporting to the public. The maximum value of profitability is 4.9337.

Table 4.1 Statistic descriptive of all variables

	FV	SDI	LEV	SIZE	LIQ	ROE
Panel balance data in the period 2013 – 2015						
Mean	1,8617	0,6905	0,4999	17,3083	1,7791	0,6931
Maximum	3,3281	0,9277	0,8401	19,3185	6,1481	4,9337
Minimum	0,6452	0,2874	0,1364	16,2731	0,4500	-0,0787
Std. Dev.	0,6531	0,1474	0,1906	0,8485	1,3291	1,0935
Observation	42	42	42	42	42	42
Cross - sectional analysis of the year 2013						
Mean	1,9055	0,7174	0,4961	17,1800	1,9315	0,1663
Maximum	2,9553	0,9122	0,8401	19,1815	6,1481	0,2621
Minimum	0,8918	0,4670	0,1364	16,2731	0,4500	0,0320
Std. Dev.	0,6090	0,1229	0,2011	0,8805	1,5944	0,0729
Cross - sectional analysis of the year 2014						
Mean	2,0046	0,6883	0,4943	17,3179	1,8035	1,8035
Maximum	3,3281	0,9254	0,8364	19,2795	4,9337	4,9337
Minimum	0,9197	0,4167	0,1419	16,4973	0,5847	0,5847
Std. Dev.	0,7064	0,1358	0,1955	0,8720	1,3282	1,3282
Cross - sectional analysis of the year 2015						
Mean	1,6751	0,6657	0,5093	17,4268	1,6022	0,1095
Maximum	3,1100	0,9277	0,7605	19,3185	4,8866	0,2496
Minimum	0,6452	0,2874	0,1365	16,5370	0,4816	-0,0787
Std. Dev.	0,6435	0,1830	0,1892	0,8377	1,0981	0,0918

This table presents descriptive statistics of all variables tested. FV is firm value which is measured by Tobin's Q. SDI is Sustainability Disclosure Index. LEV is financial leverage, measured by total debt to total assets ratio. SIZE is firm size which is measured by natural logarithm of total assets. LIQ is liquidity, measured by current assets to current liabilities ratio. ROE is return on equity. It is used as an indicator for profitability.

Based on cross – sectional analysis, the characteristics of financial performance, sustainability disclosure index, and fair value of the companies listed on the JII are varied. Mean of all variables is fluctuated year by year. Mean of firm value in 2014 (200.45%) is higher than mean of fair value in 2013 (190.55%) and in 2015 (167.51%). Mean of sustainability disclosure index in 2013 (71.74%) is higher than mean of sustainability disclosure index in 2014 (68.83%) and in 2015 (66.57%). Mean of leverage in 2015 (50.93%) is higher than mean of leverage in 2013 (49.61%) and in 2014 (49.43%). Mean of liquidity in 2013 (193.15%) is higher than mean of liqudity in 2014 (180.35%) and in 2015 (160.22%). Mean of profitability in 2014 (180.35%) is higher than mean of profitability in

2013 (16.63%) and in 2015 (10.95%). Sustainability disclosure of the companies listed on the JII is relatively high. It is more than 50%. In 2013, the companies communicate 71.74% information about their sustainability performance in their sustainability reporting. In 2014, the companies express 68.83% information regarding their sustainability performance. In 2015, the companies communicate 66.57% information of their sustainability performance in their sustainability reporting.

Hypothesis Testing Result of Substructure I

The effect of financial performance: leverage, size, liquidity and profitability on sustainability disclosure index reveals in Table 4.2. The effect of financial performance on sustainability disclosure index simultaneously is not significant. However, partially, liquidity positively significant affects the sustainability disclosure. The result support the H1c. The effect of leverage, size, and profitability is not significant on the sustainability disclosure index. The result does not support the H1a, H1b, and H1d.

Table 4.2 Coefficient, T – Stat., and F – Stat. of all Variables in Substructure I

	LEV	SIZE	LIQ	ROE	SDI	C
Coefficient	0,1171	-0,0417	0.0440*	-0,0105	2.1492***	1.2830**
T-Statistic	(0.7465)	(-1.5426)	(1.8657)	(-0.4622)	(3.507931)	(2.6321)
F-statistic 1.4625						

This table presents the results of multiple regression of all variables tested. FV is firm value which is measured by Tobin's Q. SDI is Sustainability Disclosure Index. LEV is financial leverage, measured by total debt to total assets ratio. SIZE is firm size which is measured by natural logarithm of total assets. LIQ is liquidity, measured by current assets to current liabilities ratio. ROE is return on equity. It is used as an indicator for profitability. * denote to significance level of 10%, ** denote to significance level of 5%, and *** denote to significance level of 1%.

Hypothesis Testing Result of Substructure II

The effect of sustainability disclosure index on firm value is positively significant on firm value at level 1%. It indicate that the fluctuation of firm value is caused by the level of sustainability disclosure index. The result is succeeded to support the H2.

Mediation Hypothesis Testing Results

Analysis on direct effect, indirect effect and total effect are used to see the power of influence between constructs, either directly, indirectly, or the total effect. Direct effect is the coefficient of all lines with one end dart. While the indirect effect is the effect that arises through mediating variable. Mediating variable in this research is sustainability disclosure index (SDI). The total effect is the influence of the various relationships. The direct, indirect and total effects are presented in Table 4.3 below.

Table 4.3 Parameter Estimation Value

	Direct Effect	Indirect Effect	Total Effect	P – Value	Explanation
LEV → SDI	0.151	0	0.151	0.432	Not Significant
SIZE → SDI	-0.078	0	-0.078	0.104	Not Significant
LIQ → SDI	-0.240	0	-0.240	0.050	Significant
ROE → SDI	0.397	0	0.397	0.627	Not Significant
SDI → FV	0.485	0	0.485	0.001	Significant
LEV → FV	0	0.073	0.073	-	Indirect
SIZE → FV	0	-0.038	-0.038	-	-
LIQ → FV	0	-0.116	-0.116	-	-
ROE → FV	0	0.192	0.192	-	Indirect

This table presents parameter estimation value to determine the indirect effect of financial performance on firm value. FV is firm value which is measured by Tobin's Q. SDI is Sustainability Disclosure Index. LEV is financial leverage, measured by total debt to total assets ratio. SIZE is firm size which is measured by natural logarithm of total assets. LIQ is liquidity, measured by current assets to current liabilities ratio. ROE is return on equity. It is used as an indicator for profitability.

The effect of leverage, size, and profitability on sustainability disclosure is not significant. While, liquidity negatively significantly affects the sustainability disclosure at level 5%. The value of liquidity direct effect is -0.240, meaning that the direct impact of liquidity on sustainability disclosure is as much as 24%. Sustainability disclosure positively significantly affects firm value at level 1% as much as 48.5%. The indirect effect value of leverage and profitability is more than the direct effect value. It means that leverage and profitability have indirect effects on firm value. The path diagram result is exhibited in Figure 4.2 below. The results indicate the support to H3.

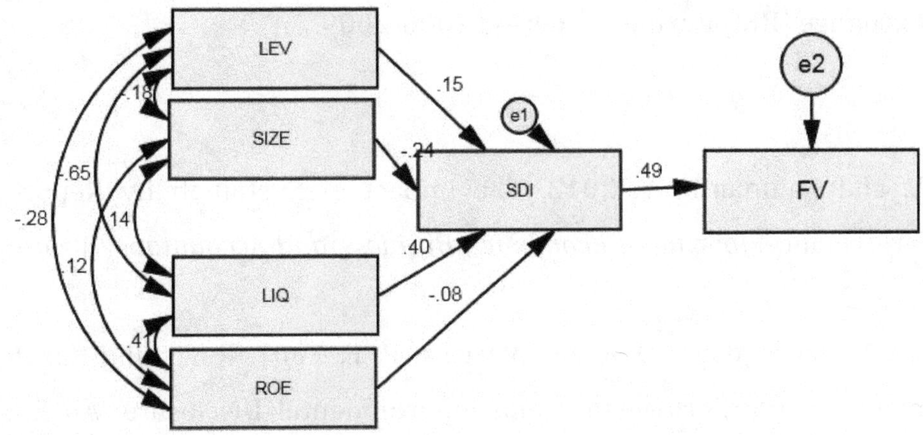

Figure 4.2 Path Diagram Result

Conclusion

The results show that the financial performance effect is not significant on sustainability disclosure simultaneously. However, partially, liquidity has a positively significant effect on sustainability disclosure at level 10%. The company with higher liquidity ratio has higher motivation to reveal their sustainability disclosure.The result supports H1c but does not support H1a, H1b, and H1d. This result indicates that the companies with a strong financial position tend to disclose sustainability disclosure. The effect of sustainability disclosure on firm value is positively significant at level 1%. It supports the H3.

Regarding the indirect effect of financial performance on firm value, the results show that leverage and profitability have positively indirect effect on firm value, but size and liquidity have no indirect effect on firm value. This means that the increase of leverage and profitability will encourage management to publish more sustainability disclosure and it will increase firm value of companies listed on the Jakarta Islamic Index. This result is in line with Wang (2017) and Li et al. (2013) who state that higher leverage encourage management to disclose more information and it will make a fluctuation of firm value. This result is consistent with the argument of Dienes et al. (2017).

The result is also consistent with Fazzini and Maso (2016), Saka and Oshika (2014), as well as Klerk and Villiers (2012). For the Indonesian case, higher sustainability disclosure of companies listed on the JII will increase their firm value. This result also support the result of Burhan and Rahmanti (2012) who conclude that sustainability reporting had an effect on the company performance of all companies except financial companies listed on the Indonesia Stock Exchange (BEI) during the period 2006-2009.

References

Burhan, A. H. N., and Rahmanti, W. 2012. The Impact of Sustainability Reporting on Company Performance. *Journal of Economics, Business, and Accountancy Ventura.* Vol. 15 No.2: 257-272.

Clarkson, M. P., Li, Y., Richardson, D.G., and Vasvari, P. F. 2007. Revisiting the Relation between Environmental Performance and Environmental Disclosure: An Empirical Ananlysis. *Accounting, Organizations, and Society, Vol. 30.*

Dienes, D., Sassen, R., and Fischer, J. 2016. What are the drivers of sustainability reporting? A systematic review. *Sustainability Accounting, Management and Policy Journal*, Vol. 7 Iss 2.

Dilling, P. 2010. Sustainability Reporting In A Global Context: What Are the Characteristics of Corporations that Provide High Quality Sustainability Reports – An Empirical Analysis? *International Business & Economic Research Journal*, Vol. 9 No. 1, pp. 19–30.

Fazzini, M. and Maso, D. L. F. M. (2016). The value relevance of 'assured' environmental disclosure. The Italian experience. *Sustainability Accounting, Management and Policy Journal*, Vol. 7 Iss 2 pp.

Gunawan, Y. and Mayangsari, S. 2015. Pengaruh Sustainability Reporting Terhadap Nilai Perusahaan dengan Investment Opportunity sebagai Variabel Moderating. *E-journal Akuntansi Trisakti*, Vol. 2 No.1: 1-12.

Haggard, K. S., Martin, X., and Pereira, R. 2008. Does Voluntary Disclosure Improve Stock Price Informativeness. *Financial Management*, 37(4), pp. 747 – 768.

Ho, L. and Taylor, M. 2007. An Empirical Analysis of Triple Bottom-Line Reporting and Its Determinants: Evidence from the United States and Japan. *Journal of International Financial Management and Accounting*, Vol. 18 No. 2, pp. 123–150.

Kend, M. 2015. Governance, firm-level characteristics and their impact on the client's voluntary sustainability disclosures and assurance decisions. *Sustainability Accounting, Management and Policy Journal*, Vol. 6 Iss 1 pp. 54 – 78.

Klerk, d. M., Villiers, d. C., and Staden, v. C. 2015. The influence of corporate social responsibility disclosure on share prices: Evidence from the United Kingdom. *Pacific Accounting Review*, Vol. 27 Iss 2 pp. 208-228.

Klerk, d. M., and Villiers, d. C. 2012. The value relevance of corporate responsibility reporting: South African evidence. *Meditari Accountancy Research*, Vol. 20 Iss 1 pp. 21 – 38.

Li, Q., Luo, W., Wang, Y. and Liansheng, W. 2013. Firm performance, corporate ownership, and corporate social responsibility disclosure in China. *Business Ethics: A European Review*, Vol. 22 No. 2, pp. 159–173.

Preacher, K. J., Rucker, D. D., and Hayes, A. F. 2007. Addressing Moderated Mediation Hypotheses: Theory, Methods, and Prescriptions. Multivariate Behavioral Research, 42 (1), pp. 185 – 227.

Saka, C., Oshika, T. (2014). Disclosure effects, carbon emissions and corporate value. *Sustainability Accounting, Management and Policy Journal*, Vol. 5 Iss 1 pp. 22 – 45.

Weber, O. (2017). Corporate sustainability and financial performance of Chinese banks. *Sustainability Accounting, Management and Policy Journal*, Vol. 8 Issue: 3

Wang, C. M. 2017. The Relationship between Firm Characteristics and the Disclosure of Sustainability Reporting. *Sustainability 9*.

7

The Impact of International Financial Reporting Standards (IFRSs) Adoption on Financial Reporting Practice in the Nigerian Banking Sector

Taibat Adebukola Atoyebi[a] Adikwu Joseph Simon[b]

[a] Corresponding Author, Department of Accounting, University of Abuja, Abuja – Nigeria, taibat.atoyebi@uniabuja.edu.ng

[b] Department of Accounting, University of Abuja, Abuja – Nigeria, agbosonjoe_simon@yahoo.com

Keywords

IFRS, Earnings Management, Capital Management, Loan Loss Provision (LLPs).

Abstract

The adoption of International Financial Reporting Standards (IFRSs) in different countries of the world has become a contemporary issue especially with respect to the reliability of financial statements. The study examined the impact of valuation of Loan Loss Provisions (LLPs) on earnings management and capital management during the pre and post-adoption of IFRS for listed deposit money banks (DMBs) in Nigeria. Using an Ex-post facto research design approach, this study utilised secondary data extracted from annual reports and accounts of fifteen (15) DMBs for the period of ten (10) years from 2006 – 2016. The results from the use of multiple regression analysis revealed a significant positive relationship between LLPs and earnings management for both pre and post-IFRS adoption. Furthermore, the study also found a positive insignificant relationship between LLPs and capital management for both pre and post IFRS adoption.

1.0 Introduction

The increasing growth in cross-border financial transactions, international trade, and investments; which unavoidably involves the preparation and presentation of accounting reports. With the increasing globalisation of the marketplace, international investors need access to financial information based on harmonized accounting standards and procedures (Beke, 2011). These reports are useful across various national borders and have brought about the development of International Accounting Standard (IAS) which was first published in 1975 by the International Accounting Standards Committee (IASC). Since then, the process for setting international accounting standards has undergone substantial evolution, culminating in the 2001 restructuring of the IASC into the International Accounting Standard Board (IASB). International Financial Reporting Standards (IFRSs) are accounting standards developed by the International Accounting Standards Board (IASB). Many countries have adopted the IFRS as their official domestic accounting standards. Each country adopting IFRS undergoes a transition process in the year of adoption. This process may be fairly disruptive for users of financial statements as accounting treatments of similar items may vary, and impair comparability and trend analysis. The IFRSs provide provision to remove allowable accounting alternatives (that existed in most countries under their respective local GAAPs) and requires accounting measurements that better reflect a firm's economic position and performance.

In Nigeria, the prudential guidelines issued by the Central Bank of Nigeria and the Statement of Accounting Standards form the Nigerian GAAP. It is mandatory for the Deposit Money Banks to comply with the stipulated guidelines in valuation of Loan Loss Provisions and loan balances in the financial statements. The Nigerian GAAP insist on loan classification into performing and non-performing (substandard, doubtful and lost) while IFRS is based on fair value measurement of loan portfolio. In essence, IFRSs are precise, admit an insufficient number of options, and prohibit hidden reserves. Based on this, the adoption of IFRS is expected to significantly reduce the ability to engage in earnings management behaviour. That is IFRS limit the opportunity for management to engage opportunistic behaviour by limiting the accounting options available to them (Barth,

Landsman & Lang 2008). International Accounting Standard (IAS) No. 39 provide guidance on how loan loss provisions (LLPs) should be established and limits the ability of managers to exercise flexibility in determining the provision (IASB, 2003). If the ability to use LLPs to manage earnings is limited, then there will be evidence of lower earnings management in post-IFRS. Prior research shows that loan loss provisions (LLPs) are primarily used as a tool for earnings management and capital management by listed banks (Ahmed, Neel & Wang, 2010; Anandarajan, Hasan & Lozano-Vivas, 2003; Anandarajan, Hasan & McCarthy, 2007; Ozili, 2015). However, the attention on the use of discretion to manage earnings received global impetus after the Enron crises and many other similar cases that followed. The main focus among the companies that were affected both in the U.S. and other parts of the world was financial irregularities, which reiterated the need for a better grasp of earnings management among practitioners, regulators and those in the academia.

Previous studies have identified that loan losses are one of the major causes of these financial crises and its provision has a direct impact on firms' cash flows and consequently the reported earnings (Chang, Shen, & Fang, 2008; Mohammad, Wasiuzzaman, & Zaini, 2011). The agenda of many regulatory bodies responding to the 2007/2008 financial crisis is the loan provisioning (EFRAG 2009). And also, the arguments of what should comprise regulatory capital varied by country with each country's regulatory body setting their respective levels and standards. To overcome this and to level the competitive conditions for banks across different countries, the Basel committee issued two accords (Busch 2009). Basel I introduced minimum capital requirements (Tier 1 and Tier II). The requirements of this accord subsequently extended to more than a hundred countries worldwide. However, Basel I inadvertently created loopholes which, according to Anandarajan *et al.* (2003) and Pérez, Salas-Fumá, and Saurina, (2008) enabled banks to engage in more aggressive earnings management. IFRS aims to ensure that loan loss provisions adequately reflect the current risk of losses, by adjusting historical provisions to prevailing economic circumstances at the time of reporting - IFRS uses the concept of discounted cash flows measurement method (KPMG, 2007). However, Bank regulators continue to stress that LLPs should be sufficient to minimise loan loss on bank loan portfolio, also emerging empirical studies suggest that bank managers may have another incentive(s) to influence or manipulate reported loan loss provision estimates other than mitigating expected credit loss. Three arguments support the reason why banks manipulate earnings: signalling argument, income smoothing or earnings management argument and capital management argument (Zhou & Chen, 2004). And also earnings management argument holds that managers increase the provision for loan losses in periods when earnings are high, under the assumption of income smoothing (Beatty, Chamberlin & Mogliolo, 1995; Collins, Shackleford & Wahlen, 1995; Rivard, Blind & Morris, 2003). This study therefore seeks to examine the impact of IFRS adoption on financial reporting practice in the Nigerian banking sector.

The main objective of this study is to examine the impact of IFRS adoption on financial reporting practice in the Nigeria banking sector. Consequently, the study hypothesized that; H_{01}: The valuation of LLPs has no significant influence on earnings management after IFRS adoption by listed banks in Nigeria.

H_{02}: LLPs has no significant impact on capital management after the IFRS adoption by listed banks in Nigeria.

2.0 Literature Review

2.1 Earnings Management

Earnings are a central part of financial statements that help a large number of stakeholders to evaluate firms' performance. Stakeholders include current investors, potential investors, creditors, suppliers, customers and other stakeholders. Stakeholders use the reported financial information to measure managers' performance, deciding compensation plans and assessing the future of the company. Reported financial information influences the investor capital allocation decisions (Xu, Taylor & Dugan 2007). Since earnings is a major and central part for management compensation decisions and investor's decision making, it create incentives for managers to practice earnings management.

Healy and Wahlen (1999) defined earnings management as a means management's use of judgment through financial reporting and structuring transactions to conceal the true economic performance of an entity. Earnings management motives are broadly classified as either opportunistic which exemplifies the classic agency problem; or signaling- which signals private information to capital markets (Beaver, 2002). Kirschenheiter and Melumad (2002) described earnings management as when a manager intentionally uses judgment and assessments to skew earnings towards a desired outcome. According to them, Managers often use manipulating activities to maximize reported earnings. Income maximization is one the more common purposes for using earnings management. However, the opposite is Big- Bath accounting where managers radically decrease earnings, providing the possibility to report positive earnings in future years.

Ahmed, Takeda & Thomas (1999) simply described earnings management as smoothing earnings while Copeland (1968) defined the concept as "the repetitive selection of accounting measurement or reporting rules in a particular pattern, the effect of which is to report a stream of income with a smaller variation from trend than would otherwise have appeared". Earnings management is a strategy employed by management of a company to deliberately manipulate the company's earnings so that the figures match a predetermined target. Income smoothing is another reason why managers manipulate earnings. Managers attempt to maintain a steady level of earnings in order to secure employment. If earnings for the current period are high and projected future earnings are low, managers intend to reserve current earnings, creating a possibility of capitalization in the future, referred to as cookie-jar accounting (DeFond & Park, 1997).

There are two methods that could be used for earnings management. First, one could use the flexibility allowed in generally accepted accounting principles (GAAP) to change reported earnings without changing the underlying (past) cash flows, which Healy and Wahlen (1999) describe as usage of managerial judgment in financial reporting. This is called accounting earnings management. Second, a manager may change operating decisions, such as delivery schedule or maintenance, in order to manage the underlying cash flows that will affect the reported income reports, which is being described as structuring of transactions by Healy and Wahlen. This kind of management is usually referred to as economic earnings management.

According to Healy and Wahlen (1999); Graham (2005) if stakeholders believe that managers possess information that is not transparent to stakeholder, they might assume and accept a degree of earnings management being exercised. This indicates that if a firm reports an earning decreases or a loss, stakeholders will assume that earnings management already has been practiced to avoid reporting a decrease in earnings or to report a loss. If a firm report a small loss, the capital markets will punish the firm severely due to the assumption of exhausted manipulation activities from the firm to meet zero earnings benchmark.

According to Roman (2009) "Earnings management occurs when firm management has the opportunity to make accounting decisions that change reported income and exploit those opportunities". He also stated that accounting for business operations requires judgment and estimates. For example, one can't measure revenue without estimating when customers will pay, how many will not pay, how many will return goods for refund and costs to the seller for fulfillment of warranty or maintenance promises. Earnings management is the premeditated dulling of variations about some level of earnings considered to be normal for the organization.

2.2 Loan Loss Provision

According to the revised Central Bank of Nigeria (CBN) Prudential Guidelines (Paragraph 12.1) 2010, licensed Deposit Money Banks (DMBs) are to make adequate provisions for perceived losses based on the credit portfolio classification system prescribed that, in order to reflect their true financial condition. Two types of provisions (that is, specific and general) are considered adequate to achieve the objectives. Specific provision are made on the basis of perceived risk of default on specific credit facilities while general provisions are made in recognition of the fact that even performing credit facility harbor some risk of loan no matter how small. Paragraph 12.3 of the Guidelines provide that, when IFRS is adopted in Nigeria, Banks were required to make provisions for loans as prescribed in the relevant IFRS Standards.

Provisions for loans recognized in the profit and loss account should be determined based on the requirements of IFRS. However, the IFRS provisions should be compared with provision determined under prudential guidelines and the expected impact/changes in general reserve should be treated as follows: Prudential Provision is greater than IFRS provision; transfer the difference from the general reserve to a non-distributable regulatory reserve. Prudential Provision is less than IFRS provision; the excess charges resulting should be transferred from the regulatory reserve account to the general reserve to the extent of the non-distributable reserve previously recognized. The non-distributable reserve should be classified under Tier 1 as part of core capital.

Grey and Clarke (2004) explained Loan loss provision as an expense on the income statement which signifies managers' assessment of expected future losses. This means that an increase in loan loss provision reduces net income, while a fall in loan losses increases net income. Since it is the result of managers' assessment of the likely loss that the company would incur should the borrower fail to repay his obligations as at when due, the provision for it is considered to have two (2) portions: non-discretionary and discretionary portions. "Non-discretionary is a function of specific quality determinants in the loan portfolio- non-accrual loans, renegotiated loans, loans past due over 90 days, specific analyses on troubled large credits, usually implying internal grading system. In order to influence earnings, banks make large provision for loan losses. It was revealed that banks in the U.S provided inadequate loan losses to understate net assets and profits. Since it is the result of managers' assessment of the likely loss that the company would incur should the borrower fail to repay his obligations as at when due, the provision for it is considered to have two (2) portions; the non-discretionary portion is the provision that is based on fair and objective analysis of the firm's economic conditions, while Mohammad et al. (2011) pointed that, the discretionary portion are those accruals that largely depend on the outcome of the managers' future expectation of uncertain events. However, the attention on the use of discretion to manage earnings received global impetus after the Enron crises and many other similar cases that followed. The main focus among the companies that were affected both in the U.S. and other parts of the world was financial irregularities, which reiterated the need for better grasp of earnings management among practitioners, regulators and those in the academia. (Chang et al. 2008 and Mohammad et al. 2011).

2.3 Capital Management

The Rules governing regulatory capital, its components and required deductions to the capital levels, shall be applied by banks for assessment of qualifying capital. Banks are required to maintain a minimum regulatory capital adequacy ratio (CAR) of 15% on an on-going basis. The Central Bank of Nigeria (CBN) will take into account the relevant risk factors and the internal capital adequacy assessments of each bank to ensure that the capital held by a bank is commensurate with the bank's overall risk profile. This would include, among others, the effectiveness of the bank's risk management systems in identifying, assessing / measuring, monitoring and managing various risks including interest rate risk in the banking book, liquidity risk, concentration risk and residual risk.

Accordingly, CBN will consider prescribing a higher level of minimum capital ratio for each bank under the Pillar 2 framework on the basis of their respective risk profiles and their risk management systems. Furthermore, in terms of the Pillar 2 requirements of the capital adequacy framework, banks are expected to operate at a level well above the minimum requirement. (see CBN Guidance Notes on Regulatory Capital 2015). Capital adequacy refers to the amount of capital held by Nigerian deposit insurance corporation (NDIC) to cover losses. The CBN currently requires capital adequacy requirements for NDIC to be based on

the Bank for International Settlements Basel Committee for Banking Supervision (1988) International Convergence of Capital Measurement and Capital Standards, commonly known as the Basel Accord. The intention of the Basel Accord was to ensure that a consistent standard be applied when determining minimum capital requirements across internationally active banks. Under the rules of the Basel Accord, capital for supervisory purposes is now considered in two tiers: Tier I and Tier II. Tier I (core capital) comprises the highest-quality capital elements. Tier I capital is defined as the sum of book value of equity (common stock and retained earnings), qualifying non-cumulative perpetual preferred stock, and minority interest in equity accounts of subsidiaries less goodwill and other intangible assets. Tier II (supplementary capital) is made up of other elements that contribute to the overall strength of a bank as a going concern but do not satisfy all of the characteristics of Tier I capital. Tier II capital is the sum of loan loss reserves (up to a maximum of 1.25% of risk weighted assets), perpetual preferred stock, hybrid capital instruments, perpetual debt, mandatory convertible debt securities, term subordinated debt, and intermediate preferred stock. A bank's capital base is the sum of its Tier I and Tier II capital less any deductions. At least 50% of a bank's capital base must be Tier I capital. The Basel Accord requires that the ratio of a bank's capital to risk weighted assets (referred to as the capital adequacy ratio) must be at least 8%.

2.4 Review of Empirical Studies

Ozili and Outa (2017) reviewed the recent academic and policy literature on bank loan loss provisioning (LLP) to identify several advances in the literature and observed that there exists some major advancement in country-specific and cross-country analyses and substantial interaction between LLPs and existing prudential, accounting, institutional firm characteristic, cultural, religious, tax and fiscal framework. Ozili (2017) investigated whether discretionary 'loan loss provisioning' by Western European banks is driven by income smoothing or credit risk considerations. The study used the ordinary least square regression to examine the relationship between loan loss provision and earnings before tax and loan loss provisions in the post-financial crisis period. The findings of the study revealed that listed banks in Western Europe carryout discretionary provisioning which is driven by income smoothing incentives in the post-financial crisis period. The study also observed that discretionary provisioning is significantly influenced by credit risk factors, mainly, non-performing loans and loan growth. Overall, the implication of the results of the study is that discretionary provisioning among Western European banks is driven by both income smoothing and credit risk considerations.

Sanyaolu, Iyoha and Ojeka (2017) examined the effect of adopted International Financial Reporting Standards (IFRS) adoption on the earning yield (EY) and earning per share (EPS) of quoted banks in Nigeria. The study made used of cross sectional data obtained for a period of 6 years from 2009 to 2014, while the panel ordinary least method of analysis was used to examine the impact of IFRS adoption on the earnings of all 15 quoted banks in the Nigerian Stock Exchange. The study found a significant and positive relationship between

IFRS adoption and the earnings yield of quoted banks in Nigeria. The study also found a significant and positive relationship between IFRS adoption and EPS of quoted banks in Nigeria. The study concludes that IFRS adoption has improved the decision making capability of the various stakeholders, thus, increasing investor confidence and the inflow of capital in the country through foreign direct investment.

Bello, Abubakar, and Adeyemi (2016) investigated the effects of IFRS adoption on earnings management of non-financial quoted companies in Nigeria. They utilized a sample of seventy-five non-financial quoted companies in Nigeria that have consistently published their audited annual financial reports between 2010 and 2014. They used a dummy variable to separate period of pre and post adoption period; before January 2012 and year-end 2014. The data collected were subjected to descriptive analysis, correlation analysis and a panel multiple regression analysis to explore both trends and possible effects of IFRS adoption on general earnings management. Their findings revealed that IFRS adoption in Nigeria does not significantly affect the tendency of Nigerian companies to manipulate earnings. Explicitly, this is contrary to the general belief that IFRS, as high quality accounting standards will reduce the possibility of earnings management.

Eneje and Paul (2016) examined the effect of IFRS adoption on the mechanics of loan loss provisioning for Nigerian Banks. Specifically, it analyzed how the change in the recognition and measurement of loan loss provision affects the accounting quality of banks thereby reducing the income smoothing behavior of the money deposit banks. Ordinary least square multiple regression analysis was used to analyse secondary data obtained from the annual reports and accounts of deposit money banks covering the period of 2005 to 2015. The findings of the study revealed that the post-IFRS has had significant effects on the mechanics of loan loss provisioning compared to the pre IFRS era in the Nigerian Money Deposit Banks. Their study recommended that banks CEO's should actively sensitize fresh accountants and auditors who are yet to be acquainted with IFRS guidelines and standards.

Nugrahanti (2015) investigated the impact of risk assessment using the risk inherent and quality implementation of quality risk management in the operational activities of banking operations to earnings management practices through loan loss provisions. The investigator used data pool from 2012 through 2014. Base on the purposive sampling method, 36 listed banks on the Stock Exchange Indonesian were selected as sample of the study. A panel data multivariate regression methodology was used. The findings of the study showed that risk assessment strengthens the decrease in the earning management implementation after the adoption of IFRS in IAS No. 39 and Basel II Accord generally evidence to improve I bank's financial report quality.

Umoren and Enang, (2015) examined whether the mandatory adoption of IFRS has improved the value relevance of financial information in the financial statements of commercial banks in Nigeria. The sample comprises of twelve listed banks in Nigeria. Specifically, financial statement figures of 2010 and 2011 (pre-adoption period) and 2012 and 2013 (post-adoption) were utilized. Descriptive statistics and least square regression were conducted to analyze the effect of IFRS adoption on the accounting quality. The result indicated that the equity value and earnings of banks are relatively value relevant to share prices under IFRS than under the previous Nigerian SAS. Results also indicate that earnings per share is incrementally value relevant during post-IFRS period while book value of equity per share is incrementally less value relevant during the post-IFRS period.

Yahaya, Kutigi, and Mohammed, (2015) investigated how the change in the recognition and measurement of banks' loan loss provision affects earnings management behavior. They investigated the post adoption off IFRS and value relevance of accounting information of quoted banks in Nigeria. Using the price model and the return model, their study found that the EPS increased in the post adoption than in the pre adoption periods. The study concluded that the restriction to incur losses under IFRS significantly reduced the ability of banks to engage in earnings manipulation. The study recommended that investors should understand the IFRS adoption process so as to avoid overvaluation of the economy when the financial markets are doing well.

Ahmed, Mohammed and Adisa (2014) explored the relationship between loan loss provision and earnings management in Nigerian DMBs. Secondary data were obtained from the 8 banks' annual reports for the period of 2006 to 2011 and robust regression was used as a tool for data analysis. The result indicated that there is a positive relationship between the provision for loan losses and earnings management in Nigerian DMBs. Trabelsi, Hamza & Chila (2013) examined the effect of IFRS on earnings quality in European Stock Market using the sample of 250 French companies listed on Euronext Paris from 2002-2007, the study found that IFRS adoption resulted in a significant improvement of value relevance of earnings. This implies that market valuation is less associated with earnings prepared in line with IFRS than those prepared under IFRS. The explanatory power of earnings improved significantly after the transition to international standards.

Tanko (2012) examined financial performance measures on some selected Nigerian banks that are quoted under the Nigerian stock market under the IFRS regime. The study used regression model to examine the banks financial performance. The study defined the change in performance based on two parameters. First, change in accounting quality (earnings management and timely loss recognition). Secondly, the performance of the firms based on changes on identified financial rations of the firms. The study test the impact of adoption as it relates to profitability, growth, leverage, and liquidity performance. Multiple logit regression and t-test were used in the analysis. The study finds that variability of earnings has decreased which suggest that there was low variability in earnings in the post IFRS adoption period. Timely loss recognition is the measure for prevalence of large negative earnings where large negative net income to be positive which signifies that IFRS firms recognize losses more frequently in the post adoption period than they do in the pre adoption period, the study conclude that accounting quality improves after the adoption of IFRS. They study also find that under IFRS, firms exhibit higher values on profitability measure, such as earnings per share (EPS). The study concludes by recommending comprehensive implementation of IFRS and that SEC and external auditors should monitor and ensure strict compliance with the adoption and provision of standards.

Leventis, Dimihopoulos and Anandaraja (2011) used a sample of 91 EU listed commercial banks covering a period of ten years (before and after implementation of IFRS), they dichotomize their sample into early and late adopters. They found that earnings management (using loan loss provisions) for both early and late adopters while significant over the estimation window is significantly reduced after implementation of IFRS. They also find that, for risky banks, earnings management behavior is more pronounced when compared to the less risky banks, but is significantly reduced in the post IFRS period. Capital management behavior by bank managers is not significant in both pre and posts IFRS regimes. Their study conclude that the implementation of IFRS in the EU appears to have improved earnings quality by mitigating the tendency of bank managers of listed commercial banks to engage in earnings management using loan loss provisions.

Outa (2011) investigated if the adoption of IFRSs in Kenya has been associated with higher accounting quality for listed companies. The study applied accounting quality measures; earnings management, timely loss recognition and value relevance. The methodology is based on prior literature definition of metrics of accounting quality mainly earnings management, timely loss recognition and value relevance. The outcomes are mixed (accounting quality had marginally improved and declined) and are very much in line with findings in other studies. Nina, Bernhard, Christopher and Ann-Kristin (2009) analyzed a large sample of German firms in the period from 1998 to 2008 found that voluntary and mandatory adopters differ distinctively in terms of essential firm characteristics. Result from their findings indicates that earnings management in the post-adoption period are mixed. While income smoothing decreases for voluntary but not for mandatory adopters, discretionary accruals only decrease for mandatory but not for voluntary adopters.

Anandarajan, Hasan and McCarthy (2005) examined whether Australian banks engage in earnings, capital management and signaling, and, if so, the extent to which loan loss provisions (LLPs) are used for this purpose. Their results indicated that banks in Australia used loan loss provisions to manage earnings. Furthermore, listed commercial banks engage more aggressively in earnings management using LLPs than other banks. Anandarajan et al (2005) also found that earnings management behavior is more pronounced after implementation of the Basel Accord. However, they did not find evidence to indicate a relationship between LLPs and capital management. This may be because loan loss reserves no longer constitute part of Tier I capital in the numerator of the capital adequacy ratio. Overall, the found a significant understating of loan loss provisions in the post-Basel period relative to the pre-Basel period. It indicated that reported earnings may not reflect the true economic reality underlying those numbers. They concluded that,

Australian banks do not appear to use LLPs for signaling future intentions of higher earnings to investors.

The concept of signaling was first studied in the context of job market by Akerlof (1970). While, Spence (1973) developed the signal equilibrium theory which provided that a good firm can distinguish itself from a bad firm by sending signal about its quality to capital markets. Signals have become useful tools for obtaining financial reports from management to potential investors. The theory also argued that a signal is a perceivable action or structure that is intended to or has evolved to indicate an otherwise not perceivable quality about the signaler or the signaler's environment. i.e., the purpose of a signal is to indicate a certain quality - Signaling by banks using Loan Loss Provision (LLPs). He also argued that the existence of information asymmetric can also be taken as a reason for good companies to use financial information to send signal to the market.

This study adopts signaling theory due to its focus on intentional disclosure of positive information. Signal is the information disclosed from the financial statements. However, bank managers known as the signalers have an incentive to manipulate the financial statements to get decision makers to act as preferred by the managers.

3.0 Methodology

The Ex-post facto research design is used in this study. The population of the study comprise of all listed deposit money banks (DMBs) in Nigeria from the period 2006–2016, taken from the Nigerian Stock Exchange (NSE) official website. Though there are 22 banks that were listed by the NSE as at 2016, 15 banks were selected for this study. The 15 banks meet the following criteria:

(i) Banks that their complete annual reports is readily available and accessible to the researcher within the period under consideration,

(ii) Banks that had their toxic assets purchased by AMCOM due to their inability to meet the CBN September 30, 2011 deadline to fully recapitalize or be liquidated, were excluded from this study.

(iii) And finally, banks that have not received any form of bailout by CBN within the period of the study.

Secondary data was used in this study and extracted from the annual reports and accounts of the banks for the periods under review. The data was collected over a period of 10 years which covers pre-IFRS adoption and post-IFRS adoption, ranging from 2006-2016, excluding 2011 which is the year of adoption. The period from 2006 – 2010 form the pre-adoption, while 2012 – 2016 form the post-adoption. The model used for testing the earnings and capital management hypotheses is a modified and extended version of the cross-sectional model used by Leventis, Dimitropoulos and Anandarajan (2011) in equations 3.1 and 3.2

$$LLP_{it} = \beta_0 + \beta_1 EBTit + \beta_2 NPL_{it} + \beta_3 SIZEit + \beta_4 AGE_{it} + \beta_5 \Delta LLA_{it} + \beta_6 CFEER_{it} + e \ldots (3.1)$$

$$LLP_{it} = \gamma_0 + \gamma_1 MCAR_{it} + \gamma_2 NPL_{it} + \gamma_3 SIZE_{it} + \gamma_4 AGE_{it} + \gamma_5 \Delta LLA_{it} + \gamma_6 CFEER_{it} + e \ldots (3.2)$$

Where: $\beta_{0\text{-}6}$ and $\gamma_{0\text{-}6}$ are the coefficient of parameters to be estimated. The dependent variable in this study is LLP (proxy for loan loss provision to total loans outstanding). The independent or explanatory variables are EBT (proxy for earnings management) and MCAR (Capital Management), while NPL, SIZE, AGE, ΔLLA and CFEER are control variables. Three models (Random effect, Fixed effect, and Pool effect model) was formulated for each scenarios; that is, model with EBT and model with MCAR both for pre-IFRS and post-IFRS.

The variables are measured thus:

LLP = ratio of loan loss provisions to total loans

EBT = ratio of earnings before taxes and LLPs to total assets

MCAR = ratio of actual regulatory capital (tier 1 capital) before loan loss reserves to the minimum required regulatory capital

NPL = ratio of loans and advances to customers divided by total bank total asset

SIZE = natural logarithm of total assets

AGE = no. of years the bank has been in operation from the date being quoted on the Nigeria Stock Exchange

ΔLLA = change in loan losses /total assets

CFEER = commission and fee income to total assets

e = error term which capture other variables not included in the model

4.0 Results

Table 4.1 Pre-IFRS and Post-IFRS Adoption MODEL with Earnings Management

Regressors	Random effect model		Random effect model	
	B	p-value	B	p-value
EBT	0.3027	0.0000	0.6570	0.0000
NPL	0.0259	0.5607	0.0496	0.2611
SIZE	-0.0046	0.1896	-0.0134	0.0002
AGE	0.0003	0.5255	-0.0003	0.6882
LLA	0.0706	0.4981	0.0520	0.6080
CFEER	1.0070	0.0404	-0.0175	0.9441
R-Squared	0.3721		0.6988	
Adj. R-Squared	0.3167		0.6722	
F-statistic p-value	0.0000		0.0000	

Source: SPSS output, 2017

As observed from the regression models selected above for the pre-IFRS and the post-IFRS performance. EBT in pre-IFRS was observed to have explained LLP at 0.3027 units with a p-value of 0.000 which is less than the 5% level of significance. While in the post-IFRS EBT is explaining the LLP at 0.6570 units with p-value of 0.000 which is also less than the 5% level of significance. The independent variables are able to explain 31.67% variation in Loan loss provision in the pre IFRS era while the variation as shown in Table 4.1 for post IFRS era is 67.22%

Table 4.2 Pre-IFRS and Post-IFRS Adoption Model with Capital Management

Regressors	Fixed effect model		Fixed effect model	
	B	p-value	B	p-value
MCAR	0.0709	0.3023	0.1157	0.0963
NPL	0.1085	0.1049	0.0709	0.3852
SIZE	-0.0037	0.4669	-0.0043	0.5586
AGE	-0.0075	0.3295	0.0173	0.0185
LLA	0.0246	0.8597	0.1022	0.6035
CFEER	0.8791	0.1876	0.6169	0.1969
R-Squared	0.1062		0.1681	
Adj. R-Squared	0.2249		0.1401	
F-statistic p-value	0.3926		0.1128	

Source: SPSS output, 2017

As observed from the regression models presented in table 4.2 for the pre-IFRS and the post-IFRS performance. MCAR in pre-IFRS was observed to have explained LLP at 0.0709 units with a p-value of 0.3023 which is greater than the 5% level of significance. While in the post-IFRS MCAR is explaining the LLP at 0.1157 units with p-value of 0.0963 which is also greater than the 5% level of significance.

This model result suggests strongly that the MCAR does not have a significant relationship with LLP both in the pre-IFRS and post-IFRS. Although, the unit of its explanation on LLP changes from 0.0709 to 0.1157 units in the pre-IFRS to post-IFRS adoption periods. This also suggests that the adoption of the IFRS increases the not significant performance of MCAR on LLP since there is an incremental variation in the MCARs explanatory coefficient for the pre-IFRS and post-IFRS adoption periods.

Since the MCAR's coefficients p-value of (pre-IFRS=0.3023 & post-IFRS=0.0963) and are both greater than 0.05(5%) level of significance, we cannot reject the null hypothesis "LLPs has no significant impact on capital management (MCAR) during the post-IFRS adoption for listed banks in Nigeria." and conclude statistically that there is no significant impact of LLPs on capital management (MCAR) during the pre-IFRS and post-IFRS adoption for listed banks in Nigeria.

5.0 Discussion

The study was carried out with the aim of achieving two specific objectives which were hitherto stated in chapter one of this study. Findings from each of the objective reveals as follows;

5.1 Earnings Management;

i. The test of hypothesis to examine whether the valuation of Loan Loss Provisions (LLPs) significantly influence earnings management under IFRS adoption for banks under consideration. The results in Table 4.1 revealed that earnings before taxes (EBT) is positive and significant at 5% level of significance in both the pre and post-adoption of IFRS. A positive and significant relationship between earnings and LLPs would mean that LLPs are used as a tool for earnings management. These findings indicate that LLPs are used as a tool for earnings management in both periods, but more aggressively so in the post-IFRS period, thus we disagree and reject hypothesis one which states that the valuation of LLPs has no significant influence on earnings management after IFRS adoption by listed banks in Nigeria.

ii. The indication is that LLPs are being used for earnings management purposes over the entire period of the analysis. The results also indicates that banks with lower earnings have an incentive to manipulate by lowering LLPs. This is possible because the expected loss approach basis for loan loss provisioning as required by IFRS may allow managers the opportunistic behavior.

iii. Despite the result showing that LLPs being used for earnings management purpose and an increase in earning management during the post-IFRS, the study also relate its findings with the prudent risk management, which states that When the economic cycle is positive, bank loans grow and bank profits tend to be relatively higher, more prudent banks may increase their loan loss provisions because these are the times when expected losses are generated and growing.

This finding corroborates the findings of other researchers (refer Ahmed et al. 1999; Anandarajan et al. 2003, 2007; Perez et al. 2008; Ozili 2015 and Leventis, et al. 2011who reported a significant and positive results relationship between LLP and EBT in the pre and post-IFRS period.

5.2 Capital Management

i. The result for the MCAR show a positive but not significant at more than 5% level in both pre and post-adoption of IFRS for listed banks in Nigeria. This indicates that there is relationship between capital management and LLPs but no sufficient evidence that LLPs are used to manage capital adequacy ratio in post-IFRS. This finding support and agreed with null hypothesis 2, the study accepts the hypothesis that states that LLPs has no significant impact on capital management after the IFRS adoption by listed banks in Nigeria. However, when CFEER*MCAR is interacted or included, the coefficient is more than 5% level of significant. This indicates insufficient evidence that LLPs will be used more aggressively to manage capital in the post-IFRS regime. Overall, we conclude that LLPs are not used as a tool for capital management.

ii. This result agrees with the studies of Anandarajan et al. (2005) and Leventis et al. (2011) that examined the use of LLPs and other related tools for capital management. They found that capital management is not significant in both pre and post IFRS regimes and banks does not use LLPs by inflating loan loss reserves when capital levels were close to violating minimum capital regulations. In Nigeria, where the CBN provide prudential guidelines for listed banks to guide in their banking operations, therefore it is difficult to violate both the IFRS and the CBN prudential guidelines.

6.0 Conclusions

The aim of this study is to examine whether loan loss provisions of IFRS has significant effect on earnings management and capital management of banks in Nigeria. We conclude that in the post-IFRS regime, there were evidence of accentuated earnings management behavior using LLPs in the sampled Nigerian listed DMBs. Furthermore, the study also found no evidence of capital management through the use of LLPs in the sampled Nigerian listed DMBs during the post-IFRS regime.

References

Ahmed, A., Mohammed, A. Y., & Adisa A. O. (2014). Loan Loss Provision and Earnings Management in Nigerian Deposit Money Banks. *Mediterranean Journal of Social Sciences, 5* (17), 250-251.

Ahmed ASC., Takeda C., & Thomas, S. (1999). Bank loan loss provisions: a reexamination of capital management, earnings management and signaling effects. *Journal of Accounting and Economics 29*, 1-25.

Ahmed, A. S., Neel M. J., & Wang D. D. (2010). 'Does mandatory adoption of IFRS improve accounting quality? Preliminary evidence.' Working paper, Texas A&M University, 2010. Retrieved January 26, 2016 from http://papers.ssrn.com/sol3/papers.cfm?abstract_id=1502909.

Ahmed, A. S., Takeda, C., & Thomas, S. (1999). Bank loan loss provisions: a reexamination of capital management, earnings management and signaling effects, *Journal of Accounting and Economics, 28*, 1-25.

Akerlof, G. U. (1970). The market for 'lemons': quality uncertainty and the market mechanism, *Quantitative Journal of Economics, 89*, 488-500.

Anandarajan, A. E., Hasan, I. E., & Lozano-Vivas, A. O. (2003). The role of loan loss provisions in earnings management, capital management and signaling: The Spanish experience, *Advances in International Accounting, 16*, 45-65.

Anandrajan, A., Hassan, I., & McCarthy, C. (2005). The use of loan loss provision for capital management and signalling by Australian banks. *Finland Discussion Papers,* Paper *22:* (2005).

Anandarajan, A. E., Hasan, I. O., & McCarthy, C. J. (2007). Use of loan loss provisions for capital, earnings management and signaling by Australian banks, *Accounting & Finance, 47* (3), 357-379.

Barth, M. E., Landsman, W. R., & Lang, M. H. (2008). International accounting standards and accounting quality. *Journal of Accounting Research 46*, 467-498.

Beatty, A. L., Chamberlain, S. L., & Magliolo, J. (1995). Managing Financial Reports of Commercial banks: the influence of taxes, regulatory capital and earnings. *Journal of Accounting Research, 333*, 231–262.

Beaver, W. (2002). Perspectives on recent capital market research. *The Accounting Review,* 453- 474.

Beke, J. U. (2011). International Accounting Standardization Practice in Hungary. *Regional and Business Studies, 3*(1), 9-24.

Bello, A., Abubakar, S., & Tesleem A. (2016). IFRS Adoption and Earnings Management in Nigerian Non-Financial Quoted Companies. International Conference on Accounting Studies (ICAS) 15-18.

Busch, A. (2009). Banking regulation and globalization. Oxford University Press, USA.

Chang, R. D., Shen, W. H.,s & Fang, C. J. (2008). Discretionary loan loss provisions and earnings management for the banking industry. *International Business & Economics Research Journal, 7*(3), 9-20.

Collins, J., Shackelford, D., & Wahlen, J. (1995). Bank differences in the coordination of regulatory capital, earnings and taxes. *Journal of Accounting Research, 33,* 263-292.

Copeland, R. (1968). Income smoothing. *Journal of Accounting Research, 6*, 101-116

DeFond, M. L., & Park, C. W. (1997). Smoothing income in anticipation of future earnings. *Journal of Accounting and Economics 23*, 115–139.

EFRAG (2009). European Financial Reporting Advisory Group. *http://www.efrag.org/homepage.asp.*

Graham, J. R., Harvey, C. R., & Rajgopal, S. (2005). The economic implications of corporate financial reporting. *Journal of Accounting and Economics, 40(1),* 3-73.

Gray, R. P., & Clarke, F. L. (2004). A Methodology for calculating the allowance for loan losses in commercial banks" *ABACUS, 40*(3), 45-48.

Healy, P. M., & Wahlen, J. (1999). A Review of the earnings management literature and its implication for standard setting. *Accounting Horizons 13*(4), 365-383.

IASB (2008). International Financial Reporting Standards. International Accounting Standards Board, London.

Kirschenheiter, M., & Melumad, N. D. (2002). Can "Big Bath" and Earnings Smoothing Co-exist as Equilibrium Financial Reporting Strategies? *Journal of Accounting Research 40,* 761–796.

KPMG (2007). Loan impairment modeling according to IAS 39 by using Basel II parameters. *KPMG Romania. April* 2007.

Leventis, S., Dimitropoulos, P. E., & Anandarajan, A. J. (2011). Loan Loss Provisions, Earnings Management and Capital Management under IFRS: The Case of EU Commercial Banks. *Journal of Financial Service Research 40*(1), 103-122.

Mohammad, W. M., Wasiuzzaman, S., & Zaini, R.M. (2011). Panel data analysis of the relationship between earnings management, bank risks, loan loss provision and dividend per share. *Journal of Business and Policy Research, 6*(1), 46-56.

Nugrahanti, T. P. (2015). Risk Assessment and Earning Management in Banking of Indonesia: Corporate Governance Mechanisms. *Global Journal of Business and Social Science Review 4*(1), 50-55.

Nina, G., Bernhard, K., Christopher, A., & Ann, K. (2009). Working Paper, International financial reporting standards and earnings Quality: the myth of voluntary vs. mandatory adoption Center for Entrepreneurial and Financial Studies

Outa, E. R. (2011). The Impact of International Financial Reporting Standards (IFRS) Adoption on the Accounting Quality of Listed Companies in Kenya. *International Journal of Accounting and Financial Reporting, 1*(1), 212-241.

Ozili, P. K. (2015). Loan Loss Provisioning, Income Smoothing, Signalling, Capital Management and Procyclicality: Does IFRS Matter? Empirical Evidence from Nigeria, *Mediterranean Journal of Social Science 6*(2), 224-232.

Ozili P. K. (2017). Discretionary Provisioning Practices among Western European Banks, *Journal of Financial Economic Policy, 9*(1), 109-118.

Ozili P. K., & Outa, E. R. (2017). Bank Loan Loss Provisions Research: *A Review Munich Personal RePEc Archive (MPRA) Paper*

Pérez, D., Salas-Fumás, V., & Saurina, J. (2008). Earnings and capital management in alternative loan loss provision regulatory regimes, *European Accounting Review, 17,* 423-445.

Rivard, R., Bland, E., & Morris, G. (2003). Income Smoothing Behavior of U.S. Banks under Revised International Capital Requirements, *International Advances In Economic Research,* 9(4), 288-294

Sanyaolu, O. A., Iyoha, F. O., & Ojeka, S. A. (2017). International Financial Reporting Standards Adoption and Earnings of Quoted Banks in Nigeria, *International Journal of Economics and Financial Issues,* 7(1), 279-284

Spence, M. (1973). Job Market Signaling, *Quality Journal of Economics, 87,* 355-374.

Tanko, M. E. (2012). The effect of International Financial Reporting Standards (IFRS) Adoption on the Performance of Firms in Nigeria. Paper Presentation, IFRS Conference-Challenges and Opportunities Organized by College of Business and Economics, Qassim University – Saudi Arabia

Trabelsi, N. S., Hamza, S. E., & Chila, H. (2013). The effects of IFRS on earnings quality in European stock markets: evidence from France. *Interdisciplinary Journal of Research in Business, 2*(12), 35-47.

Umoren, A. O., & Enang, E. R. (2015), IFRS adoption and value relevance of financial statements of Nigerian banks. *International Journal of Finance and Accounting, 4*(1), 1-7.

Xu, Z., Taylor, G., & Dugan, M. (2007). Review of Real Earnings Management Literature. *Journal of Accounting Literature,* 26, 195-228

Yahaya, O. A., Kutigi, U. M., & Mohammed, A. (2015). International financial reporting standards and earnings management behavior of listed deposit money banks in Nigeria. *European Journal of Business and Management, 7*(18).

Zhou, J., & Chen, K.Y. (2004). Audit committee, board characteristics and earnings Management by commercial banks. *Retrieved May 21, 2016 from aaahq.org/audit/midyear/05midyear/.../ZHOU_CG_EM_DEC16A.pdf*

Appendices

Table 1: Descriptive Statistics

VAR	N	PostIFRS	PreIFRS	PostIFRS	PreIFRS	PostIFRS	PreIFRS	PostIFRS	PreIFRS	PostIFRS	PreIFRS
		Range	Range	Minimum	Minimum	Maximum	Maximum	Mean	Mean	Std. Deviation	Std. Deviation
LLP	75	0.430	0.390	0.000	0.000	0.430	0.390	0.044	0.034	0.088	0.063
EBT	75	0.510	0.640	-0.010	0.000	0.500	0.640	0.069	0.064	0.106	0.094
MCAR	75	1.160	0.770	-0.160	-0.130	1.000	0.640	0.208	0.172	0.223	0.173
NPL	75	0.560	0.620	0.000	0.000	0.560	0.620	0.404	0.334	0.149	0.148
SIZE	75	9.650	9.250	0.000	0.000	9.650	9.250	7.695	7.314	2.224	1.872
AGE	75	38.000	47.000	7.000	0.000	45.000	47.000	19.867	14.307	11.377	12.676
LLA	75	0.390	0.410	0.000	0.000	0.390	0.410	0.017	0.029	0.060	0.060
CFEER	75	0.190	0.070	0.000	0.000	0.190	0.070	0.016	0.021	0.023	0.014

Source: SPSS output, 2017

Correlation Analysis
Table 2 Correlation for the Pre-IFRS Variables

		LLP	EBT	MCAR	NPL	SIZE	AGE	LLA	CFEER
Pearson Correlation	LLP	1							
Sig. (2-tailed)									
Pearson Correlation	EBT	.562**	1						
Sig. (2-tailed)		0.000							
Pearson Correlation	MCAR	0.096	-0.012	1					
Sig. (2-tailed)		0.415	0.920						
Pearson Correlation	NPL	0.208	.230*	.309**	1				
Sig. (2-tailed)		0.073	0.047	0.007					
Pearson Correlation	SIZE	-0.109	-0.080	0.219	.270*	1			
Sig. (2-tailed)		0.351	0.496	0.059	0.019				
Pearson Correlation	AGE	0.111	0.154	-0.221	0.064	-0.019	1		
Sig. (2-tailed)		0.344	0.187	0.056	0.583	0.868			
Pearson Correlation	LLA	0.201	0.183	0.132	0.212	0.083	-0.014	1	
Sig. (2-tailed)		0.083	0.116	0.258	0.068	0.480	0.904		
Pearson Correlation	CFEER	.353**	.261*	0.162	.271*	0.169	-0.150	0.153	1
Sig. (2-tailed)		0.002	0.023	0.164	0.019	0.147	0.199	0.189	
**. Correlation is significant at the 0.01 level (2-tailed).									
*. Correlation is significant at the 0.05 level (2-tailed).									

Source: SPSS output, 2017

Key:

***LLP**: Loan loss provision. ***EBT**: Earnings before Taxes.

***MCAR**: is the ratio of actual regulatory capital (Tier 1 capital) before loan loss reserve to minimum required capital.

***NPL**: is ratio of ratio of loans and advances to customers divided by total bank total asset (LOAN).

***SIZE**: the natural logarithm of total assets capturing the effect of bank size,

***AGE**: is the No. of years the bank has being operating from the date being quoted on the Nigerian Stock Exchange (NSE).

***LLA**: is measure as ratio of loan loss to total assets. ***CFEER**: is the ratio of commission and fee income to total asset.

Table 3 Correlation for the Post-IFRS Variables

		LLP	EBT	MCAR	NPL	SIZE	AGE	LLA	CFEER
Pearson Correlation	LLP	*1.000*							
Sig. (2-tailed)									
Pearson Correlation	EBT	*.802***	*1.000*						
Sig. (2-tailed)		*0.000*							
Pearson Correlation	MCAR	*0.158*	*0.157*	*1.000*					
Sig. (2-tailed)		*0.177*	*0.177*						
Pearson Correlation	NPL	*0.032*	*0.069*	*0.150*	*1.000*				
Sig. (2-tailed)		*0.784*	*0.557*	*0.200*					
Pearson Correlation	SIZE	*-0.215*	*-0.025*	*.230**	*.517***	*1.000*			
Sig. (2-tailed)		*0.064*	*0.829*	*0.047*	*0.000*				
Pearson Correlation	AGE	*0.003*	*0.004*	*-.363***	*-0.151*	*-0.198*	*1.000*		
Sig. (2-tailed)		*0.978*	*0.975*	*0.001*	*0.195*	*0.088*			
Pearson Correlation	LLA	*-0.057*	*-0.050*	*0.154*	*0.006*	*0.142*	*-0.161*	*1.000*	
Sig. (2-tailed)		*0.628*	*0.668*	*0.186*	*0.962*	*0.223*	*0.169*		
Pearson Correlation	CFEER	*-0.094*	*-0.039*	*-0.226*	*0.090*	*0.179*	*-0.044*	*0.039*	*1.000*
Sig. (2-tailed)		*0.424*	*0.741*	*0.051*	*0.445*	*0.125*	*0.708*	*0.742*	
**. Correlation is significant at the 0.01 level (2-tailed).									
*. Correlation is significant at the 0.05 level (2-tailed).									

Source: SPSS output, 2017

Hausman Test

Table 4 Hausman Test for pre-IFRS Adoption

Output for Pre-IFRS Adoption (Earnings Management)		**Output for Pre-IFRS Adoption (Capital Management)**
> phtest (pre.fixed1, pre.random1)		> phtest (pre.fixed1,pre.random1)
Chi Sqauare	8.414	Chi Sqauare 12.283
Df	6	df 6
F-statistic p-value	0.2093	F-statistic p-value 0.05594

Source: SPSS output, 2017

Table 5 Hausman Test for Post-IFRS Adoption

Output for Post-IFRS Adoption (Earnings Management)		**Output for Post-IFRS Adoption (Capital Management)**
> phtest (pre.fixed2, pre.random2)		> phtest (pre.fixed2,pre.random2)
Chi Sqauare	9.996	Chi Sqauare 8.1935
Df	6	df 6
F-statistic p-value	0.1248	F-statistic p-value 0.2243

Source: SPSS output, 2017

Table 6 variance Inflation Factor

Model		Collinearity Statistics	
		Tolerance	VIF
1	LLP	.880	1.136
	NPL	.704	1.420
	SIZE	.609	1.643
	AGE	.831	1.203
	LLA	.943	1.060
	CFEER	.880	1.137

Source: SPSS output, 2017

Table 7 Pre-IFRS Adoption Model with Earnings Management

Dependent Variable: LLP						
Regressors	Random effect model		Fixed effect model		Pool effect model	
	B	p-value	B	p-value	β	p-value
EBT	0.3027	0.0000	0.3011	0.0001	0.3018	0.0001
NPL	0.0259	0.5607	0.0554	0.3510	0.0226	0.6131
SIZE	-0.0046	0.1896	-0.0034	0.4355	-0.0045	0.1876
AGE	0.0003	0.5255	-0.0011	0.8327	0.0004	0.4597
LLA	0.0706	0.4981	-0.0336	0.7777	0.0874	0.4023
CFEER	1.0070	0.0404	0.3045	0.6055	1.1010	0.0234
R-Squared	0.3721		0.3055		0.3882	
Adj. R-Squared	0.3167		0.0483		0.3342	
F-statistic p-value	0.0000		0.0024		0.0000	

Source: SPSS output, 2017

Table 8 Pre-IFRS Adoption Model with Capital Management

Dependent Variable: LLP						
Regressors	Random effect model		Fixed effect model		Pool effect model	
	B	p-value	B	p-value	β	p-value
MCAR	0.0264	0.5383	0.0709	0.3023	0.0263	0.5388
NPL	0.0470	0.3620	0.1085	0.1049	0.0469	0.3628
SIZE	-0.0075	0.0524	-0.0037	0.4669	-0.0075	0.0520
AGE	0.0008	0.1341	-0.0075	0.3295	0.0008	0.1330
LLA	0.1416	0.2259	0.0246	0.8597	0.1422	0.2240
CFEER	1.6069	0.0028	0.8791	0.1876	1.6091	0.0027
R-Squared	0.2245		0.1062		0.2252	
Adj. R-Squared	0.1561		0.2249		0.1568	
F-statistic p-value	0.0068		0.3926		0.0066	

Source: SPSS output, 2017

Table 9 Post-IFRS Adoption Model with Earning Management

Dependent Variable: LLP						
Regressors	Random effect model		Fixed effect model		Pool effect model	
	B	p-value	B	p-value	B	p-value
EBT	0.6570	0.0000	0.6830	0.0000	0.6537	0.0000
NPL	0.0496	0.2611	0.0335	0.4595	0.0629	0.1847
SIZE	-0.0134	0.0002	-0.0184	0.0001	-0.0100	0.0027
AGE	-0.0003	0.6882	0.0006	0.8827	-0.0003	0.6381
LLA	0.0520	0.6080	0.0853	0.4495	0.0205	0.8393
CFEER	-0.0175	0.9441	0.0617	0.8187	-0.1137	0.6690
R-Squared	0.6988		0.7256		0.6915	
Adj. R-Squared	0.6722		0.6240		0.6643	
F-statistic p-value	0.0000		0.0000		0.0000	

Source: SPSS output, 2017

Table 10 Post-IFRS Adoption Model with Capital Management

Dependent Variable: LLP						
Regressors	Random effect model		Fixed effect model		Pool effect model	
	B	p-value	B	p-value	B	p-value
MCAR	0.1027	0.0747	0.1157	0.0963	0.0922	0.0781
NPL	0.0896	0.2445	0.0709	0.3852	0.1093	0.1711
SIZE	-0.0117	0.0511	-0.0043	0.5586	-0.0139	0.0138
AGE	0.0007	0.5712	0.0173	0.0185	0.0003	0.7459
LLA	-0.0215	0.9028	0.1022	0.6035	-0.0549	0.7488
CFEER	0.2044	0.6476	0.6169	0.1969	0.0342	0.9421
R-Squared	0.0957		0.1681		0.1199	
Adj. R-Squared	0.0159		0.1401		0.0423	
F-statistic p-value	0.3176		0.1128		0.1771	

Source: SPSS output, 2017

Table 11 Pre-IFRS and Post-IFRS Model Comparison (Earning Management)

Pre-IFRS vs Post-IFRS Adoption MODEL with EBT

Regressors	Random effect model		Random effect model	
	B	p-value	B	p-value
EBT	0.3027	0.0000	0.6570	0.0000
NPL	0.0259	0.5607	0.0496	0.2611
SIZE	-0.0046	0.1896	-0.0134	0.0002
AGE	0.0003	0.5255	-0.0003	0.6882
LLA	0.0706	0.4981	0.0520	0.6080
CFEER	1.0070	0.0404	-0.0175	0.9441
R-Squared	0.3721		0.6988	
Adj. R-Squared	0.3167		0.6722	
F-statistic p-value	0.0000		0.0000	

Source: SPSS output, 2017

Table 12 Pre-IFRS and Post-IFRS Model Comparison (Capital Management)

Pre-IFRS vs Post-IFRS Adoption MODEL with Capital Management

Regressors	Fixed effect model		Fixed effect model	
	B	p-value	B	p-value
MCAR	0.0709	0.3023	0.1157	0.0963
NPL	0.1085	0.1049	0.0709	0.3852
SIZE	-0.0037	0.4669	-0.0043	0.5586
AGE	-0.0075	0.3295	0.0173	0.0185
LLA	0.0246	0.8597	0.1022	0.6035
CFEER	0.8791	0.1876	0.6169	0.1969
R-Squared	0.1062		0.1681	
Adj. R-Squared	0.2249		0.1401	
F-statistic p-value	0.3926		0.1128	

Source: SPSS output, 2017

8

Corporate Governance and Financial Performance Relationship: Case for Oman Companies

İlker Yılmaz[a]

[a] College of Commerce and Business Administration, Department of Accounting, Dhofar University, Salalah, OMAN, iyilmaz@du.edu.om

Keywords
Corporate governance, financial performance, disclosure, Oman.

Abstract
The article aims to investigate the relationship between corporate governance and financial performance by using the data of 61 Oman companies traded at Muscat Securities Market for a four-year period from 2013 to 2016. The models are divided into two groups. The first group constructed a corporate governance score which is the dependent variable; the second group used the components of the score separately as dependent variables. As independent variable, two types of indicators are used; market-based and accounting-based. To reflect the market performance, Tobin's q is used and as accounting-based indicators; return on assets, gross profit margin, EBIT margin and net profit margin are used. The results showed that there are significant results between financial ratios and characteristics of corporate governance, but the overall relationship is weak in Oman context. Even though individual effects of some components of corporate governance are not significant, most models produced overall significant results.

Introduction

Corporate governance has become an important topic in developed countries after some events such as frauds and company collapses. In recent years, it has also attracted a great attention in developing countries. Many stock exchanges and regulatory bodies issued directives regarding corporate governance mechanisms and disclosures about them.

The Cadbury report (1992) simply defines corporate governance as 'the system by which companies are directed and controlled'. In a report written for OECD, Iu and Batten (2001) defined corporate governance as follows; "Corporate governance refers to the private and public institutions, including laws, regulations and accepted business practices, which together govern the relationship, in a market economy, between corporate managers and entrepreneurs (corporate insiders) on one hand, and those who invest resources in corporations, on the other". Corporate governance is especially important for publicly held companies with a large shareholders group who are not engaged in the day-to-day operations and have no direct access to inside information. Corporate governance is a framework which specifies the responsibilities and rewards of the parties involved. Although some authors cite different theories as the background of corporate governance, agency theory (Jensen, Meckling 1979) is regarded as the theoretical base of the concept of corporate governance. There is an agency relationship between shareholders (owners) and board of directors, corporate governance refers to the mechanisms designed to resolve the problems arising in this relationship. The term 'governance' is different from 'management' and its root is 'to govern', which means the administration of the State. However, management refers to the day-to-day and long-term decisions in the fields of finance, operations, marketing and so on. Therefore, governance is like bureaucratic administration of the company. Although both of these concepts refer to different aspects of the company, the common point is that they have a great importance on the success or failure of the company. In the literature, there are many studies about the relationship between different fields of management and performance of the company. Similarly, the question of whether corporate governance has any positive or negative effects on the performance of the company has been a concern in the literature.

This paper aimed to investigate the corporate governance-financial performance relationship in Oman context. Oman is the first country which adopted and applied a code of corporate governance in Gulf region. Oman is a member country of Gulf Cooperation Council which was established in 1981. Similar to other member countries, Oman generates a significant amount of revenue from oil reserves. In recent years, several sectors have started to develop such as tourism, manufacturing, services, and finance. The companies in Oman have some features which make corporate governance more important. Firstly, family businesses have a significant proportion in private sector. Secondly, government has shareholdings in many companies. Due to all these reasons, this study is significant.

Another factor which makes the study significant and original is that it constructed a corporate governance index for Oman companies. With reference to previous studies and rating methodologies, a content analysis was undertaken for corporate governance reports issued by the companies.

The rest of the paper is organized as follows; in the next section, we review the literature especially with a focus on the relationship with financial performance. It is followed by a short overview of the corporate governance environment in Oman. Then, we present the data and methodology. After that, we analyze the results and findings. The last section concludes.

Literature Review

There are many studies about different aspects of corporate governance, in this section we limit the review of literature with only studies focusing on the financial performance relationship. Regarding the relationship, some broad classifications can be made for both financial performance variables and corporate governance variables. The variables used to measure financial performance can be grouped as market-based and accounting-based. The most famous one in market-based group is Tobin's Q, besides some stock market return measures. In the accounting-based group, there are several ratios such as return on assets (ROA), return on equity (ROE), net profit margin (NPM) etc. For corporate governance variables, some studies used and analyzed different characteristics separately such as board size, board independence, ownership concentration etc., while some others calculated an overall measure composed of the similar characteristics. In addition, some studied employed the professional ratings measured by rating institutions.

We can broadly categorize the studies on corporate governance-financial performance relationship into two groups with respect to the measurement of corporate governance characteristics. The first group search for a relationship between a specific dimension or variable of corporate governance and financial performance. For example, board size, the proportion of independent directors, etc. The second group employs an overall corporate governance measure, either developed by the authors or measured by rating institutions.

Boehren and Oedegaard (2003) stated that relating corporate performance to only one dimension of corporate governance may not reveal the true relationship unless that the aspect used is controlled for other aspects of governance. Depending on this argument, many researchers constructed a single governance index, which is a scorecard that measures the corporate governance over a variety of aspects.

Gompers et.al (2003) built a governance index to proxy the balance of power between managers and shareholders by using 24 corporate-governance provisions. The sample used employed the data of 1500 large firms during 1990s. They empirically analyzed the relationship of this index with corporate performance. They concluded that firms with stronger shareholder rights had better results such as higher sales growth, higher profits and higher firm value. In addition, those firms made lower capital expenditures and made fewer acquisitions.

Bebchuk et.al searched for the correlations of 24 provisions used in Gompers' index and offered an entrenchment index based on six provisions. The four of them are "constitutional" provisions that prevent a majority of shareholders from having their way and the two are "takeover readiness" provisions that boards put in place to be ready for a hostile takeover. They found that increases in the level of the index are monotonically associated with economically significant reductions in firm valuation which was measured by Tobin's Q.

Klapper and Love (2004) used firm-level corporate governance ratings from 14 emerging markets and searched for the relationship between firm-level governance and the country's legal system. They also tested whether there is a correlation between corporate governance and operating performance and market valuation of the firm. Their study showed that there is a positive correlation between corporate governance and operating performance and market valuation. The results also showed that this correlation is higher in countries with weaker legal systems.

Ashbaugh-Skaife et al. (2006) searched for the importance of corporate governance on the firm's risk profile by examining the relationship between corporate governance and credit ratings. They measured corporate governance by using several attributes such as block shareholding, CEO power, accrual quality, etc. They investigated whether there is a relationship between quality of corporate governance and credit ratings and found e negative relationship.

Larcker et.al (2007) developed multi-indicator indices by using principal component analysis in order to mitigate measurement error and to have a comprehensive representation of corporate governance and used these indices to test whether they can explain abnormal accruals, accounting restatements, future operating performance, and future stock returns. According to the results of their study, the indices have a relationship with future operating performance, and excess stock returns. The relationship with abnormal returns is modest and mixed, and there is no relation with accounting restatements.

Bhagat and Bolton (2008) attempted to answer the question of what is the relationship between corporate governance and performance by considering the endogeneity of the relationships among corporate governance, performance, capital structure, and ownership structure. They concluded that better corporate governance is positively correlated with better contemporaneous and subsequent operating performance. Specifically, they found a positive relationship for stock ownership of board members and CEO-Chairman separation, however a negative relationship for board independence.

Lusk et.al (2008) classified companies into three groups based on their corporate governance index scores as autocratic, middle, and democratic. Due to the fact that GIM CGI scores are available for even years, they used also financial performance measures for the years 2000, 2002 and 2004 and analyzed the corporate governance financial performance relationship for the three groups. As financial performance, they used both market measures and accounting-based measures. They found that autocratic form of governance serve better the firm in the markets, but stockholders prefer democratic form.

The relationship of corporate governance and financial performance is affected by several factors. The legal system and financial structure of a country may have significant impacts on this relationship. Anderson and Gupta (2009) performed a cross-country analysis to analyze whether financial structure and legal system matter. They used a sample 1736 firms from 22 countries and concluded that financial structure and legal system of any given country have a joint effect on the relationship. This result is not surprising because stability and confidence in both legal and financial system affect positively performance and governance of companies.

Berthelot et.al (2010) pointed out the attention of capital market participants to corporate governance, particularly their need to identify situations that may cause earnings management and opportunistic behavior. One of the most important information sources about governance practices of firms is rankings published by several institutions. The authors hypothesized that if the market participants use the rankings, there must be a significant positive relationship between the rankings and stock prices. For a three-year period from 2002 to 2005, they used a sample of 796 observations from 289 Canadian firms. They used the rankings published by Canadian newspaper Globe and Mail and found that the rankings have an effect on investors; however the rankings are at least partly reflected in accounting results.

Baxter (2014) investigated the relationship between the corporate governance ratings of Australian publicly listed companies and their financial performance for the years 2006 to 2008. He used the Horwath Corporate Governance Report (HCGR) to measure the variable for corporate governance, which is the mostly known rating in Australia. The companies were allocated a star rating out of a maximum of 5 depending on the extent to which they met the best practice standards and given a ranking relative to the other companies. As the financial performance variables, he used Tobin's Q, ROA and ROE. The results of the study showed that both stars and rankings are positively associated with financial performance.

Ueng (2016) investigated the relationship between the quality of corporate governance policy and the firm financial performance by using a sample of 3068 firms from Corporate Library database. The results of the study showed that firms with a better corporate governance policy are more likely to have a better financial performance.

Some authors searched for the corporate governance-financial performance relationship by considering and focusing on board characteristics such as size and independence. Regarding the board size, which is the number of board members, there are mixed results in the literature. Some studies claimed that larger boards are better, some others claimed the opposite. Empirical findings also produced conflicting results.

Lipton and Lorsch (1992) suggested a proposal covering many aspects for improving corporate governance and they claimed that smaller boards are better than larger boards, even they advised to limit the number of members with a maximum of ten. A smaller board allows members to have more effective discussions. Yermack (1996) analyzed 452 US industrial companies for the period from 1984 to 1991 and found an inverse relationship between board size and firm value which is measured by Tobin's Q. The results also showed that smaller boards are associated with better financial ratios and such companies provide stronger CEO incentives. Coles et al. (2008) examined the effects of board size and board composition on Tobin's Q for the period 1992-2001 and they found that larger boards may be beneficial especially for the cases in which board has important advisory roles, such as the companies which are diversified across industries, large in size and with a high leverage ratio. Some studies found that there is no significant relationship between board size and financial performance. Kumar and Singh (2013) found insignificant results between board size and Tobin's Q in their study covering 2008-2009 period and 176 publicly-held companies from Indian Stock Exchange. ALJifri and Moustafa (2007) investigated the impact of internal and external governance mechanisms on financial performance in United Arab Emirates (UAE). Even though they found significant results for some mechanisms such as government ownership, the impact of board size was found to be insignificant. Arouri et.al conducted a study in banking sector of GCC countries to measure the impact of corporate governance mechanisms on performance. They found that board size had no significant impact on the performance of banks.

Zakaria et.al examined the relationship of board governance and firm performance for a sample of 73 trading and services sector listed at Malaysian stock exchange for the period of 2005-2010. They found that a positive association between board size and firm performance by controlling for investment opportunities, firm age, leverage and firm size.

Regarding board independence and foreign board members, they found insignificant results.

The proportion of independent directors, also known as board independence, is another important characteristic of corporate governance. The empirical studies which searched for the relationship between board independence and financial performance produced mixed results. (Yermack, 1996, Weir and Laing 2001, Bhagat and Black, 2002; Perry and Shivdasani,2005, Pham,P.K. et al,2011, Shan and Mclver, 2011).

Another indicator used to evaluate the corporate governance of a firm in both ratings and empirical studies is the number of board meetings. It is argued that as the number of meetings increases, it improves the decision-making efficiency of the board and then it positively affects firm performance. Although this line of reasoning seems logical and acceptable, some studies found opposing results. (Vafeas, 1999; Brown and Caylor,2006.)

Institutional ownership is also one of the aspects affecting corporate governance. It is argued that as the proportion of institutional shareholding in the ownership structure, the financial performance of the company is affected positively. Similar to other aspects, empirical findings about the institutional ownership are mixed.

Block ownership is one of the indicators which may affect corporate governance and it is also known as ownership concentration, meaning that how the shareholdings of the company are distributed and how many blockholders are there. Laeven and Levine (2008) examined the relationship between ownership structures and valuations in Europe. They found that the market value of the companies with multiple blockholders is significantly different from those with a single blockholder and from widely held companies. Blockholders are mostly institutional investors, however there is a distinction between institutional ownership and block ownership. Block ownership refers to the biggest shareholder regardless of that it is individual or institutional. The results of empirical studies searching for the effect of block ownership on financial performance produced mixed results. (Ben- Amar and Andre,2006; Laeven and Levine, 2008; Pham,P.K. et al,2011; Kang and Kim, 2012)

Bozec and Dia (2014) investigated the governance-performance relationship for Canadian companies over the period 2002-2005, with respect to shareholders' proximity which is defined based on ownership concentration and whether or not the dominant/controlling shareholder holds top executive positions in the firm. They found a positive relationship between governance indices and Tobin's Q. They also showed that ownership concentration and holding key positions by controlling shareholder do not have any impact on the relationship.

There are two positions at companies which are important both for corporate governance and management of the operations; chairman of the board and CEO. In some companies, they are separate, in some others the same person holds both positions. This aspect of governance is known as CEO Duality and it is widely searched in empirical studies. There are two opposite arguments for CEO Duality; the first one claims that when these positions are held by different persons, it will affect positively the decision making and therefore financial performance. On the other hand, the second one claims that when the positions are held by the same person, it will decrease bureaucratic procedures and produce better results. The empirical studies also produced conflicting results. (Brickley et.al, 1997; Coles and Hesterly,2000; Bhagat, S. and Bolton, B.,2002; Elsayed, K.,2007; Chahine and Tohmé, 2009; Cheng.2013; Duru et.al, 2016)

Corporate Governance In Oman

Among Gulf countries, Oman is the first to adopt corporate governance for publicly held companies. The process of modernization for Oman dates back to 1970s. His Majesty Sultan Qaboos bin Said initiated the process after he assumed power in 1970. Regarding the companies and corporate governance, the first step was the promulgation of the Commercial Companies Law which sets the legal mechanisms of all types businesses. The next milestone was the establishment of the Muscat Securities Market which opens the era of 'public' companies. Similar to all other countries, the need for the mechanisms to solve problems of public companies such as internal control and transparency issues, conflicts of interest among shareholders and management and so on. In 2002, the Capital Market Authority issued corporate governance standards for publicly held companies, known as Corporate Governance Code (CGC). The CGC was updated in 2010 and 2015. The New Code which become effective as of 22 July 2016 included 14 principles and the explanations regarding the corporate governance mechanisms and clarified many issues such as board composition and its roles, the concepts of "independence" and "related party" and provisions about the committees.

The CGC applies to all public joint stock companies listed on the Muscat Securities Market and accordingly it is compulsory to publish a Corporate Governance Report together with yearly financial statements and independent audit report. In addition to CGC report, some companies disclose more detail about their corporate governance mechanisms in the annual reports.

Code of Corporate Governance in Oman has 14 principles which are summarized below:

First Principle - Purpose of Corporate Governance: It presents the purpose of CG as setting out the processes by which firms are directed enabling them to contribute national economy, stakeholders and local community. It determines main pillars of CG as transparency, accountability, fairness and responsibility.

Second Principle- Board of Directors' Formation, Roles and Responsibilities: It states that all firms must be directed by a Board of Directors which leads and controls operations, and is responsible for long term success. This principle also clarifies the requirements, duties and rights of the members of BoD.

Third Principle - Board of Directors' Authority and Competences: This principle requires the articles of association approved by general assembly to set out authority and competences of BoD and it must be accessible to the public.

Fourth Principle -Chairperson: It specifies the profile, role and responsibilities of the chairperson, emphasizing his/her role in the implementation of corporate governance.

Fifth Principle - Company Secretary: It requires BoD to appoint a secretary to assist the board in complying to CGC and other applicable legislation.

Sixth Principle - Executive Management: It emphasizes the role of executives in implementation of strategic plans and procedures.

Seventh Principle - Professional conduct of Directors and Executives: It states the importance of professional conduct and ethics for executives in performing the duties.

Eighth Principle - Independent Director: It states that BoD members must have complete independence from management and major shareholders. Independence covers two dimensions; financial and opinion. It also specifies the cases in which independence is violated.

Ninth Principle - Rules for Related Party Transactions: It emphasizes the necessity of transparency and clarity regarding the related party transactions and requires the review of the transactions by audit committee and approval by BoD or general assembly.

Tenth Principle - Audit Committee and Internal Controls: It emphasizes the role and importance of audit committee and internal control systems and states that BoD ensure the existence and functioning of them to safeguard the interests of shareholders.

Eleventh Principle - Nomination and Remuneration Committee: It states the importance of nomination and remuneration policies and requires a balance of the remuneration to attract competent directors and the rights of shareholders.

Twelfth Principle - External Auditors: This principle states that the BoD is responsible for accurate presentation of financial statements through external auditors and therefore specifies the requirements for appointing the external auditors.

Thirteenth Principle - Corporate Social Responsibility: This principle requires the integration of corporate social responsibility into firm's activities and to exercise the roles as a good citizen and prevent adverse impacts on stakeholders.

Fourteenth Principle - Annual Reports: This principle states the role of the annual reports published by the firm with respect to the implementation of corporate governance and requires annual reports to indicate the practices are in line with principles and standards of corporate governance.

Data and Methodology

Sample

The sample used in this study includes 61 industrial and service companies traded at Muscat Securities Market for a four-year period from 2013 to 2016. It is a balanced panel with 244 observations.

Models and Variables

Panel data regressions were run to search for the relationship between corporate governance and financial performance. Two groups of models were developed depending on the independent variable. In the first group, the independent variable is corporate governance which is measured by using a scoring index. We constructed the scoring index by using the parameters used in previous studies and methodologies of rating institutions.

The construction of the index is explained in the next section. In the second group, the components of the corporate governance score are included separately as independent variables. In both groups, the dependent variable is the financial performance which is measured by one market-based indicator, Tobin's Q, and four accounting-based measures, namely EBIT, Net Profit Margin (NPM), Return on Assets (ROA) and Return on Equity (ROE). Therefore, ten models were run in total.

We used three control variables for size, gearing and growth. Size is measured as the natural logarithm of total assets. Gearing is measured as the ratio of total liabilities to total assets. Growth is measured as the percentage change in sales in each year compared to the previous year.

We constructed the following models by using all the variables mentioned above. Each model uses one of the financial performance indicators as the dependent variable and overall corporate governance score as the independent variable.

Model 1: $\text{Tobin's Q}_{it} = \alpha_0 + \text{CG Score}_{it} + \text{CV} + \varepsilon_{it}$

Model 2: $\text{EBIT Margin}_{it} = \alpha_0 + \text{CG Score}_{it} + \text{CV} + \varepsilon_{it}$

Model 3: $\text{Net Profit Margin}_{it} = \alpha_0 + \text{CG Score}_{it} + \text{CV} + \varepsilon_{it}$

Model 4: $\text{Return on Assets}_{it} = \alpha_0 + \text{CG Score}_{it} + \text{CV} + \varepsilon_{it}$

Model 5: $\text{Return on Equity}_{it} = \alpha_0 + \text{CG Score}_{it} + \text{CV} + \varepsilon_{it}$

In the second group of models, the components of CG score were used as independent variables.

Model 6: $\text{Tobin's Q}_{it} = \alpha_0 + \text{BS}_{it} + \text{BIND}_{it} + \text{NOMT}_{it} + \text{INSO}_{it} + \text{BLCO}_{it} + \text{CV} + \varepsilon_{it}$

Model 7: $\text{EBIT Margin}_{it} = \alpha_0 + \text{BS}_{it} + \text{BIND}_{it} + \text{NOMT}_{it} + \text{INSO}_{it} + \text{BLCO}_{it} + \text{CV} + \varepsilon_{it}$

Model 8: $\text{Net Profit Margin}_{it} = \alpha_0 + \text{BS}_{it} + \text{BIND}_{it} + \text{NOMT}_{it} + \text{INSO}_{it} + \text{BLCO}_{it} + \text{CV} + \varepsilon_{it}$

Model 9: $\text{Return on Assets}_{it} = \alpha_0 + \text{BS}_{it} + \text{BIND}_{it} + \text{NOMT}_{it} + \text{INSO}_{it} + \text{BLCO}_{it} + \text{CV} + \varepsilon_{it}$

Model 10: $\text{Return on Equity}_{it} = \alpha_0 + \text{BS}_{it} + \text{BIND}_{it} + \text{NOMT}_{it} + \text{INSO}_{it} + \text{BLCO}_{it} + \text{CV} + \varepsilon_{it}$

where BS: Board Size, BIND: Board Independence, NOMT: Number of meetings,

INSO: Institutional Ownership, BLCO: Block Ownership, CV: control variables.

Methodology

We run panel (longitudinal) data regressions to test the significance levels of the models constructed in the study. Panel data is defined as a data set consisted of repeated cross sections over time. With a balanced panel, the same units are observed in each time period. With an unbalanced panel, some units do not appear in each time period, often due to attrition. (Wooldridge, J.M, 2002). We have data for all variables during the study period, there is no missing value, then it is a balanced panel data.

We used Stata software to run the data analyses. For each of the models, panel regression with fixed effects and panel regression with random effects were run. Depending on the results, a comparison made among the regressions to determine which model must be chosen. Hausman test is performed in order to decide between fixed and random effects. The model chosen at this step must be tested for heteroscedasticity. In the regression models, there is an assumption that the variance of the error term is constant and it is defined as homoscedasticity. If the error terms do not have constant variance, they are called as heteroscedastic. Errors may increase as the value of an independent variable increases. Breusch-Pagan / Cook-Weisberg (estat hottest) test is designed to detect any linear form of heteroscedasticity.

Corporate Governance (CG) Index

This study constructed a corporate governance index by using the previous studies in the field and methodologies of rating institutions. The data for the index are collected through the content analysis of corporate governance reports published by the companies. It is compulsory to publish a corporate governance report according to the requirements of the Capital Market Authority. The reports are audited by independent audit firms. The items included in the index are board size, board independence, number of board meetings, institutional ownership, and block ownership (ownership concentration). The index covers 5 items, all of which is scored out of 10, which makes a total score of 50. Therefore maximum score is 50. We constructed CG score by giving points out of 10 to the five characteristics of the companies. The rationale underlying the scoring for each item is explained in the following paragraphs and summarized in Table 1.

Although there are opposing studies in the literature about ideal number of board members, in other words, whether smaller boards or larger boards are better, we assumed that larger boards are more effective and helps make better managerial decisions and results in better financial performance. Accordingly, we attached a higher score to the companies with a larger board. Board independence is measured as a percentage of independent members to the total number of members. We assumed that a higher percentage of board independence is better, so we attached a higher score to the companies with higher board independence level. Number of board meetings is scored by the assumption that meeting more frequently helps increase the coordination among members and make more effective decisions, so we attached a higher score to the companies with a higher number of board meetings. For institutional ownership, we used ascending scoring method; as the percentage of shares held by institutional investors increases, the score also increases. We assumed that this characteristic is positively related to financial performance. So, for each increment of 10 %, we attached 1 point, for example if the institutional ownership is between 51% and 60 %, the company receives 6 points. For ownership concentration, we used the percentage of shares held by the largest shareholder. As this percentage increases, we attached a higher score with the increments of 10 %. Another characteristic of corporate governance used in scoring in previous studies is CEO duality. We did not include it in our scoring, because all companies in the sample has CEO duality, which means CEO and Chairman of the Board positions are represented by different people. Therefore, this feature of corporate governance is not also included in second group of models as an independent variable.

After calculating the scores, we converted them into percentages. For example, if the score is 20, it is divided by the maximum score, that means 20/50 = 0.40 = 40%.

Analysis of The Results

Descriptive Statistics

Descriptive statistics for all the variables used in the study are presented in Table 2, categorized as financial, corporate governance and control variables. It shows mean values and standard deviations, minimum, maximum values which are reported as overall, between, and within for panel data. The standard deviations of financial variables are not high except TQ whose standard deviation is 0.64, with a maximum of 3.15 and a minimum of 0.07. For CG Score, maximum is 78 % and minimum is 27 %, and overall standard deviation is 0.11. Average score for the sample is 55%. This score shows that adoption and implementation of corporate governance mechanisms are not at expected levels. Board sizes range from 5 to 12, with an average of 7.36. Board Independence is 1 at maximum, which means that all board members are independent directors; and 0 at minimum, which means there is no independent director at the board. Almost half of the companies in the sample have BoD composed of all independent directors. Number of Meetings is 15 at maximum and 4 at minimum, with an average of 5.86.Institutional Ownership ranges from 99% to 0 %, with an average of 56 %. Similarly, block ownership which shows the ownership percentage of the largest shareholder ranges from 99% to 9 %, with an average of 40%.

Table 1: Definitions of Corporate Governance Items

Item	**Definition**	**Expected Relationship**	**Scoring Scale**
Board size	Number of members at BoD	The larger BS, the higher the score	from 1 to 10
Board Independence	The proportion of independent directors at BoD	The higher the BI, the higher the score	from 1 to 10
No of meetings	Number of BoD meetings in a year	The higher the no of meetings, the higher the score	from 1 to 10
Institutional ownership	The percentage of ownership by institutional investors	The higher the percentage, the higher the score	from 1 to 10
Block ownership	The percentage of ownership by the largest shareholder	The higher the percentage, the higher the score	from 1 to 10

Table 2: Descriptive Statistics for the Variables

		TQ	EBITM	NPM	ROA	ROE	CGS	BS	BI	NM	IO	BO	SZ	GE	SG
Mean		0.89	0.11	0.09	0.06	0.09	0.55	7.36	0.70	5.86	0.56	0.40	3.37	0.43	0.23
Std. Dev.	overall	0.64	0.20	0.19	0.08	0.23	0.11	1.51	0.28	1.90	0.26	0.22	1.38	0.24	2.76
	between	0.60	0.18	0.16	0.07	0.22	0.11	1.49	0.26	1.56	0.26	0.22	1.38	0.23	1.41
	within	0.22	0.09	0.10	0.04	0.08	0.03	0.30	0.11	1.10	0.03	0.02	0.13	0.06	2.38
Min	overall	0.07	-0.89	-0.90	-0.27	-1.66	0.27	5.00	0.00	4.00	0.00	0.09	0.78	0.09	-0.75
	between	0.09	-0.68	-0.70	-0.18	-1.20	0.28	5.00	0.22	4.00	0.00	0.11	0.88	0.10	-0.15
	within	-0.14	-0.34	-0.63	-0.12	-0.37	0.41	4.36	-0.06	2.87	0.40	0.32	2.67	0.15	-10.66
Max	overall	3.15	0.93	0.63	0.38	0.58	0.78	12.00	1.00	15.00	0.99	0.99	6.73	1.37	43.00
	between	2.44	0.51	0.45	0.25	0.40	0.76	12.00	1.00	12.00	0.99	0.99	6.69	1.28	11.02
	within	1.80	0.77	0.70	0.23	0.51	0.63	8.36	1.02	10.87	0.76	0.54	3.91	0.60	32.21

The Results of the Models

The results of the models are summarized in the following tables. Table 3a shows the panel regression results for the models in which overall corporate governance score (CG Score) is independent variable and financial performance indicators are dependent variable. With respect to overall significance of the model, all models found significant results, except model 5 in which ROE is dependent variable. With respect to the relationship of CG score on financial performance indicators, only ROA has a significant relationship, but it is negative. Other financial variables do not have any significant relationship with CG score. This result can be interpreted in the way that corporate governance mechanisms do not contribute to financial performance. The previous studies also produced conflicting results. All models in Table 3a, Size and Sales Growth have significant effects. Gearing is significant for only model 3 and 4, in which net profit margin and return on assets are dependent variables respectively.

Table 3a: Panel Regression Results for the Models 1-5

	Model 1	**Model 2**	**Model 3**	**Model 4**	**Model 5**
Dependent Variable	Tobin's Q	EBIT Margin	NPM	ROA	ROE
Constant	3.643*** (0.725)	0.119 (0.0923)	0.196** (0.0847)	0.146*** (0.0394)	0.108 (0.112)
CG Score	-0.275 (0.5578)	-0.196 (0.171)	-0.224 (0.1805)	-0.118** (0.058)	-0.193 (0.217)
Size	-0.774*** (0.226)	0.0363** (0.0127)	0.0305*** (0.0107)	0.0124** (0.0061)	0.0504* (0.0289)
Gearing	0-.0022 (0.318)	-0.0454 (0.088)	-0.212*** (0.066)	-0.136*** (0.0252)	-0.1801 (0.133)
Sales growth	-0.0031*** (0.0006)	-0.0046*** (0.0009)	-0.0002 (0.0009)	-0.00014 (0.0004)	-0.0001 (0.0009)
R^2	0.23	0.096	0.14	0.26	0.19
F-Test	12.68***	-	-	-	
Wald Chi^2	-	45.32***	28.61***	31.09***	3.53
Observations	244	244	244	244	244

*, **, *** represent significance levels for 10%, 5%, and 1%, respectively. Robust standard errors are shown in parentheses. Depending on the model adopted, F-test or Wald Ch^2 is reported.

Table 3b summarizes the results of the models in which components of corporate governance score are included as independent variables and the same financial indicators as dependent variable in each model. Similar to first group of models, these models also produced significant results with respect to overall significance except model 10 in which ROE is dependent variable. Board Size is found to be insignificant in all models. It can be interpreted that number of members in the BoD has no relationship with financial performance of the firm. In the literature, there are similar studies with the same result. (e.g, ALJifri and Moustafa (2007), Arouri et.al (2011), Kumar and Singh (2013)). Board independence is significant in only model 8 in which net profit margin is dependent variable. The coefficient is negative, meaning that there is an inverse relationship between financial performance and board independence. Number of meetings is significant for only model 9 in which ROA is dependent variable. Although it is very weak, there is a negative relationship between number of meetings and financial performance. Institutional Ownership produced significant results for three models in which EBIT margin, net profit margin and ROA are dependent variables. The directions of the relationships are positive, which means institutional ownership affects financial performance positively. Block ownership showed significant results for three models in which EBIT margin, net profit margin and ROE are dependent variables. The directions of the relationships are negative, which means there is an inverse relationship between block ownership and those financial indicators. Size produced significant results for all models, which means firm size is an important variable in corporate governance-financial performance relationship. Gearing produced significant results only for two models in which net profit margin and ROA is dependent variable respectively. Similarly, Sales growth showed significant results only for two models in which Tobin's Q and EBIT margin are dependent variables, respectively.

Table 3b: Panel Regression Results for the Models 6-10

	Model 6	**Model 7**	**Model 8**	**Model 9**	**Model 10**
Dependent Variable	Tobin's Q	EBIT Margin	NPM	ROA	ROE
Constant	3.51*** (0.597)	0.173 (0.1333)	0.279** (0.139)	0.1424*** (0.0455)	0.0963 (0.0951)
Board Size	0.0404 (0.0512)	-0.0198 (0.0182)	-0.0266 (0.0204)	-0.0031 (0.0049)	0.0073 (0.0126)
Board Independence	-0.024 (0.148)	-0.0588 (0.0577)	-0.0556* (0.0329)	-0.0112 (0.0183)	0.0646 (0.0797)
Number of Meetings	-0.0178 (0.0132)	0.0003 (0.006)	-0.0063 (0.0066)	-0.0038* (0.003)	-0.0050 (0.0038)
Institutional Ownership	-0.497 (0.535)	0.2148*** (0.077)	0.2588*** (0.0693)	0.0579* (0.0324)	0.0017 (0.0728)
Block Ownership	0.3340 (0.7935)	-0.3297** (0.1304)	-0.3255** (0.1324)	-0.1214 (0.0483)	-0.3596** (0.1744)
Size	-0.7881*** (0.1433)	0.0426*** (0.0118)	0.0423*** (0.0116)	0.0135** (0.0055)	0.0421* (0.0225)
Gearing	-0.0111 (0.278)	-0.0099 (0.097)	-0.1778** (0.0906)	-0.1295*** (0.0261)	-0.1608 (0.111)
Sales growth	-0.003*** (0.006)	-0.0048*** (0.0010)	-0.0005 (0.001)	-0.00021 (0.0004)	-0.0003 (0.0009)
R^2	0.25	0.28	0.34	0.32	0.33
F-Test	12.79***	-	-		
Wald Chi^2	-	47.53***	38.69***	47.16***	9.11
Observations	244	244	244	244	244

*, **, *** represent significance levels for 10%, 5%, and 1%, respectively. Robust standard errors are shown in parentheses. Depending on the model adopted, F-test or Wald Ch^2 is reported.

Conclusion

In this study, we aimed to search for the relationship between corporate governance and financial performance of Oman companies at Muscat Securities Market. We constructed two groups of models. In the first group, we used a corporate governance index score as the independent variable to measure the level of corporate governance. In the second group, we used the components of the corporate governance index as separate independent variables. In both groups, we used one market-based indicator of financial performance, which is Tobin's Q, and four accounting-based indicators of financial performance, EBIT margin, net profit margin, ROA and ROE.

In the first group, all models produced significant results except ROE (model 5), according to overall significance value of the model. However, only ROA (model 4) found a significant result for Corporate Governance score. Similarly, in the second group, all models produced significant results except ROE (model 9), according to overall significance value of the model. When looked at the details for components of corporate governance, we found different results for each model. The model 6 showed that none of the components have a significant effect on Tobin's Q. The model 7 showed that Institutional Ownership has a positive relationship with EBIT margin, while Block Ownership has a negative relationship with the same indicator. The model 8 aimed to find the relationship between the components and net profit margin (NPM), it showed that there is a negative relationship between Board Independence and NPM, and a negative relationship between Block Ownership and NPM. It also showed that there is a positive relationship between Institutional Ownership and NPM. The model 9 showed that there is a weak negative relationship between Number of Meetings and Return on Assets (ROA) and also that there is a positive relationship between Institutional Ownership and ROA.

These results show that the relationships between financial performance indicators and corporate governance, as overall score and separate components, are weak in Oman. One potential reason might be the poor adoption and application of corporate governance regulations. Although the Code of Corporate Governance is applicable for all public companies and they publish the standard format report, the results raised the question of whether the companies internalized the principles of corporate governance and whether they have effective governance mechanisms, rather than reporting the minimum requirements.

This study relied on the content analysis of corporate governance reports. Those reports have some advantages. One of the advantages is that the reports are audited by independent auditors, and secondly there is a standard content determined by CMA. This makes it easier to calculate the scores.

There are some future research areas. The study covered non-financial companies, a similar study can be conducted for financial sector companies in Oman. In addition, a multi-country study can be conducted covering, for instance, GCC countries by using a more-detailed scoring index.

References

Aljifri, K. & Moustafa, M. (2007).The impact of corporate governance mechanisms on the performance of UAE firms: an empirical analysis. *Journal of Economic and Administrative Sciences, Vol. 23 No. 2, pp. 71-93.*

Anderson,A. & Gupta, P.P.(2009). A cross-country comparison of corporate governance and firm performance: Do financial structure and the legal system matter? *Journal of Contemporary Accounting & Economics 5 (2009) 61–79*

Arouri, H., Hossain, M. & Muttakin, M.B. (2011). Ownership structure, corporate governance and bank performance: evidence from GCC countries. *Corporate Ownership and Control, Vol. 8 No. 4, pp. 365-372.*

Ashbaugh-Skaife H, Collins DW, LaFond R. (2006). The effects of corporate governance on firms' credit ratings. *Journal of Accounting and Economics 42(1):203–243*

Baxter, P. (2014). Corporate governance ratings and financial performance: evidence from Australia. *Int. J. Corporate Governance, Vol. 5, Nos. 3/4, pp.178–196.*

Bebchuk, L., Cohen, A., Ferrell, A.(2004). What matters in corporate governance? *Working paper. Harvard Law School.*

Ben-Amar, W. & Andre, P. (2006). Separation of ownership from control and acquiring firm performance: The case of family ownership in Canada. *Journal of Business Finance & Accounting, 33 (3/4), 517-543.*

Berthelot,S., Morris,T., Morrill,C., (2010). Corporate governance rating and financial performance: a Canadian study. *Corporate Governance: The international journal of business in society, Vol. 10 Iss 5 pp. 635 – 646*

Bhagat,S. & Black B (2002). The non-correlation between board independence and long-term firm performance. *Journal of Corporation Law 27: 231–273.*

Bhagat, S. & Bolton, B. (2008). Corporate Governance and Firm Performance. *Journal of Corporate Finance, Vol. 14, No. 3, pp. 257-273.*

Boehren, O. & Oedegaard, B.(2003). Governance and performance revisited. *Working Paper No. 28/2003. European Corporate Governance Institute.*

Bozec,R. & Dia,M.(2014). Governance practices and firm performance: Does shareholders' proximity to management matter? *International Journal of Disclosure and Governance (2015) 12, 185–209. doi:10.1057/jdg.2014.3*

Brickley, J.A., Coles, J.L., Jarrell, G. (1997). Leadership structure: separating the CEO and chairman of the board. *Journal of Corporate Finance 3 (3), 189–220*

Brown, L.D. & Caylor.M.L. (2006). Corporate governance and firm valuation. *Journal of Accounting and Public Policy 25 (2006) 409–434*

Cadbury, A. (1992). The report on the financial aspects of corporate governance. available at http://www.ecgi.org/codes/documents/cadbury.pdf

Chahine, S. & Tohmé,N.S. (2009). Is CEO Duality Always Negative? An Exploration of CEO Duality and Ownership Structure in the Arab IPO Context. *Corporate Governance: An International Review, 17(2): 123–141*

Cheng, M-T. (2013). The moderating effects of chief executive officer (CEO) duality on the relationship between research and development (R and D) spending and firm performance. *African Journal of Business Management Vol. 7(8), pp. 631-640*

Code of Corporate Governance for Public Listed Companies, Capital Markets Authority, Oman, available at: https://cma.gov.om/Home/CircularFileDownlad/5308

Coles, J. & Hesterly, W. (2000). Independence of the chairman and board composition: firm choices and shareholder value. *Journal of Management, Vol. 26 No. 2, pp. 195-214.*

Coles, D., Daniel, N., Naveen, L. (2008). Boards: does one size fit all? *Journal of Financial Economics 87, 329–356.*

Duru, A., Iyengar,R.J., Zampellic,E.M, (2016). The dynamic relationship between CEO duality and firm performance: The moderating role of board independence. *Journal of Business Research, Vol: 69, Issue: 10, Page: 4269-4277*

Elsayed, K. (2007). Does CEO duality really affect corporate performance? *Corporate Governance: An International Review, Vol. 15 No. 6, pp. 1203-1214.*

Gompers,P.A, Ishii, J.L, Metrick,A.(2003). Corporate Governance and Equity Prices. *Quarterly Journal of Economics 118(1),107-155*

Jensen, M.C. & Meckling, W.H. (1979). Theory of the firm: Managerial behavior, agency costs, and ownership structure. Springer, Netherlands

Iu, J., & Batten, J. (2001). The implementation of OECD corporate governance principles in postcrisis Asia. *Journal of Corporate Citizenship, 2001(4), 47-62.*

Kang, Y.S. & Kim, B.Y. (2012). Ownership structure and firm performance: evidence from the Chinese corporate reform. *China Economic Review, Vol. 23 No. 2, pp. 471-481.*

Klapper, LF. & Love, I. (2004). Corporate governance, investor protection, and performance in emerging markets. *Journal of Corprate Finance 10(5):703–728*

Kumar N. & Singh J.P. (2013). Effect of Board Size and Promoter Ownership on Firm Value: Some Empirical Findings from India. *Corporate Governance, 13(1), 88-98.*

Laeven, L. & Levine, R. (2008). Complex ownership structures and corporate valuations. *Review of Financial Studies, Vol. 21 No. 2, pp. 579-604.*

Larcker DF., Richardson, SA. & Tuna, I. (2007). Corporate governance, accounting outcomes, and organizational performance. *Account Rev 82(4):963–1008*

Lipton, M. and J. W. Lorsch, (1992).A modest proposal for improved corporate governance. *Business Lawyer, 1, 59-77*

Lusk, E.J., Halperin, M. and de Palma, G.C. (2008). An investigation of the relationship between Corporate Governance and firm performance: the market emergence of the Autocratic firm. *Int. J. Corporate Governance, Vol. 1, No. 2, pp.135–145.*

Perry,T. & Shivdasani,A.(2005). Do Boards Affect Performance? Evidence from Corporate Restructuring. *The Journal of Business, Vol. 78, No. 4, 1403-1432*

Pham,P.K., Suchard,J. and Zein,J. (2011). Corporate governance and alternative performance measures: evidence from Australian firms. *Australian Journal of Management, Volume: 36 issue: 3, page(s): 371-386*

Yermack, D., (1996). Higher market valuation of companies with a small board of directors. *Journal of Financial Economics, 40, 185-212*

Yuan George Shan & Ron P. McIver (2011). Corporate governance mechanisms and financial performance in China: panel data evidence on listed non-financial companies. *Asia Pacific Business Review, 17:3, 301-324, DOI: 10.1080/13602380903522325*

Ueng,C. J. (2016). The analysis of corporate governance policy and corporate financial performance *J Econ Finan (2016) 40:514–523 DOI :10.1007/s12197-015-9316-8*

Vafeas, N. (1999). Board meeting frequency and firm performance. Journal of Financial Economics, Vol. 53 No. 1, pp. 113-142.

Weir,C. & Laing,.D. (2001). Governance structures, director independence and corporate performance in the UK. *European Business Review 13: 86–95.*

Wooldridge, J.M., (2002). *Introductory Econometrics. A Modern Approach*, 2nd Edition, Thomson Learning, pp.430-432

Zakaria,Z., Purhanudin,N., Palanimally,Y.R.(2014). Board Governance and Firm Performance: A Panel Data Analysis. *Journal of Business Law and Ethics, Vol. 2(1), 1-12.*

9

Dynamic Adjustment Towards Target Capital Structure: Panel Evidence of Listed Firms in Kenya

Leonard K. Maina[a] Tobias Olweny[b] Kenneth L. Wanjau[c]

[a] Corresponding Author, Karatina University, mainaleonard9@gmail.com
[b] Jomo Kenyatta University of Agriculture and Technology
[c] Karatina University

Keywords
Dynamic Capital Structure, Speed of Adjustment, Target Leverage, Listed Firms.

Abstract
Trade-off theory of capital structure uses static and dynamic approach. The use of static approach has been prevalent. Despite the importance of dynamic capital structure the debate in Kenya is so far inconclusive. Therefore, to fill this gap, there was need to assess the speed & of adjustment from target capital structure of listed non-financial firms in Kenya. Causal research design was used. The population for this study was 65 listed firms with only 35 non- financial firms sampled due to exclusion of financial sector which has highly regulated capital structure. Dynamic Partial Adjustment model (DPA) was used to estimate target leverage in each industry and the study found out that, there exist a target leverage level which is different from observed leverage for each sector. Further, the study showed that, listed firms adjusted to target level with a speed of 51% meaning that, the adjustment costs are relatively low.

1. Introduction

Capital structure is possibly at the core of modern corporate finance. The debate on capital structure was triggered by the seminal contribution by Modigliani and Miller (1958,1963) which has seen a tremendous development in literature on the same (Hovakimian, Hovakimian, & Tehranian, 2004). However the debate on capital structure remains a puzzle more than half a century after Modigliani and Miller contribution (Berens & Cuny, 1995). The debate has been informed by four key approaches; the trade-off theory, pecking order theory, free cash flow theory and market timing theory (Deangelo & Roll, 2015) but the two main theories are trade-off and pecking order theories (Haas & Peeters, 2006).

Myers (1977), modelled the trade-off theory into static and dynamic framework. The static framework emphasizes that firm's trade-off between cost and benefits of debt, and this trade-off can explain the cross-section variation in leverage ratio across firms. The framework implicitly assumes the existence of target leverage but believe that all firms are already at their targets. However, the static framework is faced with two limitations. The first shortcoming is the use of observed debt as the optimal debt, which may not necessarily be the case and secondly is the use of non-dynamic approach of empirical analysis, while the firms' leverage ratios move overtime and may adjust towards target (Graham and Harvey, 2001; Drobetz and Wanzenried, 2007).

Unlike the static framework, the dynamic framework approach suggests that firms have their target debt but due to market imperfections and cost associated with adjustment, they may not operate at target, and therefore observed debt level may not be the optimal debt (Mukherjee & Mahakud, 2010). Realizing the fact that capital structure decisions are not static, recent researches of capital structure are taking in account the dynamic perspective of the capital structure and have used dynamic adjustment models (Oztekin, 2013).

The prevailing empirical studies on capital structure has shown that literature has remained pegged to static trade-off framework which assumes that observed and target leverage level are similar (Deesomsak, Paudyal & Pescetto ,2004 ; Huang & Song ,2006). This approach can only apply in developed markets with no market imperfections. However, developing securities markets like Kenya are characterized by market imperfection and economic shocks. Therefore, a more realistic approach need to be applied to determine whether in Kenyan securities market, there exists a target leverage level, and if so, the speed & cost at which firms adjust to the target level.

2. Literature Review

The first issue of dynamic capital structure was documented by Jalilvand and Harris (1984) and proposed that there exists a firm's target debt ratio characterized by partial adjustment to long- run financial targets (Fama and French, 2002; Guney, Ling & Fairchild, 2011). To prove Jalilvand and Harris work, Pindado (2001) by endogenzing target capital structure model and concluded that firms adjust their capital structure towards an optimum level. In similar context, 81 percent of the firms sampled by Graham and Harvey (2001) reported that they either had a target range of debt ratio or a "strict" target debt ratio. This observation was consistent with the suggestions of Myers (1984) that with the presence of adjustment cost, firms may take a longer time to adjust towards their target capital structure. This results were later confirmed by Leary and Roberts (2005) who concluded that firms do rebalance their capital structure infrequently in the presence of adjustment costs.

Using a partial adjustment model, Flannery and Rangan (2006) investigated debt targeting behavior of firms and concluded that indeed firms identify a target debt level and adjust towards it. However, firms within the same industry have tax status, debt ratios and risk behaviors therefore they may have different adjustment costs and adjustment behavior towards target capital structure (MacKay and Phillips, 2005; Ovtchinnikov, 2010).

Similar to Flannery and Rangan (2006), Sulagna (2010) studied dynamic of capital structure in the context of Indian manufacturing firms using a partial adjustment framework during the periodn1993-2008. Using GMM estimation technique, he found out that manufacturing firms in India adjust to target capital structure with factors like asset tangibility, size and profitability determining target capital structure. The results had implications to financing managers in India to consider adjustment cost while altering financing decision on firms.

In addition, Gwatidzo (2012) in South Africa studied "Dynamics in capital structure determinants in South Africa." The research focused on 178 firms listed in Johannesburg Securities Exchange for the period 1998-2008. Using a GMM estimation technique, the results showed that South African firms adjusts relatively fast towards a target capital structure with size, asset tangibility and growth affecting leverage positively. Similarly Naveed, Ramakrishnan, Ahmad & Maryam (2015) focusing on listed firms at Johannesburg Stock Exchange concludes that South African firms adjust relatively fast towards a target leverage level. However, they lack inter- industry results regarding adjustment cost and behavior towards target capital structure.

2.1. Speed of Adjustment towards Target Capital Structure.

The second line of research in capital structure dynamics has concentrated on the determination of the speed of adjustment to target capital structure. Researchers have concluded that not only do firms adjust towards a target capital structure, but the adjustment cost enhance the speed at which firms adjust their capital structures towards the optimum Faulkender &Petersen, 2012; Banerjee, Heshmati & Wihlborg, 2004; Gaud, Jani, Hoesli & Bender, 2005; Drobetz and Wanzenried, 2006; Flannery and Rangan, 2006; Huang and Ritter, 2009; Frank and Goyal, 2009).

The adjustment speed towards target capital structure varies across periods and firms because of the diversity of adjustment costs Sulgana, 2010). Using US and UK data Banerjee, Heshmati & Wihlborg (2004) postulated that the speed of adjustment depended on the absolute difference from the target debt ratio, growth opportunities and firm size therefore concluding that larger firms adjusted to target capital structure more readily compared to firms with higher growth opportunities. Similarly, Loof (2004) concluded that firms in countries that equity capital dominated adjusts faster to target leverage in comparison to debt dependent countries. Investigating Taiwanese listed companies, Yeh (2011) concluded that the speed of adjustment depends on the economic cycles of the country. During boom or recovery stages the speed of adjustment is higher than during recession stages. This was confirmed by Drobetz and Wanzenried (2006) using Swiss firms Qian, Tian & Wirjanto (2007) using Chinese firms.

There are two schools of thought regarding the relationship between distance from leverage and speed of adjustment The first argument states that the speed of adjustment is expected to be positively related to the distance from target. However, Drobetz and Wanzenreid (2006), argues that this is applicable only when firms are significantly deviated from target capital structure and they strive to adjust once only. This is consistent with findings by Mahakud and Mukherjee (2011). On the other hand, second argument claims a negative relationship between distance from leverage and speed of adjustment. According to this argument, firms adjust frequently toward their desired leverage if their actual debt is not far from target debt.

The rationale that triggers behind these arguments is fixed cost of adjustment (legal fee and investment bank fee). If fixed cost of adjustment is high, most adjustments may take place without transactions in external capital markets (Drobetz and Wanzenried, 2006). In this situation, if the firms adjust internally, as opposed to employing external debt, a negative relationship is expected to exist between distance from leverage and speed of adjustment. The uniqueness or specialization of firms may also influence the speed of adjustment.

Besides understanding the speed of adjustment researchers has raised fundamental question on what factors causes/ hinders the adjustment speed towards target capital structure Faulkender &Petersen (2008). Firm level factors affecting the speed of adjustment that are commonly cited in research include profitability, firms growth, size, asset tangibility, liquidity and distance between observed and desired target capital structure (Naveed, Ramakrishnan, Ahmad & Maryam, 2015).

In relation to profitability, firms having positive cash flows reduces costs related to external financing which consequently affect positively the adjustment process towards target debt. Given their need to raise capital, they are likely to issue securities that will move them towards their target capital structure. Therefore , the firms with large positive or negative cash flows are likely to confront a relatively low marginal cost of adjusting leverage and , hence ,manifest relatively rapid adjustment speeds .Firms with free cash flows close to zero are unlikely to be issuing or repurchasing ,and will therefore confront the largest incremental costs .They have found that adjustment speeds to be faster for the firms for whom incremental adjustment costs have been lower and the speed has been lower for the firms for whom the incremental costs have been higher (Flannery and Hankins, 2007; Faulkender &Petersen, 2008). Likewise, Mahakud and Mukherjee (2011) concluded that profitability reduces need for external financing hence facilitating fast speed of adjustment.

With respect to size Harris and Raviv (1991) postulates that firm's size is positively correlated to leverage. Since large sized firms have smaller fixed costs, are less symmetrical, employing greater amount of debt hence they can adjust to target debt faster compared to smaller firms (Mukherjee and Mahakud, 2010; Loof, 2004). Contrary to these findings there is an inverse relationship between size and speed of adjustment (Haas and Peters, 2006; Banerjee, Heshmati & Wihlborg, 2004) whereas Gonzalez and Gonzalez (2012) found no significant difference in adjustment speed between small and large sized Spanish firms.

In view of growth opportunities growth firms are usually young firms in need of external financing and Drobetz and Wanzenried (2006) concluded that such growing firms adjust faster towards target capital structure since it easier to alter their existing debt structure. Consistent with these findings are findings by Banerjee, Heshmati & Wihlborg (2004) suggesting that growing firms tend to have more flexibility in choosing the sources of finance than no-growth firms which can only change their capital structure by swapping debt against equity however they also differed in the sense that Banerjee findings show a slower adjustment speed. This could be due to the methodology used to analyze the data (least square estimation technique) which usually leads to inconsistent estimators.

In regard to distance between target leverage and observed leverage, Drobetz and Wanzenried (2006) argues that the speed of adjustment is positively related to distance from target however this argument could only be applicable when firms have deviated significantly from target capital structure and endeavor to adjust one time only. However, a negative relationship between the variables can exist when firms frequently adjust towards their target capital structure and their actual debt is not far from the target. This caused by fixed cost e.g. legal fees and investment bank fees which constitute a major portion of the rebalancing cost hence only firms that move significantly far away from the optimal capital structure will change their capital structure (Tesfaye, 2014). In conclusion, factors affecting speed of adjustment towards target capital structure varies from country but the common firm specific factors play a major role.

However, several studies have contradicted with the dynamic capital structure model results arguing that firms "time" their market conditions so as to take advantage of different conditions hence adjusting to optimal debt ratios is not a concern for firms (Baker and Wurgler ,2002). In support Welch (2004) added that the dynamics in debt ratios are caused by various shocks rather than an attempt to adjust to target level. Using Indonesian non- financial firms Reinhard and Li (2010) used a GMM approach to determine if target capital structure models can explain the dynamic behavior of firms to adjust to target levels. Their results were negative suggesting that capital structure models whether dynamic or static cannot be used to discriminate trade-off theory from other capital structure theories.

2.2. Cost of Adjustment

Dynamic trade-off theories explicitly emphasize the idea that firms have a target that maximizes its value and deviations from target are costly. The adoption of dynamic trade-off raises pertinent questions on what is the speed of adjustment and the related cost of adjustment (Frank and Goyal, 2007).Flannery & Hankins (2013) posits that the adjustment speed towards target capital structure purely depends on the adjustment costs and the costs of deviating from target capital structure. The adjustment costs are dependent on the transaction costs and the market values of stock. Firms deviating away from target leverage may have an incentive to undertake quick adjustment, especially when they face a fixed adjustment cost. However, if the cost function is proportional rather than fixed, firms with a large deviation from target leverage may have a slower speed of adjustment than those with a small deviation(Leary & Roberts, 2005)

Assuming a fixed adjustment cost function, firms should adjust their capital structure more frequently, at the lower or upper boundaries of the target leverage range. The larger the deviation from the target, the faster the speed of adjustment(Getzmann & Lang, 2010). However, when firms have a proportional adjustment cost function an opposite prediction can be reached. In this case, firms with actual leverage deviating away from the target leverage may find it costly to revert to the target, so that their adjustment is small in magnitude and takes place more slowly (Drobetz & Wanzenried, 2015).

From the foregoing review of relevant literature, it is clear that there remain issues that are yet to be resolved. For instance, on adjustment to target capital structure, Byoun (2008) looking into whether firms adjust to target leverage level found out that though they adjust to target level, they do not do so rapidly. This was consistent with Yeh & Liu (2011) on their study on "Investigation of target capital structure for electronic listed firms in Taiwan". However, Drobetz and Wanzenried (2006) studying "What determines the speed of adjustment to the target capital structure" and Gwatidzo (2014) examining "Firm's debt choice in Africa" concluded that the adjustment speed to target level should be fast. This shows that the speed of adjustment results cannot be generalized to firms in other countries and therefore need to be determined in the case of Kenya and then compared to others.

Among the studies that have supported positive relationship between firms specific variables and financial performance include Huang & Song (2006), Lin & Chang (2011), Nieh, Yau, & Liu (2008) and Kodongo, Mokoaleli-mokoteli, & Maina (2015) among others. However, contrasting results by Lambrinoudakis, (2016), Mule & Mukras (2015) and Mwangi, Onyango &Amanya (2012) shows that growth opportunities have a negative effect on financial performance.

Furthermore, on the issue of whether to embrace the static framework or dynamic framework of capital structure has been a puzzle. The argument of static framework proponents in developed markets is that there is no difference between actual and optimal target levels (Titman & Wessels (1988); Deesomsak, Paudyal & Pescetto (2004) ; Huang & Song (2006) and Shyam-sunder & Myers (1999). This has been echoed in developing markets (Abor & Biekpe, 2007; Antwi, Fiifi, Atta, Polytechnic, & Kf, 2012 ; Chen, 2002;).

The dynamic trade-off framework has received robust support in capital structure literature mostly in developed markets: (Hovakimian, Hovakimian, & Tehranian, 2004; Leary and Roberts, 2005; Flannery and Rangan, 2006; Faulkender &Petersen,2008; Huang and Ritter, 2009; Ramakrishnan, 2012). However, there is limited work relating to dynamic trade-off framework in developing markets. In South Africa for example, Tsefaye (2014) confirms that capital structure in developing markets adjusts to a target debt level but also at varying adjustment costs and speed. However, he noted that these findings could not be generalized in other developing markets due to industrial differences. Therefore, it's key to test the dynamic framework of capital structure on listed firms in Kenya.

3. Methodology

The study population was 35 non-financial sector firms out of the 65 firms listed at the NSE, Kenya for the period 2006-2015. This was due to the exclusion of banking and insurance industry since they have a regulated debt level (Antwi, Fiifi, Atta, Polytechnic, & Kf, 2012; Chen, 2002; Deesomsak, Paudyal & Pescetto ,2004).The secondary data was collected from the audited financial statements of the listed firms in the NSE. This involved using only the audited reports maintained at the NSE and CMA since they ensure consistency of reporting and are reliable for analysis purposes

Using secondary data, Tsefaye (2014) posits there are two distinct econometric models that stands out in the study of dynamic capital structure: Two stage dynamic panel adjustment model and the dynamic partial adjustment capital structure model (DPA). Although both models are widely used in analysis, Flannery and Rangan (2006) strongly proved that the two-stage dynamic panel adjustment model is limited in that it results to unusually smaller estimates of adjustment speed than the theory predict. In addition, this model does not allow for target capital structure to vary across firms while the Dynamic Partial Adjustment (DPA) model does. Since this research required variation of target leverage over different firms listed in the NSE, the study adopted the Dynamic Partial Adjustment (DPA) model.

After Flannery and Rangan (2006) approval to use two-stage dynamic panel adjustment model, the observed leverage of a firm was used to proxy target leverage. Delcoure (2007) and Titman and Wessels (1988) argue that, observed leverage can be measured using two ways. One is by using book value of total debt and the other by using book value to long-term debt. The book value of long-term debt was used in this study since firm's leverage is largely driven by long-term debt. This measure looks at capital employed and therefore best reflects the effects of past financial decisions (Drobetz & Wanzenried, 2015).

There also exist in research the debate of whether observed leverage should be computed using book values or market value of equity. Many researcher argue that book ratios are better compared to market ratios since they reflect the target debt ratios better (Hovakimian & Li, 2012; Drobetz & Wanzenried, 2015 ; Nieh, Yau, & Liu, 2008). However, using market values is dependent on several factors which may be out of control of the organization (Nunkoo & Boateng, 2015). Memon, Rus, & Ghazali (2015) studying "Dynamism of capital structure from Pakistan" argued that the use of book value over market value was because the book value relates to financial distress cost which is important in the model.This was supported by Yinusa (2015) argument in his research on "Dynamic analysis of the impact of capital structure on firm performance in Nigeria" that book value measures are accurate and have relative ease in measurement. This study used book values to compute observed leverage.

Heshmati (2001), De Miguel and Pindado (2001) states that target leverage depends on firm's specific factors which can be expressed as follows;

$LV_{it}^{*} = \beta X_{it-1} + \varepsilon_{it}$ ... .Equation 3.0

Where LV_{it}^{*} is the target leverage ratio of firm i in time t, X_{it} are the firm characteristics determining target leverage and ε_{it} is the error term.

The equation 3.0 is estimated using the approach of Hovakimian (2009) where the β is estimated separately for each year through a historical firm fixed effect panel regression. Hence β at time t is determined by regressing leverage ratios observed in year 2 through t on firm characteristics observed in year 1 to t-1 (Lambrinoudakis, 2016). Then, the estimated coefficients are used to generate proxies for target at time t+1. This shows that the target leverage level can vary both across firms and time. Therefore, in a perfect environment, observed leverage is equal to target leverage ratio. To control for correlation between the explanatory variables, a multicolinearity test was conducted.

Ozkan (2001) argue that, since adjustment cost is high, managers find it prudent to adjust the target level partially from the previous target level to current debt level. Considering adjustment costs Gaud, Jani, Hoesli & Bender (2005) in their study on "The Capital Structure of Swiss companies: An Empirical Analysis Using Dynamic Panel Data" formalized the DPA model as follows.

$LV_{it} - LV_{it-1} = \alpha(LV_{it}^{*} - LV_{it-1}), with\ 0 < \alpha < 1$ ....Equation 3.1

Where LV_{it} is the observed leverage ratio of firm i in time$t$, LV_{it}^{*} is the target leverage ratio of firm i in time$t$, α is the speed of adjustment between two periods. The speed of adjustment is inversely related to cost such that when $= 1$, the adjustment process is completed within one period and the firm at time t is at its target leverage level. If < 1, the adjustment from the previous period to the current period falls short of the adjustment required to be at target level and when $\alpha > 1$, the firm has made more adjustment than it is required. As shown in equation 3.1, this model agrees with Drobetz and Wanzenried (2006) who studied 90 Swiss firms between 1991-2001 in a study titled "What Determines the Speed of Adjustment to the Target Capital Structure?" In addition, Anil & Gwatidzo (2012) who studied "Dynamic Capital Structure Determinants in South Africa" used the same model to determine speed and cost of adjustment.

With a balanced panel data and equation 3.1, Gwatidzo (2012) studying "Dynamics in Capital Structure Determinants in South Africa." and Tsefaye (2013) study titled "Determinants of the Adjustment Speed of Capital Structure: Evidence from Developing Economies" agrees that one can identify the target capital structure and the adjustment process (cost and speed).

Since the error term v_{it} in equation 3.1 may be correlated with the lagged dependent variable LV_{it-1} fixed or random effect causing bias in estimations, caution is necessary. Several estimation procedures ranging from Anderson-Hsiao (AH) to General Moments Method (GMM) exists to estimate the model. General Moments Method estimation technique uses extra instruments obtained by orthogonality conditions existing between the lagged values of dependent variables and disturbances (Ozkan, 2001). Researchers like Ozkan (2001) studying "Determinants of Capital Structure and Adjustment to Long-Run

Target: Evidence from UK Company Panel Data", Gaud, Jani, Hoesli & Bender (2005) study on "The Capital Structure of Swiss Companies: An Empirical Analysis Using Dynamic Panel Data" and Drobetz and Wanzenried (2006) study on" What Determines the Speed of Adjustment to the Target Capital Structure?" suggested using an instrumental variables (IV) estimation method where the variables that may be correlated with the error term are controlled. However, the instrumental variables IV estimation does not necessarily lead to efficient estimates of the model parameters as it fails to utilize all of the available moment conditions.

Therefore, this study adopted GMM by Arellano and Bond (1991) since it's more appropriate in estimating dynamic capital structure model. This was adopted by scholars like Anil & Gwatidzo (2012) in their study on "Dynamic Capital Structure Determinants in South Africa", Tsefaye (2014) study on "Determinants of the Adjustment Speed of Capital Structure: Evidence From Developing Economies" and Naveed, Ramakrishnan, Ahmad & Maryam (2015) studied "Factors Affecting Speed of Adjustment under Different Economic Conditions: Dynamic Capital Structure Sensitivity Analysis."

However, this estimation method is faced by misspecification on some test statistics that may make it inappropriate to treat firm -specific factors as exogenous but assumes all explanatory variables as endogenous (Drobetz & Wanzenried, 2015). This led to use of second lag of all dependent variables where the two-step GMM estimator suggested by Arellano and Bond (1991) was used. However, Miguel and Pindado (2001) states that due to endogeneity of the explanatory variables, which according to Ozkan (2001) arises due to economic shocks that could affect some regressors, all variables should be treated as endogenous. This study therefore, treated all variables as endogenous.

4. Results

4.1. Estimation of Target Leverage

To estimate for target leverage, equation 3.0 was estimated by two step Generalized Method of Moments (GMM) estimation technique for each firm across the years. The measures of leverage used were total debt ratio and long-term debt ratio. The firm characteristics used for estimation were size, growth and asset tangibility in tandem with Hovakimian and Guangzhong (2011) on their study on "Determinants of target capital structure: the case of dual debt and equity issues", Drobetz and Wanzenried (2006) focusing on "What determines speed of adjustment to the target capital structure?" and Nunkoo and Boateng (2010) on their study on "Empirical determinants of target capital structure and adjustment to long-run target: evidence from Canadian firms". These studies also estimated target leverage using long-term debt ratio as a measure of leverage.

The econometric analysis of the coefficients in tables 4.19 & 4.20 showed that asset tangibility was significant at all levels with coefficient of 0.33 and 0.14 respectively. These results are consistent with the findings of Gwatidzo & Ojah (2012) in their study on "Corporate capital structure determinants" and Haas & Peeters (2004) studying "Dynamic adjustment towards target capital structures of firms in transition economies" who had asset tangibility significant at all levels. This confirms the trade-off theory that as proportion of tangible assets increase, the more collateral a firm can offer hence the more debt it can take. Further, firms that invest heavily in tangible assets tend to have higher financial leverage as they can borrow at lower interest rates if their debt is secured with such assets (Laeven & Perotti, 2010).

The study also finds a positive coefficient between firm size and the TDR while a negative coefficient with LDR at all levels and 10 % respectively. This is consistent with findings of Sulgana (2010) on his study on "Dynamic adjustment towards target capital structure: Evidence from Indian companies. This confirms the argument that larger firms may have access to financial markets for long-term debt as compared to small firms. In addition, large firms may have a lower ratio of bankruptcy cost to firm value compared to small firms since bankruptcy cost include fixed costs which is minimal for the former (Anil & Gwatidzo, 2012).

Regarding growth, the results further shows a positive coefficient of 0.01 and 0.02 with the leverage metrics (LDR &TDR) at 10% level of significance. This means firms listed at the NSE with substantial growth opportunities prefer using debt to finance their activities (Drobetz, 2006). These findings further agree with the signaling theory of capital structure that firms with high growth options tend to use high debt to signal good performance. On the contrary, Laeven & Perotti (2010) poses that firms with high growth prospects issue less debt because underinvestment problem leads firms to issue only risky debt that can be supported by asset-in-place. If not, managers acting on behalf of shareholders may decide not to undertake positive net present value investments to avoid the possibility of payoffs going to debt holders.

The GMM estimations in Table 1 & 2 provided target leverage for each firm and sector respectively as shown in table 3. Using LDR as a measure of leverage to estimate target capital structure, the target leverage was negative at -0.25, -0.12, -0.09, -0.15, -0.18, -0.06 and -0.17 for commercial &services, investments, manufacturing, telecommunication, construction & allied and energy &petroleum sectors respectively. However, it was uniquely evident that agricultural sector had a positive target leverage of 0.06 using LDR. This means that LDR is not adequate measure to estimate target leverage as confirmed by findings of Anil & Gwatidzo (2012), Tsefaye (2014), Naveed, Ramakrishnan, Ahmad & Maryam (2015). They conclude that Total Debt ratio best estimates the target leverage since it accommodates short-term debt. On average Construction and Allied Sector has the highest target leverage of 21.3 % as compared to the Investments sector and Telecommunication with 6%. This means for the firms in Construction and Allied Sector, their financing using debt should be 21% so as to maximize their profits.

This finding in table 3 confirms the dynamic trade-off theory that firms have a target capital structure and will tend to deviate from it depending on the cost of adjustment and market imperfections (Mukherjee and Mahmund, 2010). The presence of target capital structure is in tandem with the findings of Flannery and Rangan (2006), Huang and Ritter (2009), Ramjee and Gwatidzo, (2012), Oztekin (2013). The discussion of target capital structure has prevailed in developed markets over the years (Ramjee and Gwatidzo, 2012) leaving the developing markets behind. Lemma and Negash (2014) attributes this to the inefficiency and incompleteness of the capital markets in the developing markets, causing financing decisions to be subject to irregularities.

Table 1: Estimation of Target Leverage using Lagged LDR

```
. xtreg LDR ASSET size growth

Random-effects GLS regression                   Number of obs      =       350
Group variable: countryid                       Number of groups   =        35

R-sq:                                           Obs per group:
     within  = 0.0674                                         min =         10
     between = 0.5215                                         avg =       10.0
     overall = 0.3633                                         max =         10

                                                Wald chi2(3)       =     50.01
corr(u_i, X)   = 0 (assumed)                    Prob > chi2        =    0.0000
```

LDR	Coef.	Std. Err.	z	P>|z|	[95% Conf.	Interval]
ASSET	.3330333	.0569921	5.84	0.000	.2213309	.4447358
size	-.0218344	.0032349	-6.75	0.000	-.0281747	-.015494
growth	.001575	.001885	0.84	0.403	-.0021195	.0052695
_cons	.0260067	.0433722	0.60	0.549	-.0590012	.1110147
sigma_u	.12306122					
sigma_e	.12254341					
rho	.50210829	(fraction of variance due to u_i)				

Table 2: Estimation of Target Leverage using Lagged TDR

```
. xtreg TDR ASSET size growth

Random-effects GLS regression                   Number of obs      =       350
Group variable: countryid                       Number of groups   =        35

R-sq:                                           Obs per group:
     within  = 0.1286                                         min =         10
     between = 0.5251                                         avg =       10.0
     overall = 0.3335                                         max =         10

                                                Wald chi2(3)       =     62.56
corr(u_i, X)   = 0 (assumed)                    Prob > chi2        =    0.0000
```

TDR	Coef.	Std. Err.	z	P>|z|	[95% Conf.	Interval]
ASSET	.1387451	.0329706	4.21	0.000	.0741239	.2033663
size	.003234	.001842	1.76	0.079	-.0003763	.0068442
growth	.0022688	.0010606	2.14	0.032	.00019	.0043477
_cons	.0313741	.0257342	1.22	0.223	-.0190641	.0818122
sigma_u	.08662847					
sigma_e	.07101446					
rho	.59808446	(fraction of variance due to u_i)				

Table 3: Sector Target Leverage

SECTOR	Firms	LDR	TDR
Agriculture	6	0.065595	0.173902
Automobile & Accessories	3	-0.25012	0.078671
Commercial & Services	7	-0.12148	0.16515
Investment	2	-0.09208	0.059014
Manufacturing	7	-0.15532	0.109871
Telecommunication	1	-0.18465	0.061225
Construction & Allied	5	-0.05547	0.212592
Energy and Petroleum	4	-0.17461	0.187674

4.2. Estimation of Speed and Cost of Adjustment

Firms listed at the Nairobi Securities Exchange have proved to have a target leverage level that is different from the observed leverage between 2006 and 2015. This confirms the dynamic trade-off theory and rejects the static trade-off that assumes observed leverage equals the target leverage (Mukherjee & Mahakund, 2010). This therefore means that firms listed at the Nairobi Securities Exchange may move toward the target or away the target leverage at a certain speed.

Using General Methods Moment dynamic panel estimation suggested by Arellano and Bond (1991) equation 3 was estimated to determine the speed of adjustment for each firm from the observed leverage to target leverage as show in Table 4.

Table 4: Determining Speed of Adjustment

Dependent Variable: Leverage	All Equities
Leverage: Lag 1	0.4918***
	(0.0284)
Asset Tangibility	0.017
	(0.045)
Size	0.01*
	(0.005)
Growth	0.002***
	(0.0002)
Constant	-0.063
	(0.05)
Observations	296
Wald Chi^2 test (df=4)	3038.3***
Autocorrelation Test: AR(1)	-2.52**
AR(2)	1.22
Sargan test (df=175)	30.99
*** p<0.01, ** p<0.05, * p<0.1	

The coefficient of lagged leverage is 0.49 or 49% which is significant at 1% level. This suggest that on average about 51% leverage gap (Target leverage- observed leverage) is covered within a year by firms listed at the Nairobi Securities exchange.

The speed at which firms adjust from target leverage varies from study to study and from firm to firm with part of the reason have to do with the econometric methods used and the cost related to adjustment (Sulgana, 2010). Studies showing a low speed of adjustment include Reinhard and Li (2010) in Indonesia with 4%, Mukherjee and Mahakud (2010) in India with 41%, Getzmann, Lang, and Spremann (2010) in Asian firms with 39% and Getzmann, Lang, and Spremann (2010) with 41%.This high speed of adjustment is consistent with Tsefaye (2014) results which suggest two things. First, is that there exists a heterogeneity of adjustment speed across countries and second, is that the speed of adjustment tends to be higher on developing countries as compared to developed countries. This high speed is comparable to South African firms with a speed of 66% (Gwatidzo, 2014). Since the speed of adjustment is inversely related to cost, the adjustment cost towards the target level is relatively low in Kenya and in South Africa. This could be due to the underdeveloped derivatives market in Kenya, leaving banks as a major source of corporate debt. Therefore, due to cheap financing on deposit, banks offer lower cost of corporate debt thereby lowering the transaction cost.

Further, the results shows that there exists negative first order autocorrelation as shown by significant AR(1) but there was no second order autocorrelation as shown by AR(2) statistic. According to Tsefaye (2014) this results are consistent because presence of first order correlation is expected but higher order autocorrelation should not be present. Wald test of 3038.3 was significant at 1 % proving the dependent variables are jointly significant and therefore explain the dependent variable. Sargan test of over-identification was not significant at 10 percent proving that the instruments used are valid.

The results in table 4 further shows the influence of firm characteristics on the speed of adjustments. Growth shows a significant positive effect on the speed of adjustment at 1% level. This agrees with the findings of (Authors, 2014b; J. Chen, Jiang, & Lin, 2014; Nunkoo & Boateng, 2015; Ramakrishnan, 2012). This shows that it is easier to change the debt of growing firms since they can avail alternative sources of funds as compared to small firms (Drobetz & Wanzenried, 2015).

In relation to size, the results shows that size has a positive significant effect on the speed of adjustment. These results are consistent with (Hovakimian & Li, 2012; Lambrinoudakis, 2016; Nunkoo & Boateng, 2015) that large firms will adjust more since adjustments of capital structure may require fixed costs which are less for large firms as compared to small firms (Getzmann & Lang, 2010).

With respect to tangibility the results shows a weak positive relationship. Most studies shows a positive relationship since it's easier to use tangible assets as collateral thereby reducing debt related agency costs (Leary & Roberts, 2005). This means firms with more tangible assets at the Nairobi Securities Exchange can use them as collateral hence borrowing at a lower rate of interests.

5. Discussion

The results showed that firms listed at Nairobi Securities Exchange have a target debt level where they can maximize their profitability. It was evident that firms in different sectors have different levels of target leverage that they can utilize hence, it cannot be generalized to all sectors. This conforms to the trade-off theory, which states that there is an advantage of financing using debt though it should be used prudently to avoid bankruptcy. The positive relationship between target leverage and performance means that if firms operate at that level, their performance will be maximized. It was however noted that firms listed at the NSE operates below the target level hence they have more room to increase their debt level. There is therefore a crucial role that capital markets should play in setting appropriate target leverage for each sector which will enhance firms listed at the NSE are competitive and operates as a going concern.

With a target leverage, the findings shows that firms listed at the NSE do not operate at the target leverage level. Therefore, they adjust at a certain speed and cost. The study documents that firms with high growth rate adjust fast compared to slow growing firms. This findings conforms with Drobetz & Wanzenried (2015) in their study on " What determines speed of adjustment to the target capital structure". In addition, it's notable from the findings that the speed of adjustment varies from one sector to the other.

6. Conclusion

The study recommends that firms listed at the NSE should make effort to operate at the target level so that they can maximize the wealth of their shareholders. However, because of random events or other changes, firms may temporarily deviate from their target capital structure and then only gradually work back to the target level. In fact, in the presence of adjustment costs, the study recommends that it might be cheaper for firms not to fully adjust to their targets even if they recognize that their existing leverage ratios are not optimal. Therefore, firm managers need to influence the adjustment speed prudently in cognizant of the adjustment cost.

The dynamic partial adjustment model used in this study takes into account the speed of adjustment and cost of adjustment when determining whether to operate at the target leverage level. However, corporate financial managers are concerned with future investment need and expected cash flows when setting their financial policy. Therefore, future research can be conducted to extend the empirical models which takes into account future expectations that influence financing policy.

References

Abor, J., and Biekpe, N. (2005). What determines the capital structure of listed firms in Ghana? *African Finance Journal*, 7(1), 37.

Abor, J., and Biekpe, N. (2007). Corporate governance, ownership structure and performance of SMEs in Ghana: Implications for financing opportunities. *Corporate governance*, 7(3), 288-300.

Abdeljawad, I., Nor, F. M., Ibrahim, I., & Abdul, R. (2013). Dynamic Capital Structure Trade off Theory : Evidence from Malaysia. *Proceedings of 3rd Global Accounting, Finance and Economics Conference*, 1–10.

Akhtar, S. (2012). Relationship between Financial Leverage and Financial Performance : Evidence from Fuel & Energy Sector of Pakistan, *4*(11), 7–18.

Akintoye, I. R. (2009): "Sensitivity of Performance to Capital Structure," Banking and Finance Letters, 1, pp. 29 – 35.

Antwi, S., Fiifi, E., Atta, E., Polytechnic, K., & Kf, P. O. B. (2012). Capital Structure and Firm Value: Empirical Evidence from Ghana, *3*(22), 103–111.

Baum, C. F., & Econometrics, E. C. A. (2013). Dynamic Panel Data estimators, 1–50.

Bauer, P. (2004). Determinants of capital structure empirical evidence from the Czech republic. *Finance a Uver - Czech Journal of Economic and Finance*, *54*(1–2), 2–21.

Banerjee, S., Heshmati, A. and Wihlborg, C. (2004), "the dynamics of capital structure", *Research in Banking and Finance*, Vol.4, pp.275-97

Berens, J. L., & Cuny, C. J. (1995). The Capital Structure Puzzle Revisited. *The Review of Financial Studies*, *8*(4), 1185–1208. http://doi.org/10.1093/rfs/8.4.1185

Berger, A. N., Klapper, L. F., and Udell, G. F. (2001). The ability of banks to lend to informationally opaque small businesses. *Journal of Banking and Finance*, 25(12), 2127- 2167.

Bradley, M., Jarrell, G.A .and Kim, E. H. (1984), "On the existence of an optimal capital structure: theory and evidence", *Journal of Finance*, Vol.39 No.3, pp .857.

Buvanendra, S., Sridharan, P., & Thiyagarajan, S. (2017). Firm characteristics, corporate governance and capital structure adjustments: A comparative study of listed firms in Sri Lanka and India. *IIMB Management Review, 29*(4), 245–258. https://doi.org/10.1016/j.iimb.2017.10.002

Chen, J. J. (2002). Determinants of capital structure of Chinese listed companies. *Journal of Business Research*, 57(12), 1341-1351.

Chen, J. (2004). Determinants of capital structure of Chinese-listed companies. *Journal of Business Research* 57 (2004) 1341– 1351.

Cheng, Y., Liu, Y., & Chien, C. (2010). Capital structure and firm value in China: A panel threshold regression analysis. *African Journal of Business ..., 4*(12), 2500–2507. http://www.academicjournals.org/AJBm/PDF/pdf2010/18Sept/Cheng et al.pdf

Chinaemerem, O. C. (2012). Impact Of Capital Structure On The Financial, *1*(12).

Deangelo, H., and Masulis, R. (2015). Optimal capital structure under corporate and personal taxation. Journal of Financial Economics, 8(1), 3-29.

De Miguel, A. D. and Pindado, J. (2001), "Determinant of capital structure: evidence from Spanish panel data", Journal of Corporate Finance, Vol.7 No.1, pp.77-99.

Deesomsak, R., Krishna, P., and Pescetto, G. (2004). The determinants of capital structure: Evidence from the Asia Pacific region. Journal of Multinational Financial Management, 14, 387-405.

Drobetz, W. and Wanzenried, G. (2006), "What determines the speed of adjustment to the target capital structure?" Applied Financial Economics, Vol.16 No.13, pp.941-958

Fama E., and French K. (2002). Testing trade-off and pecking order predictions about dividends and debt. *Review of Financial Studies*, 15, 1-33.

Fama, E. F., & French, K. R. (2011). First draft: September 2006 This draft: September 2011 Capital Structure Choices Eugene F. Fama and Kenneth R. French*, (September).

Faulkender, M. and Petersen, M. A. (2006). Does the source of capital affect capital structure?, *Review of financial studies*, 19(1), 45-79.

Faulkender, M., Flannery, M.J., Watson Hankins, K. and Smith, J.M. (2012),"Cash flows and leverage adjustments", *Journal of Financial economics*,Vol.103 No.3,pp.632-646

Flannery, M. J. and Rangan, K. P. (2006). Partial adjustment towards target capital structure., *Journal of Financial Economics*, 79(3), 469-506.

Flannery and Hankins (2007), A Theory of Capital Structure Adjustment Speed, Working Paper, University of Florida, United States.

Frank, M.Z. and Goyal, K.V. (2009), "Testing the pecking order theory of capital structure", *Journal of Financial Economics*, Vol.67No.2, pp.217-248.

Gaud, P., Jani, E., Hoesli, M., and Bender, A. (2005). The capital structure of Swiss companies: An empirical analysis using dynamic panel data. *European Financial Management*, 11(1), 51-69.

Getzmann, A., & Lang, S. (2010). Determinants of the target capital structure and adjustment speed – evidence from *Asian, European and U. S. -capital markets*, (February), 1–41.

Ghosh, A. and Jain, P. C. (2000): "Financial leverage changes associated with corporate mergers," *Journal of Corporate Finance*, 6, pp. 377 – 402.

Gujarati, D. (2013). Basic Econometrics (5th Ed.). New York: McGraw Hill.

Gonzalez, V.M. and Gonzalez, F. (2012), "Firm size and capital structure: evidence using panel data", *Applied Economics*, Vol.44No.36, pp.4745-4754.

Graham, J. R. (2000), "How big are the tax benefits of debt?" *Journal of Finance*, Vol .55 No.5, Pp.1901 -1941.

Graham, J. R., and Harvey, C. R. (2001). The theory and practice of corporate finance: Evidence from the field. *Journal of financial economics*, 60(2), 187-243.

Guney, Y., Ling, L. and Fairchild, R. (2011), "The relationship between product market competition and capital structure in Chinese listed firms", *International Review of Financial Analysis,* Vol.20 No.2011, pp.41-51.

Gwatidzo, T. and Ojah, K. (2012), "Corporate Capital Structure Determinants", *African Finance Journal*, Vol.11 No.1, pp.1-23.

Gwatidzo, T. and Ojah, K. (2014): "Firms' debt choice in Africa: Are institutional infrastructure and non-traditional determinants important?" *International Review of Financial Analysis*, 31, pp. 152 – 166.

Haas, R . and Peeters, M. (2004), "The dynamic adjustment towards target capital structures of firms in transition economies", DNB Staff Report Number 123, DeNederlandsche Bank NV, Amsterdam.

Harris, M., and Raviv, A. (1990). Capital structure and the informational role of debt. *Journal of Finance*, 45(2), 321-349.

Hassan, L. (2016). Capital Structure and Firm Performance : Did the Financial Crisis Matter ? - A cross-industry study.

Hadlock, C. and James, C. (2002): "Do banks provide financial slack?" Journal of Finance, 57, pp. 1383 – 1419.

Hovakimian, A., Opler, T. and Titman, S. (2001). The debt-equity choice. Journal of Financial and *Quantitative Analysis*, 36(1), 1-24.

Hovakimian, A., Hovakimian, G. and Tehranian, H. (2004), "Determinants of target capital structure: the case of dual debt and equity issues", *Journal of Financial Economics*, Vol.71 No.3, pp.517-540.

Hove, R. (2017). The Impact Of Capital Structure On Company Profitability Of Industrial Companies Listed On The Johannesburg Stock Exchange. Dissertation by Magister Commercial in Financial Management Sciences, (March).

Huang, R. and Ritter, J. (2009), "Testing theories of capital structure and estimating the speed of adjustment", *Journal of Financial and Quantitative Analysis*, Vol.44, pp.237-71

Huang, G., and Song, F. M. (2006). The determinants of capital structure: evidence from China. *China Economic Review*, 17(1), 14-36.

Hutchinson, R. W. (1995): "The capital structure and investment decisions of the small owner managed firm: some exploratory issues," *Small Business Economics*, 7, pp. 231 – 239.

Hutten, E. (2014). The influence of leverage on firm performance: a corporate governance perspective, 1–30. Retrieved from http://essay.utwente.nl/65216/

Igbinosa, S. (2015). Another Look at Capital Structure and Corporate Performance in Emerging Markets: The Case of Nigeria. *Asian Journal of Business Management*, 7(1), 1–12. https://doi.org/10.19026/ajbm.7.5163

Ismail, M. (2016). Effect of Financial Leverage on Financial Performance of Non-Financial Firms Listed At the Nairobi Securities Exchange (November).

Jalilvand, A., and Harris, R. S. (1984). Corporate behavior in adjusting to capital structure and dividend targets: An econometric study. *Journal of Finance*, 39(1), 127-145.

Jensen, M. (1986), "Agency costs of free cash flow, corporate finance, and takeovers", *American Economic Review*, Vol.76 No.2, pp. 323 -329.

Jensen, M. and Meckling, W. (1976), "Theory of the firm, managerial behavior, agency costs and ownership structure", *Journal of Financial Economics*, Vol.3 No.4, pp.305

Kajananthan, R., & Nimalthasan, P. (2013). Capital structure and its impact on firm performance : A study on Sri Lankan listed manufacturing companies. Merit Research *Journal of Business and Management*, 1(2), 37–44.

Kiogora, G. M. (2000): "Testing for variations in the capital structure of companies quoted at the Nairobi Stock Exchange," Unpublished MBA thesis. University of Nairobi.

Kodongo, O., Makoteli, M., and Maina, L. (2015), "Capital structure, profitability and firm value: panel evidence of listed firms in Kenya. *The African Finance Journal*, Volume 17 Part 1, 2015.

Lambrinoudakis, C. (2016). Adjustment Cost Determinants and Target Capital Structure, 20(1), 1–39.

Laeven, R. J. A., & Perotti, E. C. (2010). Optimal Capital Structure for Insurance Companies Optimal Capital Structure for Insurance Companies.

Leary, M.and Roberts, M. (2005), "Do firms rebalance their capital structure?", *Journal of Finance,* Vol. 60, pp.2575-619.

Levin, D. M. (1988). The opening of vision: Nihilism and the postmodern situation. London: Routledge.

Lin, F.L. and Chang, T. (2009), "Does debt affect firm value in Taiwan? A panel threshold regression analysis", *Applied Economics*, Vol.43No.1, pp.117-128.

Loof, H. (2004), "Dynamic optimal capital structure and technical change", Structural Change and Economic Dynamics, Vol.15 No.4, pp.449-468.

MacKay, P.and Phillips, M.G. (2005), "How does industry affect firm financial structure", The *Review of Financial Studies*, Vol.18 No.4, pp.1434-1466.

Maghanga, E. N., & Kalio, D. M. (2014). Effect of Leverage on Financial Performance of Parastatals: A Case of Kenya Power. *International Journal of Science and Research*, 5.

Modigliani, F.and Miller, M .H. (1958), "The cost of capital, corporation finance and the theory of investment", *American Economic Review*, Vol.48, pp .261 -297.

Modigliani, F. and Miller, M .H. (1963), "Corporate income taxes and the cost of capital: a correction", *American Economic Review*, Vol.53 No.3, pp.433 -443.

Mule, R. K., & Mukras, M. S. (2015). Financial leverage and performance of listed firms in a frontier market: Panel evidence from Kenya. *European Scientific Journal*, 11(7), 547–563.

Mwangi, C. I., Anyango, O. M., & Amenya, S. (2012). Capital Structure Adjustment, Speed of Adjustment and Optimal Target Leverage among Firms Quoted on the Nairobi Stock Exchange, 2(9), 100–114.

Myers, S. (1977), "Determinants of corporate borrowings", *Journal of Financial Economics*, Vol.5 No.2, pp. 147- 175.

Myers, S. (1984), "The capital structure puzzle", *Journal of Finance*, Vol.39 No.3, pp. 575-592.

Myers, S. (2001). Capital structure. *Journal of Economic Perspectives* 15 (2), 81–102.

Nassar, S. (2016). The impact of capital structure on Financial Performance of the firms : Evidence from Borsa Istanbul Business & Financial Affairs, 5(2), 5–8. https://doi.org/10.4172/2167-0234.100017

Naveed, M., Ramakrishnan, S., Ahmad, M., Maryam, A., Naveed, M., Ramakrishnan, S., Studies,F. T. (2015). Article information: Retrieved from http://dx.doi.org/10.1108/JCEFTS-08-2014-0015.

Nieh, C. C., Yau, H.Y. and Liu, W.C. (2008), "Investigation of target capital structure for electronic listed firms in Taiwan", Emerging Markets Finance and Trade, Vol.44 No.4, pp. 75-87.

Nunkoo, P. K .and Boateng, A. (2015), "The empirical determinants of target capital structure and adjustment to long run – target: evidence from Canadian firms", *Applied Economics*, Vol.17, pp.983-90.

Onaolapo, A. A. and Kajola, S. O. (2010): "Capital structure and firm performance: evidence from Nigeria," *European Journal of Economics, Finance and Administrative Sciences*, 25, pp.70 – 82.

Ovtchinnikov, A.V. (2010), "Capital structure decisions: evidence from deregulated industries", Journal of Financial Economics, Elsevier, Vol.95 No.2, pp.249-274.

Oztekin, O. (2013). Capital Structure Decisions Around the World: Which Factors are Reliably Important? *Journal of Financial and Quantitative Analysis* (JFQA).

Ozkan, A. (2001), "Determinants of capital structure and adjustment to long run target: evidence from UK company panel data", *Journal of Business Finance and Accounting*, Vol.28No.2, pp.175-198

Paudyal, K. (2004). The Determinants of Capital Structure: Capital Market-Oriented versus Bank-Oriented Institutions. *Journal of Financial and Quantitative Analysis*, 43(1), 59-92.

Pervaiz Ahmed Memon, Rohani Bt Md Rus, Zahiruddin B. Ghazali. 2015. Firm and Macroeconomic Determinants of Debt: Pakistan Evidence. *Procedia - Social and Behavioral Sciences* 172, 200-207

Qian, Y., Tian, Y.and Wirjanto, T.S. (2009), "Do Chinese publicly listed companies adjust their capital structure toward a target level?" *China Economic Review*, Vol.20, pp.662-76.

Roden, D. and Lewellen, W. (1995): "Corporate capital structure decisions: evidence from Leveraged buyouts," Financial Management, 24, pp. 76 – 87.

Salim, M., & Yadav, R. (2012). Capital Structure and Firm Performance: Evidence from Malaysian Listed Companies. *Procedia - Social and Behavioral Sciences*, 65(ICIBSoS): 156–166. https://doi.org/10.1016/j.sbspro.2012.11.105

Sulgna Mukherjee Jitendra Mahakud, (2010),"Dynamic adjustment towards target capital structure: evidence from Indian companies", *Journal of Advances in Management Research,* Vol. 7 Issue 2 pp. 250 – 266.

Shyam-Sunder, L., and Myers, S. C. (1999). Testing static trade-off against pecking order models of capital structure. *Journal of Financial Economics*, 51, 219-244.

Titman, S., and Wessels, R. (1988). Capital structure choice. *Journal of Finance,* 43(1): 1-19.

Titman, S., and Wessels, R. (2004). The determinants of capital structure choice. *Journal of Finance,* 43(1), 1-19.

Tsefaye T. Lemma, (2014),"Determinants of the adjustment speed of capital structure", *Journal of Applied Accounting Research*, Vol. 15 Issue 1 pp. 64 – 99.

Yeh, H.H. (2011), "Adjustment behaviour of capital structure over the business cycles: evidence from the construction industry of Taiwan", *Construction Management and Economics,* Vol.29, pp.329 -40.

Yinusa, O. G (2015) Dynamic analysis of the impact of capital structure on firm performance in Nigeria. Unpublished thesis

Zeitun, R., & Tian, G. G. (2007). Capital structure and corporate performance : evidence from Jordan. *Australasian Accounting Business and Finance Journal,* 1(4), 40–61.

Zhang, L. (2013). Capital structure, profitability and firm value: panel evidence of listed firms in Kenya, (47061).

10

Economic Value Added Approach in Measurement of Financial Performance: An Investigation on Economic Added Values of Holdings and Investment Companies Processed in BIST 100 in Turkey

Feden Koç[a]

[a] Lecturer, Usak University, Karahalli Vocational School, Dept. of Office Management and Administrator Assistantship, feden.koc@usak.edu.tr

Keywords

Value-Based Financial Performance Measurement, Economic Value Added (EVA), Holding and Investment Companies, Stock Exchange Istanbul (BIST).

Abstract

Objective of this study is to examine the economic value added (EVA) approach, which is a value-based performance measurement method, and the calculation of this approach from the methods used to measure financial performance. In this context, an application has been presented for the examination and comparison of holdings and investment companies in terms of economic value, using annual financial statement data for holding companies and investment companies traded in Stock Exchange Istanbul 100 index in Turkey in 2016. In the application part, 9 holding and investment companies were examined and compared in terms of economic added value. In the practice part of the study, companies that can access paid dividend data for the last five years are included in the holding companies and investment companies sector, while the other companies are excluded from the research. According to the findings of the study, when the holdings and investment companies examined in the study are evaluated in general for 2016, Hacı Ömer Sabancı Holding Joint Stock Company, which has the highest EVA value and the best financial performance. (-787.415.407,65) and Eczacıbaşı Investment Holding Partnership Joint Stock Company (-117.686.290,15) cannot create value for their shareholders with EVA value, whereas the existing Have consumed their capital. It has been found that they cannot create shareholder value with EVA value and consume their existing capital instead of creating value.

1. Introduction

It is obligatory nowadays for companies to survive in the face of increasing competition conditions and to measure their performance in financial investment decisions via various analyzes correctly. This obligation has put value-based financial performance measurement methods at the forefront of performance measurement, taking account of market capitalization value and shareholder expectations, as well as accounting information and non-accounting data, instead of traditional accounting-based traditional approaches focusing on company and performance. Value-based measurement methods to determine the company's value can be classified as periodic value measures and measures that express a certain time point of the values of the periods. Among these periodic value measures, economic profit, economic added value (EVA), shareholder value added and cash value added measures can be considered. The value of firms at a certain time point consists of market value, net present value and market value added (Ehrbar, 1998: 194). Among these value-based measurement methods, the economic value added approach provides information on whether companies create economic value and whether the shareholders' capital increases. There are some studies in the literature on the economic value added (EVA) approach. Houle (2008: 3, 30), economic value added approach that implements the companies in the study that compared with this approach, application companies, shareholder value of companies that applied the correct approach, strategic thinking, capital investment, which affected in areas such as daily work decisions, value creation has become visible in the institutions of the importance Has reached the end. He also noted that the economic value added approach represented much more of a performance measure than the focal point of the management system and mind. Susan et all. (2002: 59) Economic Value Added (EVA) of the relative effectiveness of future accounting gains and predicting earnings per share and the work that they deal with the development of their accuracy, EVA's have reached the conclusion that include information on increasing earnings per share in predicting future earnings. In addition, although EVA adds an increased value without anticipating future earnings, analysts have come to the conclusion that the information obtained from EVA has not been appropriately used. Woods et all. (2012) The importance of the economic value in determining the cost targeted in the electronics industry, their study has analyzed over multinational companies in Europe, EVA and strategic product profitability method, the attribution and the calculated target cost stated that quite difficult. He also noted that it is very difficult to use the EVA approach to calculate the targeted cost-of-return when the accounting costs are complex and the capital is large. Farsio et al. (2000: 115) Standard & Poor's 500 (S & P 500) and the Dow Jones Industrial Average (DJIA) stock indices in companies involved in their study examined the relationship between EVA and stock returns, EVA's stock is not a good indicator of performance and stock In this aspect, which explains only a part of the variability of the surplus fluctuation of the sen, the economic value added approach has been criticized by reaching the result that it is missing. Young (1997: 335, 342) also stated that the economic value added method is easy to conceptualize but requires information on market risk, company premiums, company-specific and forward-looking estimates. Young has also criticized the economic value added approach in this respect by arguing that the evaluation of investor requests at auction for past returns always leads to imperfect results in estimating the cost of self-capital.

In the study, general information regarding the literature on the concept of economic value added and the equations for calculating the economic value added were provided first. Following to that, an application was given to examine the holding companies and investment companies traded on the BIST 100 index in terms of economic value added.

1.1. Objectives of the Study

The main objective of this study is to examine the EVA measure, a value-based performance criterion. The specific objectives that support the main objective are;

- Investigation of whether the companies listed in Table 1 operating in the BIST 100 index create value for shareholders and, together with this,

Companies listed in Table 1;

- Comparison of weighted average capital costs,
- Comparing the cost of self-capital,
- The comparison of the dividend growth values of next year,
- Comparing the values of the dividend growth,
- Comparison of growth rates,
- Comparisons of self-referrals,
- Comparison of re-investment rates,

- Comparison of profit distribution ratios,
- It is aimed to compare the total share prices.

1.2. Scope and Limitations of the Study

Briefly, scope of the study consists of 9 holding and investment companies that are traded at BIST 100 in Turkey and can access the dividend payments paid for the last five years. Other holdings and investment companies that have not been able to access the paid dividend data for the last five years are excluded from the survey. In addition, the financial information used in this study is based solely on the information provided by the companies to BIST.

1.3. Data and the Methodology Used in the Study

Data of the companies included in the study were obtained from the data published by BIST in Turkey. The related 9 BIST holding and investment companies that are able to access the annual (12-month) balance sheet and income table data announced by the companies for the years 2012-2016 and to be able to access the dividend tax paid for the last five years were included in the analysis and their EVA values and financial performances were compared. In comparison, TL, the national currency of Turkey, is used.

Companies considered in the scope of the study are presented in Table 1 as below.

Table1. Companies considered in the study.

No	Company Name	Process Code
1	Alarko Holding Joint Stock Company	ALARK
2	Borusan Investment and Marketing Joint Stock Company	BRYAT
3	Eczacıbaşı Investment Holding Partnership Joint Stock Company	ECZYT
4	EIS Eczacıbaşı Phar., Indus. and Finan. Inv. Ind. and Trade JSC.	ECILC
5	Hacı Ömer Sabancı Holding Joint Stock Company	SAHOL
6	Hedef Venture Capital Investment Trust Joint Stock Company	HDFGS
7	TAV Airports Holding Joint Stock Company	TAVHL
8	Tekfen Holding Joint Stock Company	TKFEN
9	Verusaturk Venture Capital Investment Trust Joint Stock Company	VERTU

In the application section of the study, the total EVA values created by the companies listed in Table 1 in the BIST 100 index in Turkey were calculated and compared. In this context, in terms of EVA values, companies were asked to answer questions such as which companies create value for their shareholders, which companies generate the highest and lowest value, or create no value.

2. Investigation and Calculation of Economic Value Added Concept

2.1. Economic Value Added (EVA) Concept

The concept of economic value added was first developed in 1896 by Alfred Marshall, who came to the concept of "surplus profit" and made some adjustments on capital (Bayrakdaroğlu and Ünlü, 2009: 290). According to Marshall, the concept of "surplus profit", which can also be expressed as "economic profit", is calculated by subtracting the amount of interest to be paid by the capital invested from the total net earnings over the current interest rates applied (rep. Öztürk, 2004: 352).

here are many definitions of EVA in the literature. For example; Joel M. Stern and his partner Bennett Stewart, who are considered creators of EVA, describe EVA as "the difference between economic profit and the alternative cost of investing at similar risk levels of investors" (Stewart, 1991: 118). According to Weissenrieder (1997: 10), the economic value added is simply the portion of the net profit after tax that exceeds the total annual capital cost. Walker (1999: 2) also defines EVA as an instrument that is used or should be used in an organization, especially in decisions related to the cost of capital equipment. According to Öztürk (2004: 353), EVA measures whether the company's earnings meet the weighted average capital cost and is defined as the difference between the post-tax return on the capital invested by the company and the cost of capital. The common definition of EVA is that economic value added is a measure of the company's value as a performance tool.

2.2. General Information about EVA

The amount of profit calculated according to Generally Accepted Accounting Principles is called accounting profit, but this does not take into account the opportunity cost of capital investments. The economic profit is calculated by subtracting the total income from the total cost, where the total cost also includes the opportunity cost of the production factors. In this context, Generally Accepted Accounting Principles are generally insufficient to measure the financial performance of a company. For this reason, according to Stewart, the value created by an enterprise should be measured by economic profit rather than accounting profits. In addition, according to Stewart, in order to adequately reveal the financial performance of a company, it is necessary to make 164 corrections that are caused by the inadequacies in the generally accepted accounting principles, so that the distortions in the company's after-tax profits and capital can be eliminated (rep. Otlu and Karaca, 2011: 142).

The economic value added approach also examines the value created by the company, the value created by the company and the profitability of the companies, which are developed in the 1980s and which do not take into account the inflation effect and the operating cost of the enterprise. In this method, it is argued that the revenues of the companies as a result of their activities should meet the cost of the capital invested in these activities (Gücenme and Arsoy, 2006: 72).

The most important goal of profit-making organizations is to create acceptable earnings in terms of shareholders (Otlu and Karaca, 2011: 142). The economic value added approach is based on the idea that an operator should make at least as much profit as the cost of capital. However, the economic value added approach helps to make strategic decisions about the company as a performance measurement tool and points out where the shareholder wealth is being created or destroyed (rep. Otlu and Karaca, 2011: 142).

2.3. Calculating the Economic Value Added (EVA)

EVA is an accounting-based method for measuring company performance. However, EVA calculations use variables not included in accounting reports as well as accounting data. The EVA method is measured in terms of financial performance, net operating profit after tax and investment assets (weighted average capital cost) needed for obtaining these profits, taking into account the cost of capital (Brewer et al., 1999: 11). There are many equations in the literature regarding the calculation of economic value added. Young (1997: 334), however, has formulated the EVA as follows.

Net Sales

– Activity Expenses (including the tax)

= Activity Profit

– Capital Fees

= EVA

The economic value added can also be obtained by multiplying the difference between the total capital contribution and the capital cost by the committed capital amount. In this context, another equation for the calculation of economic value added is expressed as below (Stewart, 1991: 136):

EVA = Capital x (r - c)

In the equation above;

r: means total capital return.

c: means capital cost.

With a clearer presentation, it is possible to express EVA, which measures the increase in the activity of a company during the year concerned, as below (Topal, 2008: 254):

EVA = [Profit before interest and tax x (1-tax ratio)] – [Capital invested x Weighted average capital cost] (1)

In the functionalization of the EVA model, it is first necessary to estimate some of the key determinants listed as below (Firer, 1994: 57):

- Profit before interest and tax,
- Tax rate,
- Growth in income,
- Investment required for the operating capital,
- Fixed capital investments,

- The life of the predicted strategy,

The determinants of the discount rate (or cost of capital) as:

- Self-capital cost,
- Cost of debt,
- Leverage.

In this context, measuring EVA value as well as some other values of companies that are presented in the equations below will make the EVA model functional and provide better health outcomes in the measurement of financial performance. Some equations for the measurement of EVA and some other financial performance indicators are also presented below.

According to the EVA approach, one of the most important factors in determining firm value is the weighted average capital cost (Gücenme and Arsoy, 2006: 72). However, in order to calculate the EVA, the weighted average capital cost, which expresses the actual capital costs of firms, must be calculated (Başçı, 2008: 11). The weighted average capital cost can be formulated as follows (Yılmaz and Bastı, 2013: 87);

$$\text{Weighted Average Capital Cost (WACC)} = \frac{De}{S + De} \times C_b \times (1\text{-}T) + \frac{S}{S + De} \times C_c \quad (2)$$

In the equation above;

WACC: is the Weighted average capital cost,

S: is the book value of the self-capital

De: is the book value of debt,

C_c: is the cost of self-capital,

C_b: is the pre-tax cost of borrowing and

T: is the tax rate.

In order to calculate the WACC cost, capital costs of the companies have to be firstly calculated. According to the Gordon Growth Model, the cost of self-capital in ordinary shares can be calculated as follows (Başçı, 2008: 4);

$$\text{Cost of self-capital } (C_c) = D_1 / P_0 + g \quad (3)$$

In the equation above;

D_1: is the dividend growth for the next year,

P_0: is the total share price,

g: is the growth rate.

Another equation for calculating the cost of self-capital is presented as below (Sharma and Kumar, 2010: 201);

$$\text{Cost of self-capital } (C_c) = R_i + b_s \times (R_m - R_i)$$

In the equation above;

Cc : is the cost of self-capital,

R_i : is the risk-free interest rate,

R_m : is the expected return of the market,

b_s : is the beta coefficient of the stock.

In order to calculate the cost of self-capital, it is necessary firstly to calculate the dividend growth value of the next year. The dividend growth of the next year can be calculated by using the equation provided as below (Şahin, 2017);

$$\text{Dividend growth of the next year } (D_1) = D_0 \times (1+ g) \quad (4)$$

The average growth of the dividends paid in the past is obtained by subtracting the dividend payment of the previous year from the dividend payment of the current year and dividing the difference into dividend payment of the previous year. This expression can be formulated as follows (Şahin, 2017);

$$\text{Average Dividend Growth} = D_1 - D_0 / D_0 \quad (5)$$

It is necessary to also have growth rate for calculating the cost of self-capital. The growth rate can be formulated as follows (Doğanay and Aktaş, 2005: 10);

$$g = \text{Return on Self-capital} \times (1\text{- Profit Distribution Ratio}) \quad (6)$$

The return on self-capital, which is included in the equation of growth rate, can be calculated as follows (Saraç, 2015: 19);

$$\text{Return on Self-capital} = \text{Net Profit} / \text{Self-capital} \quad (7)$$

The reinvestment rate can be calculated as follows, by using the growth rate equation;

$$\text{Reinvestment Rate} = (1 - \text{Profit Distribution Ratio}) \quad (8)$$

The profit distribution ratio, which is included in the reinvestment rate equation, is measured with sum of the price the investor will pay for the stock and the present value of the profit share amounts to be obtained. According to this expression, the profit distribution ratio can be calculated by using the equation given as below (Brealey, 2001: 448-449);

$$P_0 = \sum_{t=1}^{\infty} \frac{D_t}{(1+C_c)^t} \quad (9)$$

In the equation above;

P_0 = Stock market price at t_0,

D_t = Amount of profit expected to be earned per year till t. year,

C_c = Cost of self-capital,

If the total share price in the profit distribution ratio formula is in other words the stock market price, the profit distribution ratio formula can be used to formulate as follows:

Total Share Price = Value per Share x Total Share Value (10)

3. An Application of Holding Companies and Investment Companies Treated in BIST 100 in Turkey

3.1. Alarko Holding Joint Stock Company

The five-year average dividend growth value of Alarko Holding Joint Stock Company can be calculated as given below by using the Equation 5;

2016: average dividend growth in 2016 = 31 - 26 / 26 = 0,19
2015: average dividend growth = 26 - 6,18 / 6,18 = 3,21
2014: average dividend growth = 6,18 - 6,80 / 6,80 =(-0,09)
2013: average dividend growth = 6,80 - 5,40 / 5,40 = 0,26
2012: average dividend growth = 5,40 - 2,67 / 2,67 = 1,02

4,59 / 5 = 0,918

The future dividend growth value of 2018 can be calculated by using the Equation 4, as follows;

Dividend growth of the next year (D_1) = 31 x (1+ 0,918) = 59,458 TL

The return on self-capital is calculated by using Equation 7, as follows;

Return on Self-capital = 151.469.315 / 223.467.000 = 0,68

The total share price can be calculated as follows, by using Equation 10;

Total Share Price = 0,260 x 223.467.000 = 58.101.420 TL

The profit distribution ratio is calculated as follows, by using Equation 9;

Profit distribution ratio = 58.101.420 / 29.743.134 = 1,95

The reinvestment rate is calculated as follows, by using Equation 8;

Reinvestment rate = (1- 1,95) = 0,95

The expected growth rate is calculated as follows, via Equation 6;

Expected growth rate (g) = 0,68 x 0,95 = 0,646

The cost of self-capital is calculated by using Equation 3, as follows;

Cost of Self-capital (Cc) = (0,31 / 5,72) + (0,646) = 0,70

By using the above calculated data, weighted average capital cost is calculated via Equation 2, as follows:

$$\text{WACC} = \left[\frac{1.005.754.504}{2.343.846.633} \text{ x } (0{,}12) \text{ x } (1\text{- }0{,}20)\right] + \left[\frac{1.338.092.129}{2.343.846.633} \text{ x } (0{,}70)\right] = 0{,}40254$$

EVA is calculated via Equation 1, as follows;

EVA = [(195.095.770) x (1-0,20)] – [(2.343.846.633 x 0,40254)] =

156.076.616 – 943.492.023,65 = (-787.415.407,65)

3.2. Borusan Investment and Marketing Joint Stock Company

The five-year average dividend growth value of Borusan Investment and Marketing Joint Stock Company can be calculated as given below by using the Equation 5;

2016: average dividend growth = 35,2 - 37,33 / 37,33 = (-0,06)

2015: average dividend growth = 37,33 - 74,67 / 74,67 = (-0,50)

2014: average dividend growth = 74,67 - 53,87 / 53,87 = 0,39

2013: average dividend growth = 53,87 - 61,07 / 61,07 = (-0,12)

2012: average dividend growth = 61,07 - 33,40 / 33,40 = 0,83

0,54 / 5 = 0,108

The future dividend growth value of 2018 can be calculated by using the Equation 4, as follows;

Dividend growth of the next year (D_1) = 35,2 x (1+ 0,108) = 39,0016 TL

The return on self-capital is calculated by using Equation 7, as follows;

Return on Self-capital = 31.237.363 / 28.125.000 = 1,11

The total share price can be calculated as follows, by using Equation 10;

Total Share Price = 0,011107 x 2.812.500.000 = 31.238.437,5 TL

The profit distribution ratio is calculated as follows, by using Equation 9;

Profit distribution ratio = 31.238.437,5 / 31.237.363 = 1,00003

The reinvestment rate is calculated as follows, by using Equation 8;

Reinvestment rate = (1- 1,00003) = 0,00003

The expected growth rate is calculated as follows, via Equation 6;

Expected growth rate (g) = 1,11x 0,00003= 0,0000333

The cost of self-capital is calculated by using Equation 3, as follows;

Cost of Self-capital (Cc) = (0,35 / 43,56) + (0,0000333) = 0,0081

By using the above calculated data, weighted average capital cost is calculated via Equation 2, as follows:

$$WACC = \left[\frac{24.247.489}{798.975.498} \times (0,12) \times (1-0,20)\right] + \left[\frac{774.728.009}{798.975.498} \times (0,0081)\right] =$$

WACC = 0,010767

EVA is calculated via Equation 1, as follows;

EVA = [(38.509.347) x (1 - 0,20)] - [(798.975.498 x 0,010767)] =

= 30.807.477,6 - 8.602.569,18 = 22.204.908,42

3.3. Eczacıbaşı Investment Holding Partnership Joint Stock Company

The five-year average dividend growth value of Eczacıbaşı Investment Holding Partnership Joint Stock Comp. can be calculated as given below by using the Equation 5;

2016: average dividend growth = 1,15 - 120 / 120 = (-0,99)
2015: average dividend growth = 120 - 11 / 11 = 9,91
2014: average dividend growth = 11 - 11 / 11 = 0
2013: average dividend growth = 11 - 15 / 15 = (-0,27)
2012: average dividend growth = 15 - 15 / 15 = 0

8,65 / 5 = 1,73

The future dividend growth value of 2018 can be calculated by using the Equation 4, as follows;
Dividend growth of the next year (D_1) = 1,15 x (1+ 1,73) = 3,1395 TL

The return on self-capital is calculated by using Equation 7, as follows;
Return on Self-capital = 140.010.841 / 105.000.000 = 1,33

The total share price can be calculated as follows, by using Equation 10;
Total Share Price = 1,334 x 103.547.077 = 138.131.800,72 TL

The profit distribution ratio is calculated as follows, by using Equation 9;
Profit distribution ratio = 138.131.800,72 / 140.010.841 = 0,99

The reinvestment rate is calculated as follows, by using Equation 8;
Reinvestment rate = (1- 0,99) = 0,01

The expected growth rate is calculated as follows, via Equation 6;
Expected growth rate (g) = 1,33 x 0,01= 0,01333

The cost of self-capital is calculated by using Equation 3, as follows;
Cost of Self-capital (Cc) = (1,15 / 9,73) + (0,0133) = 0,1315

By using the above calculated data, weighted average capital cost is calculated via Equation 2, as follows:

$$WACC = \left[\frac{51.848.970}{1.565.373.455} \times (0,12) \times (1-0,20)\right] + \left[\frac{1.513.524.485}{1.565.373.455} \times (0,1315)\right] =$$

WACC = 0,130324

EVA is calculated via Equation 1, as follows;
EVA = [(152.899.300) x (1 - 0,20)] - [(1.565.373.455 x 0,130324)] =
122.319.440 - 240.005.730,15 = (-117.686.290,15)

3.4. EIS Eczacıbaşı Pharmaceutical, Industrial and Financial Investments Industry and Trade Joint Stock Company

The five-year average dividend growth value of EIS Eczacıbaşı Pharmaceutical, Indus. and Financial Inv. Industry and Trade JSC. can be calculated as given below by using the Equation 5;

2016 average dividend growth = 50 - 40 / 40 = 0,25
2015 average dividend growth = 40 - 8 / 8 = 4
2014 average dividend growth = 8 - 9,60 / 9,60 = (-0,17)
2013 average dividend growth = 9,60 - 10 / 10 = (-0,04)
2012 average dividend growth = 10 -10 / 10 = 0

4,04 / 5 = 0,808

The future dividend growth value of 2018 can be calculated by using the Equation 4, as follows;
Dividend growth of the next year (D_1) = 50 x (1+ 0,808) = 90,4 TL

The return on self-capital is calculated by using Equation 7, as follows;

Return on Self-capital = 167.557 / 685.260 = 0,24

The total share price can be calculated as follows, by using Equation 10;

Total Share Price = 0,2736 x 67.546.552.900 = 18.480.736.873,44 TL

The profit distribution ratio is calculated as follows, by using Equation 9;

Profit distribution ratio = 18.480.736.873,44 / 167.557 = 110.295,22

The reinvestment rate is calculated as follows, by using Equation 8;

Reinvestment rate = (1- 110.295,22) = (-110.294,22)

The expected growth rate is calculated as follows, via Equation 6;

Expected growth rate (g) = 0,24 x (-110.294,22) = (-26.470,608)

The cost of self-capital is calculated by using Equation 3, as follows;

Cost of Self-capital (Cc) = (0,5 / 4,75) + (-26.470,608) = (-26.470,50)

By using the above calculated data, weighted average capital cost is calculated via Equation 2, as follows:

$$\text{WACC} = \left[\frac{748.213}{3.992.703} \times (0{,}12) \times (1 - 0{,}20)\right] + \left[\frac{3.250.755}{3.992.703} \times (-26.470{,}50)\right]$$

$$\text{WACC} = 0{,}017989 - 21.551{,}59 = (-21.551.57)$$

EVA is calculated via Equation 1, as follows;

EVA = [(197.188) x (1 - 0,20)] - [(3.992.703 x (- 21.551,57)] =

157.750,4 + 86.049.018.193,71 = 86.049.175.944,11

3.5. Hacı Ömer Sabancı Holding Joint Stock Company

The five-year average dividend growth value of Hacı Ömer Sabancı Holding Joint Stock Company can be calculated as given below by using the Equation 5;

2016 average dividend growth = 20 – 15 / 15 = 0,33
2015 average dividend growth = 15 – 10 / 10 = 0,5
2014 average dividend growth = 10 – 10 / 10 = 0
2013 average dividend growth = 10 – 10 / 10 = 0
2012 average dividend growth = 10 – 10 / 10 = 0

0,83 / 5 = 0,166

The future dividend growth value of 2018 can be calculated by using the Equation 4, as follows;
Dividend growth of the next year (D_1) = 20 x (1+ 0,166) = 23,32 TL

The return on self-capital is calculated by using Equation 7, as follows;
Return on Self-capital = 5.547.146 / 2.040.404 = 2,72

The total share price can be calculated as follows, by using Equation 10;
Total Share Price = 13,04 x 204.040.393.100 = 2.660.686.726.024 TL

The profit distribution ratio is calculated as follows, by using Equation 9;
Profit distribution ratio = 2.660.686.726.024 / 5.547.146 = 479.649,67

The reinvestment rate is calculated as follows, by using Equation 8;
Reinvestment rate = (1- 479.649,67) = (-479.648,67)

The expected growth rate is calculated as follows, via Equation 6;
Expected growth rate (g) = 2,72 x (-479.648,67) = (-1.304.644,38)

The cost of self-capital is calculated by using Equation 3, as follows;

Cost of Self-capital (Cc) = (0,2 / 10,84) + (-1.304.644,38) = (-1.304.644,36)

By using the above calculated data, weighted average capital cost is calculated via Equation 2, as follows:

$$\text{WACC} = \left[\frac{263.460.496}{308.267.839} \times (0,12) \times (1-0,20)\right] + \left[\frac{44.807.343}{308.267.839} \times (-1.304.644,36)\right]$$

WACC = 0,082046 - 189.632,65 = (-189.632,57)

EVA is calculated via Equation 1, as follows;

EVA = [(6.830.104) x (1 - 0,20)] - [(308.267.839 x (-189.632,57)] =

5.464.083,2 + 58.457.622.557.916,23 = 58.457.628.021.999,43

3.6. Hedef Venture Capital Investment Trust Joint Stock Company

The five-year average dividend growth value of Hedef Venture Capital Investment Trust Joint Stock Company can be calculated as given below by using the Equation 5;

2016 average dividend growth = 1,5 – 2 / 2 = (-0,25)
2015 average dividend growth = 2 – 1,25 / 1,25 = 0,6
2014 average dividend growth = -
2013 average dividend growth = -
2012 average dividend growth = -

0,35 / 5 = 0,07

The future dividend growth value of 2018 can be calculated by using the Equation 4, as follows;

Dividend growth of the next year (D_1) = 1,5 x (1+ 0,07) = 1,605 TL

The return on self-capital is calculated by using Equation 7, as follows;

Return on Self-capital = 1.523.933 / 20.000.000 = 0,076197

The total share price can be calculated as follows, by using Equation 10;

Total Share Price = 0,076 x 20.000.000 = 1.520.000 TL

The profit distribution ratio is calculated as follows, by using Equation 9;

Profit distribution ratio = 1.520.000 / 1.523.933 = 0,99

The reinvestment rate is calculated as follows, by using Equation 8;

Reinvestment rate = (1- 0,99) = 0,01

The expected growth rate is calculated as follows, via Equation 6;

Expected growth rate (g) = 0,076197 x 0,01 = 0,00076197

The cost of self-capital is calculated by using Equation 3, as follows;

Cost of Self-capital (Cc) = (0,01 / 4,50) + 0,00076197 = 0,045761

By using the above calculated data, weighted average capital cost is calculated via Equation 2, as follows:

$$\text{WACC} = \left[\frac{71.800}{32.636.765} \times (0,12) \times (1- 0,20)\right] + \left[\frac{32.564.965}{32.636.765} \times 0,045761\right] =$$

WACC = 0,000211 – 0,045660 = (- 0,045449)

EVA is calculated via Equation 1, as follows;

EVA = [(1.523.933) x (1 - 0,20)] - [(32.636.765 x (- 0,045449)] =

1.219.146,4 + 1.483.308,3 = 2.702.454,7

3.7. TAV Airports Holding Joint Stock Company

The five-year average dividend growth value of TAV Airports Holding Joint Stock Company can be calculated as given below by using the Equation 5;

2016 average dividend growth = 68,25 – 95,67 / 95,67 = (-0,29)
2015 average dividend growth = 95,67 - 84,25 / 84,25 = 0,14
2014 average dividend growth = 84,25 - 54,78 / 54,78 = 0,54
2013 average dividend growth = 54,78 - 39,34 / 39,34 = 0,39
2012 average dividend growth = 39,34 – 25 / 25 = 0,57

1,35 / 5 = 0,27

The future dividend growth value of 2018 can be calculated by using the Equation 4, as follows;
Dividend growth of the next year (D_1) = 68,25 x (1+ 0,27) = 86,68 TL

The return on self-capital is calculated by using Equation 7, as follows;
Return on Self-capital = 399.379 / 363.281 = 1,099366

The total share price can be calculated as follows, by using Equation 10;
Total Share Price = 1,17 x 363.281.250 = 425.039.062,5 TL

The profit distribution ratio is calculated as follows, by using Equation 9;
Profit distribution ratio = 425.039.062,5 / 399.379 = 1.064,25

The reinvestment rate is calculated as follows, by using Equation 8;
Reinvestment rate = (1- 1.064,25) = (-1.063,25)

The expected growth rate is calculated as follows, via Equation 6;
Expected growth rate (g) = 1,099366 x (-1.063,25) = (-1.168,90)

The cost of self-capital is calculated by using Equation 3, as follows;
Cost of Self-capital (Cc) = (0,76 / 21,42) + (-1.168,90) = (-1.168,86)

By using the above calculated data, weighted average capital cost is calculated via Equation 2, as follows:

$$WACC = \left[\frac{8.511.246}{11.505.470} x\ (0{,}12)\ x\ (1\text{-}\ 0{,}20)\right] + \left[\frac{2.994.224}{11.505.470} x\ (\text{-}1.168{,}86)\right] =$$

$$WACC = 0{,}071016 - 304{,}188239 = (-\ 304{,}117223)$$

EVA is calculated via Equation 1, as follows;

EVA = [(702.051) x (1 - 0,20)] - [(11.505.470 x (- 304,117223)] =

561.640,8 + 3.499.011.585,71 = 3.499.573.266,5

3.8. Tekfen Holding Joint Stock Company

The five-year average dividend growth value of Tekfen Holding Joint Stock Company can be calculated as given below by using the Equation 5;

2016 average dividend growth = 30,69 – 16,24 / 16,24 = 0,89

2015 average dividend growth = 16,24 – 10,81 / 10,81 = 0,50

2014 average dividend growth = = -

2013 average dividend growth = 0 – 35,74 / 35,74 = (-1)

2012 average dividend growth = 35,74 – 18,96 / 18,96 = 0,89

1,28 / 5 = 0,256

The future dividend growth value of 2018 can be calculated by using the Equation 4, as follows;

Dividend growth of the next year (D_1) = 30,69 x (1+ 0,256) = 38,55 TL

The return on self-capital is calculated by using Equation 7, as follows;

Return on Self-capital = 330.323 / 370.000 = 0,892764

The total share price can be calculated as follows, by using Equation 10;

Total Share Price = 0,877 x 370.000.000 = 324.490.000 TL

The profit distribution ratio is calculated as follows, by using Equation 9;

Profit distribution ratio = 324.490.000 / 330.323 = 982,34

The reinvestment rate is calculated as follows, by using Equation 8;

Reinvestment rate = (1- 982,34) = (-981,34)

The expected growth rate is calculated as follows, via Equation 6;

Expected growth rate (g) = 0,892764 x (-981,34) = (-876,11)

The cost of self-capital is calculated by using Equation 3, as follows;

Cost of Self-capital (Cc) = (0,31 / 10,30) + (-876,11) = (-876,08)

By using the above calculated data, weighted average capital cost is calculated via Equation 2, as follows:

$$WACC = \left[\frac{4.289.352}{6.668.809} \text{ x } (0{,}12) \text{ x } (1- 0{,}20)\right] + \left[\frac{2.379.457}{6.668.809} \text{ x } (-876{,}08)\right] =$$

WACC = 0,061747 – 312,588752 = (- 312, 53)

EVA is calculated via Equation 1, as follows;

EVA = [(438.938) x (1 - 0,20)] - [(6.668.809 x (- 312, 53)] =

351.150,4 + 2.084.202.876,77 = 2.084.554.027,17

3.9. Verusaturk Venture Capital Investment Trust Joint Stock Company

The five-year average dividend growth value of Verusaturk Venture Capital Investment Trust Joint Stock Company can be calculated as given below by using the Equation 5;

2016 average dividend growth = 9,5 – 30 / 30 = (-0,68)

2015 average dividend growth = 0 – 30 / 30 = (-1)

2014 average dividend growth = -

2013 average dividend growth = -

2012 average dividend growth = -

(-1,68) / 5 = (-0,336)

The future dividend growth value of 2018 can be calculated by using the Equation 4, as follows;

Dividend growth of the next year (D_1) = 0,2829 x [1 + (-0,336)] = 0,1878 TL

The return on self-capital is calculated by using Equation 7, as follows;

Return on Self-capital = 22.623.917 / 52.000.000 = 0,435248

The total share price can be calculated as follows, by using Equation 10;

Total Share Price = 0,44 x 52.000.000 = 22.880.000 TL

The profit distribution ratio is calculated as follows, by using Equation 9;

Profit distribution ratio = 22.880.000 / 22.623.917 = 1,01

The reinvestment rate is calculated as follows, by using Equation 8;

Reinvestment rate = (1- 1,01) = 0,01

The expected growth rate is calculated as follows, via Equation 6;

Expected growth rate (g) = 0,435248 x 0,01 = 0,00435248

The cost of self-capital is calculated by using Equation 3, as follows;

Cost of Self-capital (Cc) = (0,1 / 2,93) + 0,00435248 = 0,038482

By using the above calculated data, weighted average capital cost is calculated via Equation 2, as follows:

$$\text{WACC} = \left[\frac{8.806.491}{139.929.552} \times (0,12) \times (1-0,20)\right] + \left[\frac{131.303.061}{139.929.552} \times 0,038482\right] =$$

WACC = 0,006042 – 0,036110= (-0,030068)

EVA is calculated via Equation 1, as follows;

EVA = [(22.623.917) x (1 - 0,20)] - [(131.303.061 x (- 0,030068))] =

18.099.133,6 + 3.948.020,44 = 22.047.154,04

Conclusions

Within the scope of measuring financial performance of companies, the economic value added (EVA) method provides information on whether a company creates economic value and whether the capital of its shareholders has increased. In this context, the annual financial state table, comprehensive income state table and the footnote data of nine companies, which can provide dividend data of the last five years and are among holding and investment companies traded in the Istanbul Stock Exchange 100 Index Turkey in 2016, were used. Considering the related data, holdings and investment companies were examined in terms of various performance indicators and finally economic value added. When the findings were evaluated, the value added by the related companies were calculated as -787.415.407,65 for Alarko Holding Joint Stock Company, 22.204.908,42 for Borusan Investment and Marketing Joint Stock Company, -117.686.290,15 for Eczacıbaşı Investment Holding Partnership Joint Stock Company, 86.049.175.944,11 for EIS Eczacıbaşı Pharmaceutical, Industrial and Financial Investments Industry and Trade Joint Stock Company, 58.457.628.021.999,43 for Hacı Ömer Sabancı Holding Joint Stock Company, 2.702.454,7 for Hedef Venture Capital Investment Trust Joint Stock Company, 3.499.573.266,5 for TAV Airports Holding Joint Stock Company, 2.084.554.027,17 for Tekfen Holding Joint Stock Company, and 22.047.154,04 for Verusaturk Venture Capital Investment Trust Joint Stock Company. Ergo, considering these data, Hacı Ömer Sabancı Holding Joint Stock Company is the one having the highest EVA and showing the best financial performance in 2016 as among holding companies and investment companies traded in Stock Exchange Istanbul 100 index in Turkey. Considering the EVA, the remaining companies rank as follows: EIS Eczacıbaşı Pharmaceutical, Industrial and Financial Investments Industry and Trade Joint Stock Company is on the second place with

86.049.175.944,11 TAV Airports Holding Joint Stock Company is on the third place with 3.499.573.266,5, Tekfen Holding Joint Stock Company is on the fourth place with 2.084.554.027,17, Borusan Investment and Marketing Joint Stock Company is on the fifth place with 22.204.908,42, Verusaturk Venture Capital Investment Trust Joint Stock Company is on the sixth row with 22.047.154,04, and finally, Hedef Venture Capital Investment Trust Joint Stock Company is on the seventh place with 2.702.454,7. On the other hand, Alarko Holding Joint Stock Company (with the EVA of -787.415.407,65) and Eczacıbaşı Investment Holding Partnership Joint Stock Company (with the EVA of -117.686.290,15) have not been able to create value for their shareholders, but they have consumed their existing capital.

It is clear that investors will reach optimal investment decisions by using EVA methodology and using high EVA value as compared to traditional valuation methods, while ultimately evaluating the financial performance of companies in the process of evaluating various investment decisions.

References

Başçı, E. Ş. (2008). Cost of Capital (In Turkish), Sakarya Univ. Center of Cont. Education, http://www.kgk.sakarya.edu.tr/FileUploads/Src/63d7ca74-4a8d-4b77-89e6-88cfe967b845/B%C3%B6l%C3%BCm%2008%20-20Sermaye%20Maliyeti%20(Sunu).pdf, (Accessed on: 17.03.2017).

Bayrakdaroğlu, A. and Ulaş, Ü. (2009). "EVA and MVA in Performance Valuation: Comparative Analysis of ISE and NYSE in Terms of These Criteria (In Turkish)", *Süleyman Demirel University Journal of Economics and Administrative Sciences, Vol.* 14, *No:* 1, *pp. 290.*

Brealey, R. A., S. C. Myers, A. J. Marcus (2001). *Fundamantals of Cooparate Finance.* Third Edition, Mc Graw-Hill Companies, New York.

Brewer, C. P., Chandra, G., Clayton, A. Hock (1999). "Economic Value Added (EVA): Its Uses and Limitations", *Sam Advanced Management Journal, Spring, pp. 11.*

Doğanay, M., Aktaş, R. (2005). Valuation of Shares (In Turkish), http://www.kgk.sakarya.edu.tr/FileUploads/Src/f6f5d823-5444-4ce4-baa0 88cfe95ed35a/B%C3%B6l%C3%BCm%2005%20-%20Hisse%20Senedi%20%20De%C4%9Ferleme%20(e-kitap).pdf, (Accessed on: 18.01.2017).

Ehrbar, A. (1998). *EVA: The Real key to Creating Wealth*, John Wiley&Sons: ABD.

Farsio, F., Degel, J., Degner, J. (2000). Economic value added (EVA) and stock returns, Spring- Winter, pp. 115, http://go.galegroup.com/ps/anonymous?id=GALE%7CA85473261&sid=googleScholar&v=2.1&it=r&linkaccess=fulltext&issn=10737340&p=AONE&sw=w&authCount=1&isAnonymousEntry=true, (Accessed on: 12.01.2017).

Firer, C. (1994). Investment Basics XXX. EVA™: The Real key to Creating Value!, Investment Analysts Journal, 23: 40, 57, http://dx.doi.org/10.1080/10293523.1994.11082342, (Accessed on: 12.03.2017).

Gücenme, Ü., ve Arsoy, A. P. (2006). "Measurement of Financial Performance with Classified Cash Flow Statement Form in Accounting Standards (In Turkish)", *Journal of Accounting and Finance, No: 30, April, pp. 72.*

Houle, M. (2008). Economic Value Added, A Senior Thesis submitted in partial fulfillment of the requirements for graduation in the Honors Program Liberty University Spring 2008, pp. 3, 30. http://digitalcommons.liberty.edu/cgi/viewcontent.cgi?article=1046&context=honors, (Accessed on: 22.03.2017).

Machuga, S. M., Jr Pfeiffer, R. J., Verma, K. (2002). "Economic Value Added, Future Accounting Earnings, and Financial Analysts' Earnings Per Share Forecasts", *Review of Quantitative Finance and Accounting, Kluwer Academic Publishers, Manufactured in The Netherlands, Volume 18, pp. 59.*

Otlu, F., Karaca S. (2011). "Integrated Activity Based Costing and Economic Value Added System via Strategic Management Perspective", *Journal of Accounting and Finance, No: 51, pp. 142.*

Öztürk, M. Başaran (2004). "An Alternative Method of Measuring Financial Performance: Economic Value Added (In Turkish)", *Atatürk University Journal of Economics and Business Administration, Vol. 18, No: 3-4, pp. 352-353.*

Saraç, M. (2015). Financial Management (In Turkish), http://content.lms.sabis.sakarya.edu.tr/Uploads/58671/28261/finans_dersnotlari-2015.pdf, (Accessed on: 24.03.2017).

Sharma, A. K. and Kumar, S. (2010), "Economic Value Added (EVA) - Literature Review and Relevant Issues", *International Journal of Economics and Finance, 2 (2), p.201.*

Stewart, G. (1991). *The Quest for Value: A Guide for Senior Managers.* New York: Harper Business.

Stewart, G. B. (1991). *The Eva Management Guide:The Quest For Value.* Usa:Harper Business Publishers Inc.

Şahin, H. (2017). Valuation of Shares (In Turkish), http://www.fhu55.com/sites/default/files/.../Ders_7_hisse%20senedi%20degerlemesi.ppt, (Accessed on: 24.03.2017).

Topal, Y. (2008), "Relationship Between Economic Value Added (EVA) and Market Value Added (MVA): Example from ISE Manufacturing Enterprises (In Turkish)", *Süleyman*

Demirel University Journal of Economics and Administrative Sciences, Vol. 13 No. 2, pp. 254.

Villiers, J. D. (1997). "The Distortions in Economic Value Added (EVA) Caused by Inflation, Journal of Economics and Business", *Elsevier, Volume 49, Issue 3, p. 286.*

Weissenrieder, F. (1997). Value Based Management: Economic Value Added or Cash Value Added?, Gothenburg Studıes In Fınancıal Economıcs, Study No. 1997: 3 https://papers.ssrn.com/sol3/papers.cfm?abstract_id=156288, (Accessed on: 24.03.2017).

Woods, M., Taylor, L. and Fang, G. C. G. (2012). Management Accounting Research, Volume 23, Issue 4, December pp. 261, 275- 276, http://www.sciencedirect.com/science/article/pii/S1044500512000443, (Accessed on: 24.12.2016).

Yılmaz, T., Bastı E. (2013). "Performance Analysis Based on Economic Value Added (EVA) and Market Value Added (MVA) of Manufacturing Industry Companies: ISE Example (In Turkish)" *Journal of Management and Economics Research, No: 21, pp. 87.*

Young, D. (1997). Economic Value Added: A Primer for European Managers , Elsevier, İnsead, Volume 15, Issue 4, pp. 334- 335, 342. http://www.sciencedirect.com/science/article/pii/S0263237397000145, (Accessed on: 08.02.2017).

Permissions

All chapters in this book were first published in JAF&AS, by Yalova University; hereby published with permission under the Creative Commons Attribution License or equivalent. Every chapter published in this book has been scrutinized by our experts. Their significance has been extensively debated. The topics covered herein carry significant findings which will fuel the growth of the discipline. They may even be implemented as practical applications or may be referred to as a beginning point for another development.

The contributors of this book come from diverse backgrounds, making this book a truly international effort. This book will bring forth new frontiers with its revolutionizing research information and detailed analysis of the nascent developments around the world.

We would like to thank all the contributing authors for lending their expertise to make the book truly unique. They have played a crucial role in the development of this book. Without their invaluable contributions this book wouldn't have been possible. They have made vital efforts to compile up to date information on the varied aspects of this subject to make this book a valuable addition to the collection of many professionals and students.

This book was conceptualized with the vision of imparting up-to-date information and advanced data in this field. To ensure the same, a matchless editorial board was set up. Every individual on the board went through rigorous rounds of assessment to prove their worth. After which they invested a large part of their time researching and compiling the most relevant data for our readers.

The editorial board has been involved in producing this book since its inception. They have spent rigorous hours researching and exploring the diverse topics which have resulted in the successful publishing of this book. They have passed on their knowledge of decades through this book. To expedite this challenging task, the publisher supported the team at every step. A small team of assistant editors was also appointed to further simplify the editing procedure and attain best results for the readers.

Apart from the editorial board, the designing team has also invested a significant amount of their time in understanding the subject and creating the most relevant covers. They scrutinized every image to scout for the most suitable representation of the subject and create an appropriate cover for the book.

The publishing team has been an ardent support to the editorial, designing and production team. Their endless efforts to recruit the best for this project, has resulted in the accomplishment of this book. They are a veteran in the field of academics and their pool of knowledge is as vast as their experience in printing. Their expertise and guidance has proved useful at every step. Their uncompromising quality standards have made this book an exceptional effort. Their encouragement from time to time has been an inspiration for everyone.

The publisher and the editorial board hope that this book will prove to be a valuable piece of knowledge for researchers, students, practitioners and scholars across the globe.

List of Contributors

Shelly Prahadian Putri
Corresponding Author, Faculty of Economics, Sriwijaya University, Palembang, Indonesia

Mohamad Adam
Prof., Faculty of Economics, Sriwijaya University, Palembang, Indonesia

Luk Luk Fuadah
Ph.D., Faculty of Economics, Sriwijaya University, Palembang, Indonesia

Ohiani Danjuma Lawal
Corresponding Author, Department of Accounting and Management, Nigerian Defence Academy, Kaduna, Nigeria

Eniola Samuel Agbi
Department of Accounting and Management, Nigerian Defence Academy, Kaduna, Nigeria

Lateef O. Mustaphac
Department of Accounting and Management, Nigerian Defence Academy, Kaduna, Nigeria

Ather Azim Khan
Dr., Faculty of Management Studies, University of Central Punjab, Pakistan

Faisal Mustafa
Dr., Faculty of Management Studies, University of Central Punjab, Pakistan

Ambreen Khursheed
Corresponding Author, Faculty of Management Studies, University of Central Punjab, Pakistan

Tiwi Aliffiani
Corresponding Author, Faculty of Economics, Sriwijaya University, Palembang

Syamsurijal
Prof., Faculty of Economics, Sriwijaya University, Palembang Indonesia

Harry Anugerah Pradana
Corresponding Author, Faculty of Economics and Business, University of Padjadjaran, Indonesia

Sulaeman Rahman Nidar
Faculty of Economics and Business, University of Padjadjaran, Indonesia

Zaenal Aripin
Faculty of Economics and Business, University of Padjadjaran, Indonesia

Yossi Diantimala
University of Syiah Kuala, Banda Aceh, Indonesia

Taibat Adebukola Atoyebi
Corresponding Author, Department of Accounting, University of Abuja, Abuja - Nigeria

Adikwu Joseph Simon
Department of Accounting, University of Abuja, Abuja - Nigeria

İlker Yılmaz
College of Commerce and Business Administration, Department of Accounting, Dhofar University, Salalah, OMAN

Leonard K. Maina
Corresponding Author, Karatina University

Tobias Olweny
Jomo Kenyatta University of Agriculture and Technology

Kenneth L. Wanjau
Karatina University

Feden Koç
Lecturer, Usak University, Karahalli Vocational School, Dept. of Office Management and Administrator Assistantship

Index

www.ingramcontent.com/pod-product-compliance
Lightning Source LLC
LaVergne TN
LVHW080716210926
848485LV00003B/473